Ryanland

A NO-FRILLS ODYSSEY ACROSS
THE NEW EUROPE

Philip Nolan was born in Dublin in 1963. An award-winning travel writer, he has also worked for most Irish national newspapers, including the *Sunday World, Sunday Press, Sunday Tribune* and *Evening Herald*, and was deputy editor of *Ireland on Sunday*. He now works as a freelance travel writer, motoring columnist and current-affairs commentator for the *Irish Daily Mail* and *Irish Mail on Sunday*. He is married to Sharon Plunkett and divides his time between Dublin and County Wexford.

Ryanland

A NO-FRILLS ODYSSEY ACROSS THE NEW EUROPE

PHILIP NOLAN

HODDER
HEADLINE
IRELAND

Contents

For Sharon

Introduction – Welcome to Ryanland

The propeller plane is weaving through a violent sky, the drone of its engines rising and falling as it battles through the murk. Suddenly, there is a break in the cloud, and, in the strong moonlight, I can tell we are maybe 10,000 feet up. Off to my right, I see a huge fire. Suddenly, I clock a flare making its way towards us, then another. Within minutes, for as far as the eye can see, shells are being lobbed into the sky, exploding in great, angry arcs of flame. Each seems to come closer than the previous one, and as the plane races to gain altitude, there is a loud bang, followed by a series of smaller explosions. My heart races, my mouth dries. There's only one thing for it.

I ring the call bell and buy another Heineken...

It is 5 November 1987, Guy Fawkes Night, and this is my first experience of a budget airline. Virgin Atlantic has started a route from Dublin to Luton and though it is billed as no-frills, I wasn't expecting to find myself on a Vickers Viscount, a plane they stopped building in 1962. The aircraft I'm sitting in is at least a year, and maybe as much as a decade, older than I am. This would be a sobering thought at the best of times, but even more so when I am flying over England on a night when the country is ablaze with bonfires and fireworks.

What's even worse is that my contraband cargo is exploding. There are two things every Irish emigrant craves above all else – Kimberley biscuits and Tayto crisps. I am ferrying twelve packets of cheese 'n' onion to my sister in Watford but, because the Viscount is not as highly pressurised like a jet, the air pressure inside the bags is greater than the pressure in the cabin. I have been watching in alarm as each has gradually expanded to the size of a football; now they have started to pop, and the bangs are drawing stares from fellow passengers. By the time one of them sends slivers of potato three rows in every direction, I am expecting to be wrestled to the ground and then locked in the loo for the rest of the flight.

Virgin is the second airline on the Luton route. The first is a maverick little carrier called Ryanair, named after its founder, Tony Ryan. At one point, he also owned a large stake in the newspaper I worked for in the early 1990s, the *Sunday Tribune*. The editor at the time, Vincent Browne, who had some legendary run-ins with staff, was fond of joking that Ryan bought into the paper instead of Aer Lingus because the *Sunday Tribune* carried more passengers.

Ryanair began operations in 1985 from Waterford, in southeast Ireland, to London Gatwick, with a fifteen-seater Embraer Bandeirante turboprop and a cabin crew who couldn't be taller than five feet two inches or they wouldn't have been able to walk up and down the aisle. A year later, with bigger planes, it started flying from Dublin to Luton, an airport then almost exclusively used for charter flights. Most Irish people had heard of it only because it became famous in a Campari commercial when Cockney model Loraine Chase was asked by a Mediterranean playboy, 'Were you wafted here from paradise?', at which point she looked at him dismissively and said, 'Nah, Luton Airport.'

Ryanair arrived at a time when air travel was still very much the preserve of the wealthy. I was fifteen when I first flew, on a school tour to Barcelona, and that happened only because we got a special rate (the flight stopped at Lourdes to decant pilgrims – we had it almost to ourselves from there to Spain). My family holidays were taken in Leeds in the north of England, and that meant taking the car-ferry from Dún Laoghaire to Holyhead and a drive over the Pennines in a Ford Anglia estate. Because there were four kids, and it was long before MPVs or SUVs arrived, I spent all those drives travelling backwards, sitting on rugs and cushions in the boot. Put it this way – no-frills travel holds few terrors for me.

The high fares that flag-carrier airlines like Aer Lingus and British Airways used to charge (IR£209 return from Dublin to London – that's €265 converted, but well over €500 adjusted for inflation) meant few working-class families ever flew, except perhaps on once-a-year charters to the Costas or the Algarve. You could track down advance-purchase tickets, so-called APEX fares, but you usually had to book them a month in advance, stay a Saturday night and observe dozens of other conditions, some of which involved fasting, self-mortification or the sale of a sibling into slavery.

I started flying on business in 1983, when I was sent to London to conduct a hugely important interview (oh, OK, then – it was the kids from *Fame*). Nursing my shattered dream of becoming an award-winning war correspondent, I spent the flight home as I would spend so many more in the 1980s, reclining at 35,000 feet above Europe on half-full planes chatting amiably across the aisle with other passengers. There would be champagne and a difficult choice between the beef or salmon, served by a woman freshly scraped from the cover of *Vogue*. I would have a Silk Cut ready the very second the sign was switched off, and chain-smoke my way home; I once managed nine cigarettes in fifty minutes between Heathrow and Dublin. It was bliss, but it was mad. It had to change.

I first flew with Ryanair in 1988, by which stage it had replaced the original forty-six-seater BAE 748 prop jobs that flew the Luton route with BAC One-Elevens owned by the Romanian airline, Tarom. The aircraft were on what is known as a 'wet' lease, which meant they came with Romanian pilots too. Those of us who flew during that period have had less difficulty deciphering the in-flight announcements of more recent times.

Over the years, Ryanair expanded its route network, and passenger numbers rose – from 592,000 in 1988 to its first million-plus year in 1993, to its first million-plus *month* in August 2001 to its first 2-million-plus month in July 2003. Driving this extraordinary growth was a man called Michael O'Leary, who joined the board of Ryanair in 1988, became deputy chief executive in 1991, and chief executive three years later. O'Leary famously studied the Southwest Airlines model in the US and returned with the zeal of the converted, paring the product back to its most basic element, moving as many people as possible between one location and another in the fastest possible time.

The frequent-flier scheme was discontinued (the biggest single catchment area for members was around Knock Airport in the west of Ireland, which was served by no other airline, so fliers had no option but to be loyal). A brief flirtation with business class came to an end – so did free newspapers, and complimentary meals and drinks. Seat allocation was ended, and once you hit the tarmac, it was every man for himself. There were no jet bridges; if it was squalling rain, you still had to make a dash in the open air for the terminal.

Over the years, the model was refined and refined again. Suppliers who didn't play ball were dumped – for a time, you couldn't even get ice on a Ryanair flight because there was a dispute with the ice-making firm. The famous twenty-minute turnarounds kept planes in the best place for them to make money – the air – but were also contingent on the passengers themselves cleaning the plane. Even that worked – we had, after all, been trained for it in McDonald's.

Airports were miles from the cities they served. The legacy of the Cold War was hundreds of now obsolete NATO and Warsaw Pact airfields, and O'Leary identified them as prime civil aviation sites. Sometimes, his geography was hilariously elastic; when he started flying to Hahn Airport in Germany, the long-time home of the United States Air Force 50th Fighter Wing, he billed it as 'Frankfurt', which is 126 kilometres distant. Lufthansa, the German national carrier, was outraged, but the fuss it made handed Ryanair an invaluable awareness boost.

Fares tumbled, even when compared with Ryanair's own recent past; after all, its Dublin–Luton launch fare was £99. A clever marketing stroke that made rivals levitate with anger saw the airline stripping out the price of the 'flight' and listing taxes and charges separately – indeed, it wasn't long before flights were advertised for 'free'. By the time the company discovered the internet and removed travel agents and proper tickets from the equation, the world was tech-savvy enough to book a flight for itself. Within months, ryanair.com was the busiest travel website in Europe, and it still is.

The only fly in the ointment was that no one really liked Ryanair very much. If you were to list sentences you knew for sure you would never hear, then 'I'm really looking forward to my Ryanair flight' would have to be in the Top Three. No other business that does things so well gets quite such a bad press. After all, check-in is usually brisk and efficient. Because of its tight schedule, the airline is almost always the most punctual on every route it flies. It loses fewer bags than any other carrier (mostly, I suspect, because so many of us cram everything we need into the 10kg carry-on allowance). It never bumps anyone from a flight because, unlike other airlines, it does not routinely overbook them in the hope that a few passengers either miss connections or simply don't show up. It never charges fuel supplements, even when oil has doubled in price from the cost-per-barrel rate it hedged at six months ago.

So what's the problem? Well, the issue seems to be the perception that Ryanair is a fair-weather friend. There is no flexibility built into the business model – when something goes wrong, passengers are left to fend for themselves. Over the years, there have been countless stories in the papers about scout groups and school tours and pregnant women sleeping on far-flung floors and waiting days to get a flight home when weather or technical problems force cancellations.

Whether it is fair or not, the corporate culture of the company is inevitably intertwined in most people's eyes with their perception of Michael O'Leary. Many people love him, and believe him to be an iconoclast who took on a protectionist cartel, sat it on a mound of Semtex and stood well back. Others detest him for turning flying, once the most civilised form of travel, into something nasty and dispiriting. He has driven demand to levels airports cannot cope with, and many have become overcrowded, nasty, stressful places, with endless security queues and the sort of facilities you thought had disappeared with 1950s bus stations.

He has forced other airlines to follow him in the death spiral down-market. Aer Lingus killed off its business-class service in Europe, it charges €12 for the snipes of champagne that once came free, and there has been a marked depreciation in the quality of service. Its most famous advertising campaign, launched in the 1980s, showed passengers being tucked in under their blankets and virtually having bedtime stories read to them by elegantly coiffed hostesses. It carried the tagline 'You're

Home'. If that is still true, we have definitely moved to a less salubrious part of town.

None of this seems to matter. For all that we grumble about no-frills service, we really don't care. The more prosperous we get, the more we seem to love cheap flights, and we have driven Ryanair to record profits. Over 42 million of us, more than the population of Poland (actually, probably the population of Poland, and a few Brits and Irish thrown in) flew with the airline in 2006, on 454 routes between twenty-four countries. In that time, the fares have been lower than ever before, but the other charges rise all the time.

Free when it was introduced, online check-in now costs €3, and is automatically billed to your ticket unless you deselect it. They try this with holiday insurance too – negotiating the site is like walking through a dark alley late at night, trying to avoid being mugged. When Ryanair started charging for checked baggage ('checked' as in handed in, not Burberry suitcases) early in 2006, you paid €3.50 per sector, so it was €7 for a return flight. By early 2007, that had gone up to €6, and €12 return. S&M novices could scarcely be so frequently tested on how much pain they could endure.

The key to Ryanair's success is endless expansion. Europe is still an underdeveloped aviation market, and rising prosperity in the eastern half of the continent will drive demand, while continued migration will mean an increasing number of flights will be taken by commuters rather than leisure travellers.

All of this is changing for ever the way we fly. Without Ryanair, it is impossible to imagine a Europe where a man from Galway and a man from Glasgow can live side by side at their summer homes in Alicante, or where a Latvian émigré can work all week at a factory in Limerick and still enjoy a few beers with his mates in Riga once a month. Europe has been redrawn as Ryanland, as airports clamour to attract the airline. It has opened up places we have never heard of, and brought us back in our millions to places we last visited long ago.

A Mexican student who was staying with us came home one day and told us she was off for a week to see Paris, Milan, Rome and Berlin. When we were her age, we slung backpacks over our shoulders and bought Inter-Rail tickets, sleeping on overnight trains to avoid accommodation costs and living on baguettes and cheese, and I asked if the itinerary wasn't a little ambitious.

'The train?' Jimena asked incredulously. 'No, we're flying with Ryanair.' She and her friends had put the trip together on the net. It had cost them buttons, and allowed them to see quarter of a continent in a week instead of a month.

Intrigued, I logged on myself and a plan formed. Before I knew it, I was on an odyssey of my own, revisiting places I hadn't been to for years, making first visits to many of the most recent EU accession states, often fetching up at airports with nothing planned and letting whimsy guide me to destinations I had never before considered.

By the time I was done, I had taken sixty-one Ryanair flights and a few with other airlines to fill in the gaps. On some, I paid to check in a bag, on others I didn't. But here's the thing – all of those flights combined cost just €2,064.29 (or £1,405.06 sterling). That's an average of just €33.84 (£26.44) per sector, which I find astonishing. For that sort of money, I can tolerate an awful lot of crap.

It is important, though, also to bear in mind that I immediately paid as much as €20 return to continue by bus or train to the city I wished to visit; and on at least three occasions (Oslo Torp, Paris Beauvais and Frankfurt Hahn), this leg of the journey took longer than the flight. Car hire at the destinations, combined with taxi fares, totalled more than the airfares. Hotel accommodation made up the bulk of my expenses; I started out modestly, but the one place I do like a few frills is in a hotel room and, as my travels progressed, the hotels got more and more upmarket. At my second destination, Beauvais in France, I stayed in a €49 two-star hotel; by the time I reached Venice, six months later, I treated myself to a room in a world-famous palazzo for €215.

It's important to mention that I paid for every flight, except in about three instances where I combined work with travel and someone else bought the ticket. All tickets were bought at standard internet rates; Ryanair itself did not know about this book and had absolutely no involvement with it whatsoever.

And so it was that, on an early summer's day in 2006, I crawled out of my pinstripe suit and into my jeans, ditched the briefcase and pulled out the rucksack (rather quickly replaced by a wheelie case – my back isn't what it used to be) and set out to take a snapshot of eight months in the life of a continent – a sprawling, historic, wild, beautiful, lively hotchpotch of lifestyles, religions and cultures.

Welcome to Ryanland.

Ryanland

1: Gothenburg City–Stockholm Skavsta
2: Paris Beauvais
3: Porto
4: Newcastle-upon-Tyne
5: Oslo Torp
6: Glasgow Prestwick
7: Salzburg
8: Frankfurt-Hahn
9: Santiago de Compostela–Santander
10: Stansted–Gatwick
11: Cork
12: Aberdeen–Edinburgh
13: Carcassonne–Marseille
14: Lübeck
15: Reus Salou
16: Biarritz–Pau
17: Knock Ireland West–London Luton
18: City of Derry–East Midlands
19: Leeds-Bradford–Birmingham
20: Blackpool
21: Brno
22: Bristol–Bournemouth
23: Girona–Alghero
24: Tampere
25: Riga–Liverpool–Manchester
26: Bratislava–Milan Bergamo
27: Wroclaw–Krakow
28: Kaunas
29: Murcia–Valencia
30: Rome Ciampino–Venice Treviso
31: Berlin Schönefeld
32: Eindhoven–Brussels South Charleroi
33: Malta Luqa

IRELAND

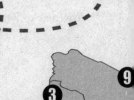

PORTUGAL

SPAIN

GOTHENBURG CITY–
STOCKHOLM SKAVSTA

FR952

Dublin (DUB) to Gothenburg City (GSE)

1,240 km

€73.13

It is an inauspicious start. I can tell from here, twenty-seven rows back, that the three Swedish boys wandering down the aisle wearing green, 40-centimetre-high, plush-velvet leprechaun hats will occupy the row in front of me and drive me mad for the entire flight. They appear unconcerned that the hats are stripping them of the aura of cool they have otherwise accrued by dressing in that modern slacker uniform of baggy cargo pants and oversized Billabong T-shirts, while adopting such a glazed, remote, Bill-and-Ted look that the collective noun for them is most likely a *perplexity* of Swedes.

Of course, maybe they're just incredibly cunning. Given Ryanair's carry-on baggage allowance (if it's over 10 kilograms, it goes in the cargo hold), perhaps they just have extra luggage under the hats. Or alcohol, secreted away for their parents, since booze is so dear in Scandinavia. What a simple ruse – just put your excess baggage on your head, stick on your leprechaun hat and pay nothing extra. Instead of weighing all my underwear to find the lightest (a pair of chain-store boxers; Calvins are a full 20 grams heavier), I could simply have decanted the entire drawer into a baseball cap and fetched up looking like a Conehead. If I'd borrowed a hat from a Smurf, I could have brought a set of golf clubs with me.

The families are already on board, after smugly brushing past us ('Look! We had sex and bunked the queue!'), but instead of congregating in a way that would be considerate to other passengers, they spread themselves around the plane like masts offering optimum coverage for a mobile-phone network, with squealing replacing ringtones. It is bedlam.

Today, there's a gurgling infant in 8D. In 11B, there's an evil three-year-old with ringlets, who smiles at her parents but, the moment they turn away, fixes me with a lopsided, *Omen*-like smirk that intimates the sacred daggers of Megiddo are about to lunge from the slot usually occupied by the oxygen mask and fillet my cerebral cortex like sushi. Back in 19E, an eight-year-old boy detached for just fifteen minutes from his Sony PSP has started to kick the seat in front of him – and across the aisle in 26C is an obese girl in a Playboy-logo crop-top who already looks faintly green and who, at cruising altitude, reminds us with some force that she had three packets of Hula-Hoops and a gallon of Fanta for breakfast.

Unsettled by the staring girl, I nurse a single can of Amstel all the way to Gothenburg City Airport. Landvetter is the city's main hub and the one still used by the airlines that give you an assigned seat and a free newspaper that really costs you ninety quid. But City is nearer to town, the landing fees are lower, the staff (I think his name was Ingmar) are much nicer – and it's a classic example of the Ryanair effect. Before the airline commenced operations here in 2001, the airport handled about 9,000 passengers a year, mostly people arriving on private jets. Now, 500,000 passengers and two more airlines (Wizzair and Germanwings) pass through, and there are flights to Dublin, Stansted, Glasgow, Frankfurt-Hahn, Cologne, Budapest and Warsaw.

Like so many such airports, the quirkiness is charming. At the end of the runway, there is a Wild West-style riding school, boasting a paddock filled with horses that whinny and bolt as the plane touches down. One wing of the terminal seems to be made from a B&Q party tent, but the practical side of not having to negotiate a big airport – nowadays, they're department stores with departure gates – is that we're off the plane, onto the Flygbussarna bus, into the central station and checked into our hotel within fifty minutes. It is amazingly quick, given that some Ryanair destinations, such as Vienna, are served by airports in different *countries* (Bratislava in next-door Slovakia), never mind within the same municipality.

The hotel, the First G at the train station, is the usual Swedish mix of blond wood, crisp cotton and dramatic accent prints and, with a full buffet breakfast, costs just €113 for a double room. I need a double because, as this is the first nervous footstep on my trek across Ryanland, Sharon, my wife, has selflessly volunteered to come along for moral support. Gothenburg is a delight and also turns out to be the McDonald's capital of the world – the golden arches pop up everywhere. In the giant Nordstan Shopping Centre alone, there are three, occupying prime sites on the cruciform crosswalks. We sadly succumb, piling in some ballast, because our next stop is an Irish pub.

Munster is playing Biarritz in the final of the Heineken European

Cup, so we dash to the Auld Dubliner on Ostra Hamngatan where the RTÉ coverage is being shown. There, we find dozens of fans wearing sweaty red nylon-and-Spandex shirts that are too tight for them, knocking back half the annual output of the Guinness brewery and cheering their vocal cords raw for the Irish side – and, in a corner, two Frenchmen in their early twenties, dressed in shirts with button-down collars, crisply creased trousers and Gucci-style loafers, urging on their own heroes. They look like two bankers who have accidentally called in at the Ballinasloe Horse Fair.

Within three minutes, Biarritz upset the script and score a try. The French boys celebrate so noisily, a man leans over to me and says, 'Fuckers! Could they not find a French pub?' But later, Munster come good and, after a nail-biting series of counter-attacks is convincingly repelled, they are champions of Europe. Leinster is my home province, but such a win by any Irish team means a night of celebration, so we move to O'Leary's Irish Bar and Restaurant, where the Eurovision Song Contest pops up on the screens.

Over the coming weeks and months, I will visit most of the countries competing here. The contest simply serves to fill me with trepidation, reminding me that Europe can also be a scary place, full of men with mullets and wearing sleeveless T-shirts bought for about €6 in Lidl.

Middle-aged men from Lithuania, sharply dressed like the cast of *Reservoir Dogs*, sing, 'We are the winners of Eurovision, vote for us' – Ireland later does just that, giving them its maximum twelve points, mostly because all of Lithuania, excepting the six on stage, now actually lives in Ireland and hijacked the phone vote.

A cheer goes up in the pub for Carola, the Swedish entrant, who won once before, fifteen years ago, with a song called 'Sturmwind', the Swedish for Stormwind. I remember her – she was a cracker then but I fear she's been at the smorgasbord ever since and spent too much time at the bread end of the trestle table and not enough at the fish. She has big, highlighted hair and her make-up is too dark. I ask the people at the next table how old she is and they say they think she's forty. 'She looks well on it,' I lie. Christ, she could play Aslan in *The Lion, the Witch and the Wardrobe*.

A stag party arrives and all the men are dressed as women. Not in that vampish, drag-queen way, but in frocks that haven't seen the light of day since, well, since Carola was in kindergarten. As I stand at the urinal, one of these grannies comes in, lifts her skirt and what appears to be a petticoat (and a petticoat, I think, crosses the fine line between fun and transvestism), and is just about to go about her business when she falls over backwards and, after muttering in a language I don't recognise, passes out cold. The view, briefly, is like *The Crying Game* remade by geriatrics. Two other grannies pick her up and take her out to play pool, where she manages to fall over again. A New Zealander who looks like Miss Marple laughs and says, 'Bloody Hungarians – can't take their drink!' and the granny is carried by two of her mates into the Gothenburg night.

Finland wins the Eurovision. A band called Lordi, dressed as cadavers, sings of 'Hard Rock Hallelujah'. We have come a long way since an eighteen-year-old Dana sat on a stool and sang about 'All Kinds of Everything' – and I imagine Lordi's definition of all kinds of everything is slightly more catholic than Dana's, who served a term as an MEP at the European parliament and showed herself to be Catholic with a *C* as big as the one that used to be on the Eiffel Tower when it bore a neon sign that spelled out Citroën.

The things that made Dana think of her sweetheart were wishing wells, wedding bells and early-morning dew. Next morning, Sharon and I are up early enough to actually see the early-morning dew as we take a boat tour of Gothenburg, which reveals itself as a very handsome city. The boat, wide and very low, with an open top, is called a *paddan*, so now I know a second Swedish word – toad. At one bridge, nicknamed the Cheese Slicer, the clearance is mere centimetres and we all have to lie on the ground to pass beneath, an unnervingly claustrophobic experience. We tour what was once the city moat and I decide I like it all so much I will return. 'You're going to dozens of cities,' Sharon cautions. 'You can't like them all.'

I put her on the bus back to City Airport while I take the train to Stockholm, almost 500 kilometres away. And I think, she's right, isn't she? I can't possibly like them all. Because even though I don't plan to be there for months yet, I already have a bad feeling about Luton…

Soon, I am reclining in my chair, surfing the internet wirelessly on my laptop and listening to a Hôtel Costes compilation on my iPod. I am on the Plateau of Chilled. In the distance, I am vaguely aware of a ringing noise. Suddenly, at least eight people are staring at me. Actually, wrong word – they're glaring at me. One of them leans into my face. 'This is a quiet zone,' he says rather loudly in perfect English. 'You must switch off your phone.'

Welcome to the X2000, Sweden's high-speed train, which travels at 200 kilometres per hour, tilts quite alarmingly as it rounds corners, and doesn't dare emit so much as a clickety-clack in case the passengers stop it and beat the living shit out of it. I bought an hour's worth of wi-fi 'internet ombord' but am now too terrified to continue using it, in case hitting the laptop keys has me reported to the quiet-zone police. What I can't quite understand is why quiet on the train is so important. Sweden is quiet anyway. Look out the window and all you see are fir trees and lakes. Not noisy, lots-of-jet-skis lakes either – just endless stretches of tranquil water. It is incredibly tedious, like spending three hours in the picture on a jigsaw puzzle, looking for the fern that completes the forest.

If I were a Swede travelling regularly to Stockholm from Gothenburg, I'd want a disco train, with thumping house music and glitter balls in every carriage, gun turrets on every railcar so I could shoot at trees and bother wildlife, and rocket launchers to lob ordnance at lakes. Instead, I see a reindeer, a field of Shetland ponies, a lot of wooden houses painted red and then the whole lot again in a different order.

I have taken the train because while I must fly either into or from Ryanland airports, my own rules of engagement do not compel me to do both. In fact, my own rules of engagement are just that – mine – and therefore are as flexible as I want to be. But here, the train is so expensive – over €90 for this one-way trip – that I could have saved money by flying from Gothenburg to Stansted and back to Skavsta. It would have been more scenic too.

I love the cities but, otherwise, Sweden is jaw-slackeningly dull. Stare out the window for too long and drool drips from your chin, like an old person plonked in a wheelchair in the conservatory of a nursing home, contemplating the world beyond. On the Ryanair website, one of the package holidays on offer is described thus: 'Six Days Tour of Historical Mining and Metal Production in Sweden. Thematic tour including visits to Sala silver mine, Avesta twentieth-century iron works, Norberg medieval mining area and the world heritages of Engelsberg Ironworks and Stora Kopparberget copper-mining area.' I would sooner invite Kathy Bates around with two blocks of wood and a lump hammer.

I arrive in Stockholm and check into the Rica Hotel Kungsgatan. I booked the room on hotels.com and, to save money, clicked yes to one without a window. The downside is that I now feel hemmed in; the upside that there is no danger of having to look at more trees.

Out on the street, what is remarkable is that Swedes in Sweden don't look like Swedes on the Costa del Sol in the summer. There, they have skin the colour of Ryvita and are enviably blonde; here, they look just like we do. Perhaps only the top 10 per cent of very fit Swedes – 'fit' in the modern sense – are allowed leave the country while the rest spend June, July and August counting Shetland ponies beside glassy lakes in the middle of nowhere and saying ssshhhh! to each other.

After a long walk, what should I happen upon but another Dubliner bar, the sister, it turns out, of the one in Gothenburg. I have two pints of Eriksberg beer, which I discover to my cost is 5.3 per cent alcohol by volume. On a big screen, Sweden are playing the Czech Republic in the final of the World Ice Hockey Championship. I'm not a hockey fan so I decide this might be a good time to eat and settle myself at the bar of TGI Friday's across the road, where the game also holds everyone rapt.

I order fajitas – 'when in Rome', I say to myself for no reason, and start giggling uncontrollably. The Eriksberg is doing its job. As a couple of pints of Carlsberg follow and Sweden go 2–0 up, life has become very pleasant. As the third goes in, hockey is my new favourite sport and I join the rest of the bar in a round of applause and order another beer. When they score a fourth, I hear a basso-profundo roar that turns into a girlish shriek, and realise to my horror I have made the noise myself…

'Where's this taking place?' I ask.

'White Russia,' says the barman.

'Ah, Belaroosh,' I say, astonished that I am now slurring.

'Actually, where's Riga?' he asks, a hint of hesitation creeping into his voice.

'Latvia.'

'Well, it's there then.'

Now forgive me, but when the Soviet Union fragmented, the future of Europe was far from assured and Sweden's proximity to the Baltic states might have left it imperilled. Yet its young people still don't know the difference between Belarus and Latvia? I wouldn't trust them with a vote in Eurovision.

Soon, Sweden has won the hockey. Jönsson is hugging Samuelsson, Lunqvist is high-fiving Holmqvist, and the restaurant empties in seconds – all that noise has them sprinting for their quiet zones.

I should go home but I remember the Berns Hotel is around the corner. I was last here in 2000 as a guest at the after-party following the MTV Europe Music Awards. Back then, we were greeted by fire-eaters and trapeze artists, and we were amused by the irony of dancing in the grand salon to the Abba tribute band, Björn Again, in the country that gave us the original. Tonight, the hotel is quiet. Built by Heinrich Berns, it opened in 1863 and enjoyed mixed fortunes until it was fully restored in the 1990s under the watchful eye of Habitat guru Terence Conran. It is effortlessly elegant in an overblown, gilded, rococo kind of way, a hybrid of chandeliered opulence and sleek irony.

On the first-floor balcony, a DJ is playing at the outdoor bar. There is only one stool and it is already occupied, so I stand and have a Spendrup's. And another. And again. I worried that I might not be tolerated in jeans, but as more people drift in from Berzelii Park, they are progressively scruffier; I suspect they have spent a lot of money dressing down, paying other people to scuff their hems for them. I'm tired of standing and beginning to feel the effects of all that beer. My eyes light on two chrome and leather stools in the distance, but as I make a bolt for one of them, the meaty forearm of a bouncer blocks my path.

'Where are you going?' he asks.

'To get one of thosh schtools.'

He looks at his pal and they crack up laughing.

'Those stools, Sir, are ice buckets.'

My shame is palpable. In Sweden's best-known designer hotel, a stopping-off point for Europe's new celebrity royalty, I have been exposed as an unsophisticated arriviste who can't identify a designer ice bucket at 20 metres. Head hung, I slink back to my windowless, lifeless, airless, joyless room and lapse into a drunken coma.

Next morning, I take the bus to Djurgården, to visit the Vasamuseet, my favourite museum in the world. The *Vasa* was a wooden warship commissioned by King Gustavus II Adolphus and designed to send terror straight to the aortas of Sweden's arch-enemies (like, doh, Latvia and White Russia, dude). But on 10 August 1628, just 1,300 metres after it left its moorings on its maiden voyage, a gust of wind blew the ship over and it sank with the loss of fifty lives. We are not talking about the high-point of maritime engineering here.

It stayed on the seabed for 300 years before it was located and raised, and it now sits in a darkened, humid, harbourside museum. It is pulse-quickeningly impressive and evocative – you can practically smell the gunpowder. Do yourselves a favour; if you have kids, postpone Disneyland in Paris and bring them here instead. No pirate of the Caribbean could compete with the awe you feel looking at a real ghost ship.

Across the road is Skansen, founded by Artur Hazelius in 1891. It's an outdoor museum that charts the history of the country through genuine period homes and public buildings transported from all over Sweden and Norway. Bringing lots of different house styles together and displaying them in one place? It's no wonder a Swede invented IKEA.

I was in Skansen before, in mid-winter, and found it deserted and spooky. There are bears and wolves in the park. What, I worried, if they escaped their enclosures and stalked me, playfully passing my extremities between them like the batons in a relay race? I ran from the place and vowed to return some distant summer – and today, it is as it should be, dappled with May sunshine, full of laughing children and adoring parents. And the bears I once feared are timid to the point of torpor, in a pen that's too small for them and betraying signs of stereotypical behaviour.

Strangely saddened, I leave for Skavsta, like so many Ryanair out-posts it's a former military airbase that is actually 100 kilometres from the city it serves. On the eighty-minute bus journey, all I can see are more bloody trees, except for one small slip-up when we flash past something that looks suspiciously like a farm. I am doubly perplexed. Why did the bin in my hotel room have three sections for recycling when there is enough wood here to gift-wrap Jupiter...? After a row over the weight of my bag (if a woman's handbag doesn't count, neither should my laptop), I bid Sweden goodbye. Changing cultures like a pair of socks, I am off to the bosom of *la douce France*.

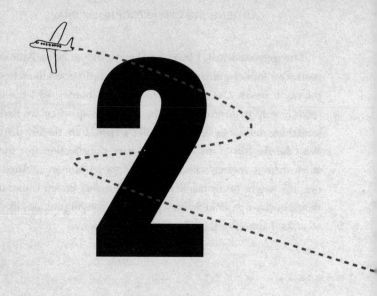

PARIS BEAUVAIS

FR9503

Stockholm Skavsta (NYO) to Paris Beauvais (BVA)

1,410 km

€43.01

I first flew to Beauvais with Ryanair in 1999. Later, when I bought a holiday home in Normandy, it became my local airport, in the way most Ryanair airports are local – which is to say it was 160 kilometres from where I would have liked it to have been. I see from my flight log (rather sadly, I meticulously have kept this since that first flight to Barcelona) that I have passed through Beauvais Airport, whether arriving or leaving, forty-two times, yet I have always driven straight past the town. Usually a *toutes directions* kind of guy, tonight I'm off to the *centre ville*...

This proves not to be a good time for wandering, though. It is chucking it down with rain, a virtually permanent state of affairs in northern France, so I take refuge in a clean if unimaginative two-star hotel, Le Cygne – a snip at €47 – and am told that the best place still open for food at nine o'clock on a Monday night is yet another Irish bar, imaginatively called l'Irlandais. I ask for a pizza and a *seize*, and the big surprise is that a 20-centimetre goat's cheese pizza, a massive side salad and, ultimately, two pints of Kronenbourg 1664 (*seize*, or sixteen, for short), cost just €14. You'd pay more than that holding on the phone for a reservation in Dublin or London.

A Frenchman at the bar starts talking to me – there are just the two of us there. When asked, I say, 'Je suis irlandais', but, like most French, he thinks I have said *hollandais* – because I can't make that phlegmy 'errrr' sound in *irlandais* convincingly unless I run out of Benylin – and starts asking about Amsterdam. Once I clear up the confusion, he gets very animated. He used to work in Dublin and loved it but cannot remember where he lived. As we chat, it becomes obvious he can't, in fact, remember anything about the city at all, in a way that suggests he actually was never there. More pertinently, he is also now looking at me in an unnerving way.

'Vous êtes de Beauvais?' I venture, unsurprised to note a slight wobble in my voice.

'Non,' he says, 'Paris.'

'Ah, mais vous travaillez ici, peut-être?'

'Non.'

We sit in silence but still he smiles at me with the unembarrassed enthusiasm of a child regarding a puppy; if he peeled back his lapel to unveil an 'I'm a serial killer' badge, I couldn't be less surprised. Even the Kronenbourg is not anaesthetising me to the fact that peril is in the air.

After making a series of grand gestures – dramatically pulling back the cuff of my sweater, deliberately widening my eyes as I look at my watch, muttering something about it being *trop tard*, in short, everything a pantomime Frenchman would do short of bellowing, '*Mon Dieu, est-ce que c'ést l'heure?*!' – I bid him *bonne nuit* and he says *à bientôt* but, as far as I'm concerned, there won't be a next time.

As I walk back to the hotel (that's actually a lie – I break several records in the inexplicably deleted Olympic discipline of Covering 200 Metres On A Deserted Street While Looking Backwards Over Your Shoulder), I bemoan the fact that the French work fewer hours than anyone in Europe yet seem to go to bed earlier than everyone excepting two-year-olds on Christmas Eve. If the nuclear reactor up the road at Paluel had just issued a red alert, the place couldn't be any more eerily devoid of what the rest of western Europe broadly categorises as normal human life. Of course, they're all inside, eating six-course meals, drinking Haut-Médoc and peering occasionally through the shutters for long enough to report to the rest of the family that another foreigner is hurtling down the street backwards – 'Champagne, maman,' a voice will say, 'ze looper has found eemself anothayre victeem.'

Oh well, at least my heart rate has gone so high it sluices the cholesterol, caffeine and alcohol from every artery in my body and I sleep soundly. I am up at seven and back at Beauvais-Tillé Airport just twelve hours after arriving. As ever, it is chaotic. The terminal is a large marquee with four departure flaps; leaving it is like running away *from* the circus. No one ever tells you which flap to queue at, so when a plane lands, there is always a stampede.

Though we are supposed to board in sequence – 1–90 first, then 91–189 – it all looks like the Maginot Line the day after the Germans snuck around it. The gate personnel affect a collective shrug that suggests they would prefer to be harvesting organs from live children instead of directing the uncivilised hordes to a plane. I take a deep breath and patiently stand my turn. It is time to go to Porto.

PORTO

FR9134

Paris Beauvais (BVA) to Porto (OPO)

1,240 km

€132.36

I am curled up in seat 29A (well, contorted would be a better word – Ryanair's non-reclining seats are the very opposite of comfortable), finishing the most fascinating book, *Citizen Coors* by Dan Baum. It's the story of the American brewing family, their almost perverse resistance to modern marketing and their slavish fondness for a brand of conservatism that saw them boycotted by just about every minority imaginable – African-Americans, trade unionists, gay men and registered Democrats (though on Planet Coors, the latter two categories seem to have been taken as synonymous). All of this is hugely diverting, though it has nothing to do with my journey – it's just that the book has been on five holidays with me already and I can no longer justify its drain on my baggage allowance.

As I read the last line, I look out the window and see Porto unfold before me. Ribeiro, the old town, sits lazily in the shadow of Téophile Seyrig's Dom Luís I steel bridge. Downriver, the white Arrábida Bridge, the last one before the Douro joins the Atlantic, glints in strong sunshine. But, soon after we overfly Boavista's football stadium and line up for landing, there is a roar and we are gaining altitude again. For five minutes, no one says a word – they are too busy counting each other's new grey hairs. My hands look like they're attached to a pneumatic drill; this whole project is, in retrospect, utterly perverse when undertaken by a man who is terrified of flying.

The captain finally comes on the blower. 'Ladies and gentlemen, as you may have noticed, we are making what we call a go-around. We were within 500 feet of the runway when an unusually large flock of birds flew across, so we will attempt to land again.' I have had maybe six go-arounds in twenty-eight years of flying (memorably, in Copenhagen in 1988, the captain couldn't be sure if the landing gear was up or down and we had to fly past the control tower so they could perform a visual – my, what fun *that* was), yet this is my second in a month. Just three weeks ago, on a Qantas flight from Sydney to Melbourne, we shot skyward and were told by the first officer that an earlier flight had, I swear to God, 'hit a rabbit' and 'we're just going round while they clean it off the runway'.

What a preposterous excuse. My eight-year-old Saab could hit a deer and reduce it to a thin film of fur on the hard shoulder, yet I'm expected to believe an Airbus 330 couldn't vaporise two buck teeth, one set of big ears and a bobbly tail? For Christ's sake, by 1910, Australia had built three rabbit-proof fences that ran for 3,256 kilometres, and you tell me that, a whole century later, they can't isolate the runway in Melbourne with a bit of chicken wire? Imagine if these people had been in charge of fencing off the paddocks at the riding school in Gothenburg – we probably would have hit a horse.

I contemplate all of this as we bank sharply over the sea and line up again. Téophile Seyrig's two-tier masterwork looks as lovely as ever, the Arrábida Bridge still thrums with reflective energy, the BFC pattern on the stadium seating alerts me to the fact that we are over Boavista once again. I am humming 'I Got You Babe' and thinking *Groundhog Day* when a chilling thought hits me. What if the birds are still there? What if the evil little bastards are *waiting* for us? What if one has rounded up all the others and is asking, right, when the big one comes round again, which of you is *man* enough to take her? I close my eyes in terror and open them only when a gentle bump says we are back on the ground.

Porto Airport is light, modern and airy. The European Under-21 Football Championship kicks off today in this northern region of Portugal, and huge infrastructure has been put in place. Sadly, the Metro line to the city is still a week away from completion and I am ready to sneer until I remind myself that Dublin's millennium project, the Spire – a 120-metre stainless-steel needle in the middle of O'Connell Street, only mildly ironic in the city that was once the heroin capital of Europe – wasn't completed until 2003. At least on the Iberian peninsula, they were sufficiently energised to actually put a name on *mañana*.

My hotel, the Dom Henrique, is typical of many built in Portugal in the 1970s, heavily influenced by Oscar Niemeyer's brutish work in Brasilia. It is all unvarnished concrete, unimaginative mosaic walls and interior décor straight from a cheap 1970s porn movie (indeed, spending a night at the finest example of the genre, Niemeyer's own Casino Park Hotel in Madeira, is like being an extra in *Boogie Nights*).

The Dom's website says it was built, and I quote, with 'input from some of Portugal's top architects'. I don't know about you, but when I see three words as vague as 'input', 'some' and 'top' in the same sentence, it makes me think the hotel was really drawn on the back of a fag packet by a man who had just lost his glasses, and the 'input' from 'some' of Portugal's 'top' architects was a collective snigger. I booked the hotel because the Bar Anrrique, 54 metres up on the seventeenth floor, enjoys views over the city – and when I get there, I feel quite sure that if I peer into the far distance, I might even see the 1980s on the horizon.

Porto (the English like to call it Oporto, as if it was an Irish surname) was once known as Portucale and gave its name to the entire country and, more famously, to port wine. It was also the birthplace of Prince Henry the Navigator, the self-same Dom Henrique who lent his name to my hotel. Henry was obsessed with sailing so far south in Africa that he would miss out the marauding Moors completely, and men under his command eventually did so, reaching present-day Sierra Leone. This was achieved thanks to the development of the caravel, a square-rigged ship with a lateen sail that could tack against the wind. Sailors had long since solved the problem of getting to anywhere they wanted – now, at last, they had found a way to come back.

Henry's sailors also colonised Madeira, Porto Santo, the Azores and the Cape Verde Islands, and this success sparked a wave of empire building that saw the royal houses of Europe break open the Crayola box and colour in the map of the world.

From the heart of the old town at Ribeiro, I board a tourist boat and we head off at a clip to the mouth of the Douro. We are sailing into the sun, and it plays on the whitecaps created when the incoming tide meets the fast-flowing river, turning the horizon into a dazzle of diamantes. It looks like the sequinned curtain about to go up on a glitzy revue; if I didn't know what lay beyond, I guess that, just like Henry, I would have investigated too.

I eat lunch in the A Marina restaurant, and resist the temptation to have the 'rice with selfish' (though given the fact that I'm dining alone, I might have got away with it). Instead, I start with six mussels on the half shell, covered in chopped tomatoes, onions and coriander, and swimming in olive oil, with crusty bread on the side. For mains, I have a whole grilled daurada with potatoes and side salad (and believe me, the last time anyone did anything this wicked with a fish, it was Tom Hanks in *Splash*), and follow it with an almond tart for dessert. I wash all this down with a half-bottle of Planalto Vinho Branco Seco, a 2004 reserva – then, because you really have to, I ask for a port to finish, and am served a bottle of Croft cunningly disguised as a glass. In Dublin, I reckon the lunch would be €40; in Porto, it costs just €23.

I wander around the old town in a very mellow frame of mind. It's a UNESCO World Heritage Site but it's not in a great state of repair. Many buildings lie empty, and most look precarious. I'm all for faded grandeur, but here it seems to have crossed that line into unfettered decay.

Porto was never conquered by the Romans or the Moors and, after repelling the Napoleonic armies, it was given the title *A Cidade Invicta* – the Unvanquished City. Now time may triumph where mortal armies failed. Saving Porto will cost a fortune, but most of the city's budget seems to have been blown on that light-rail network – and, to be fair, the living still need to get around while we try to preserve what has been bequeathed to us by the dead. Yet I still hope that Porto, a city with the power to bewitch in an instant, continues to do so for generations. And while they're preserving things, maybe they could add the bar at the top of the Dom Henrique to the list.

I go to bed early. Next day, I return directly to Dublin on a flight crewed by a first officer called Dimitri Dimoniov and his helpers Mattheus, Marika, Sada and Krystyna – it's a safe bet Ryanair's recruitment scouts have cast their net a bit farther than Ballyhaunis.

I've been away just five days and already I've flown 5,260 kilometres in a huge arc that has taken me from Scandinavia to the Atlantic seaboard of Portugal. Three countries and five airports into Ryanland, I am hopelessly – maybe naïvely – intoxicated with what lies ahead.

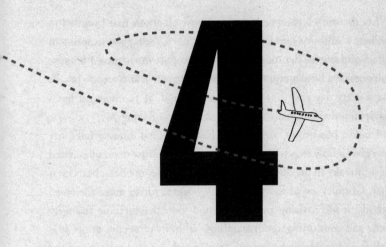

NEWCASTLE-UPON-TYNE

FR172

Dublin (DUB) to Newcastle (NCL)

346 km

€36.13

Thirty minutes after I disembark the Metro from the airport, I am feeling something I cannot put a name on – only later does it dawn on me that this is love at first sight. On this bright, sunny morning, Newcastle is luminous, with gentle hilly streets, softly buffed sandstone streetscapes, two thrilling bridges and an attitude that makes it, in my mind, the most European city in England. And before anyone starts getting shirty, I clearly include its energetic twin city of Gateshead, home to one truly beautiful building and also to one of the ugliest I have ever seen – but more of that later.

My first stop is the one attraction above all others that I wanted to visit here – Antony Gormley's *Angel of the North*, the biggest sculpture in Britain and one of the most viewed pieces of art in the world because (a) it's beside a busy motorway and railway main line and 90,000 people pass it every day and (b) it's 20 metres tall and, at 54 metres, it has a wingspan only marginally smaller than that of a Boeing 747.

I take a bus from Gateshead Exchange and, ten minutes later, my heart gives a little leap when I see the angel for the first time, silhouetted against the sky in the distance. When I get up close, my heart beats even faster. Gormley raked the wings at a 3.5-degree tilt to make the angel look like it was inviting an embrace, and there is something strangely serene and comforting about standing within its protective grasp. It is made from special weather-resistant steel which contains copper, and the original harsh red I remember from media coverage of its inauguration has mellowed. At the base, which has been rubbed by the 400,000-plus visitors who stop at the site every year, it has that deep, red-brown patina of a roasted coffee bean. It is luscious.

When the sculpture was planned, there was a lot of local opposition – some people even thought it would interfere with television reception. To me, it is a tremendous accomplishment, accessible, visible and, yes, stirring. If only all public art fulfilled such simple criteria. And, frankly, I think it would pick up TV signals, not block them – personally, I would have kept schtum, run a scart cable from the angel to my living room and sat back to watch *The Price Is Right* from Tahiti.

Touched by God (or at least one of His helpers), I am off to see mammon in the form of the Metro Centre, Europe's largest shopping mall. And large it is, with a dedicated bus and rail station, all the usual High Street suspects within its precincts and also, unexpectedly, a chapel and a mini-theme park complete with rollercoaster. But it also predates modern shopping-centre design and feels as jaded as week-old lettuce, and it holds my interest long enough only to have a haircut and to buy a few DVDs.

Back in town, I walk from the bus station to the Sage centre on Gateshead Quays, a new music venue with three auditoria, designed by Sir Norman Foster, whose gherkin-shaped HQ for Swiss Re has redefined the City of London. The Sage is bulbous, sheeted in reflective glass and it looks like a giant witchetty grub that has just overfed on a gum tree. Predictably, some Gateshead residents slated the expense of building it, and no doubt tried the same trick of claiming it would block out *Coronation Street* on days when the wind was coming from the southwest – but, yet again, Gateshead Council has got it all audaciously right. This is a brilliant, iconic building. When taken with the Baltic Art Gallery next door and the Millennium Bridge (a winner of the Stirling Prize for Architecture) out front, we're talking a triple-whammy punch with enough clout to define a region, never mind a city.

What they have done here is wonderfully far-sighted. Rivers were once the dirty little secret we had to tolerate, in the years when they were no more than thoroughfares for trade and open sewers. With so many cities now reclaiming their water frontage, whole new patterns of living are evolving. In many places, that just means overpriced apartments and offices above a ground-floor Starbucks and a smoothie bar – but with its high density of public spaces and arts venues, Newcastle/ Gateshead seems to me to be leading the way. From the clean, vertical, concrete lines of the Baltic to the bubbly curves of the Sage, from the pedestrian passenger deck arc of the elliptical bridge to the mixed-height housing development atop the hill, there is a texture here that feels unique and I'm getting higher on the genius of it all by the minute.

At the Baltic, a converted flour mill, there is no permanent collection – the vast space is taken up today by three visiting exhibitions, including one by Sam Taylor-Wood. One of her installations is a video of David

Beckham asleep – in a bed, surprisingly, and not dressed in his England kit and in the middle of a game. The showstopper, though, is her series of photographs of famous actors crying. Not all are successful: Ray Winstone looks like he has a migraine, Steve Buscemi like he forgot to pay the Visa bill. Kris Kristofferson exudes the defeated air of a man who still, three decades on, can't believe he was talked into doing the remake of *A Star Is Born* with Barbra Streisand.

The honours go to the Irish actor Gabriel Byrne, who has a wonderfully craggy face at the best of times. Gabriel looks bereft, as if he just saw a bus filled with sick kids plunge into a crocodile-infested river on the day his Lotto numbers came up but he hadn't bought a ticket because he had to take his dog to be put down. Jude Law, foetally curled up in a corner, looks like he's just been caught out with the nanny. He is crying for himself, while Gabriel looks like he has become a slice of kitchen towel with thirst pockets that are struggling to absorb the pain of the entire world. It is as neat a summary of the difference between a boy and a man as I have ever seen on a single wall and a deeply arresting contrast. I linger for ages, until hunger intrudes and I amble off in search of food.

From the ubiquitous Pitcher and Piano café bar on the Newcastle side of the Tyne, you can take in the whole dazzling quayside panorama. Well, dazzling with one exception. High on a hilltop stands the Gateshead Civic Centre car park designed in the 1960s by the high priest of Brutalist architecture, Owen Luder. There were street parties when Luder's Tricorn shopping centre in Portsmouth was demolished two years ago after being voted the ugliest building in Britain, but the net effect was simply to move his wretched car park up a rung on the ladder. Long slated to face a terminal date with TNT, it has so far been spared because do-gooders who live hundreds of miles from it are demanding that it be preserved as a defining landmark in building history. Movie history too, because it played a vital role in a seminal 1970s Michael Caine actioner and is now known to one and all as the *Get Carter* Car Park.

Its defenders should sit where I'm sitting on this sunny evening, looking at a built environment perfect in every respect except for Luder's monstrous interloper. Like a black hole, it seems to suck in the light reflected by the Sage – it may have looked good once but it has long since turned malevolent. If anyone cared to hand me a hammer, I would happily start chipping away at it myself.

After the Pitcher and Piano, where I try a Newcastle Brown Ale, or Newky Broon, for the first time ('What's it like?' I ask the barman as he pours. 'I don't know, I'm Iranian and I don't drink,' he laughs), I wander aimlessly around a few more bars before returning to my lushly purple, crypto-Gothic quayside hotel, an outpost of the modish Malmaison boutique chain. The first-floor bar windows are open and a warm breeze is blowing through. I find myself a couch covered in crushed velvet and faux fur – it is like snuggling up in Austin Powers' wardrobe. Outside, darkness has tucked Luder's wart away for the night and all that remain visible are the buildings I love. It is a dreamy end to a day of seductively satisfying surprises.

Next morning, I take a last peep at the Tyne Bridge – just like Sydney Harbour Bridge would look if you took both support piers between forefinger and thumb and squeezed the whole structure – and hail a taxi. A businessman asks if he can join me in the trip to the train station and we chat en route about my high-speed jaunt around Ryanland on flights that occasionally cost less than a euro before tax.

As we arrive, he offers me five pounds towards the fare, but I refuse. With a smile, he forces the money into my palm. 'If you won't let me pay for your taxi, then please let me pay for your flights,' he says with a warm smile.

When the English turn on the urbane charm, they are peerless, and it is hard not to love them. His gesture leaves me smiling all the way to the airport and I wonder if I will have to carry the memory even further – for I am off to Norway, a country that carries an intimidating reputation for Calvinist dourness and sky-high prices. I might be glad of the fiver yet.

OSLO TORP

FR1706

Newcastle-upon-Tyne (NCL) to Oslo Torp (TRF)

853 km

£24.30

My fears about Oslo turn out to be unfounded in one instance – and very well founded in the other. The Norwegians, the ones I meet anyway, are anything but dour. In fact, on this sunny, warm day, they are so light-hearted they seem to be skipping along the Karl Johans Gate (*gate* is Norwegian for street, as is *gata*, which applies to a feminine street, presumably one with shoe shops – I'm always terribly grateful we don't do this male–female thing in English). But by God it really is expensive.

It has taken me twenty minutes longer to get here on the coach from Torp than it did to fly to there from Newcastle. The airport in truth serves somewhere called Sandefjord, which sounded so nice I considered abandoning my intention to make for the capital and just go there instead. Now I am glad I stuck with Plan A. I discover that a walking tour of Oslo departs from City Hall at six o'clock, which leaves me just enough time to have a drink at the pavement café of the Grand Hotel. The Grand has been an Oslo institution since 1874. Nobel Peace Prize winners always stay here, as do visiting celebrities – and, indeed, a throng has gathered outside today because King Juan Carlos and Queen Sofia of Spain are in residence.

I order a beer and note the locals looking at me with concern. When I ask for a second, I swear I hear a gasp. When I ask for the bill, a woman behind me blurts out an exhortation that I deduce to be something akin to, 'Will nobody help that poor man?' But it is too late. I have seen the bottom line and I have started to swoon. Beer is the equivalent of €7 a bottle...

The crowd has deepened now, anxious for a glimpse of the royals. Norway's King Harald and Queen Sonja visited Spain in 1995 and tradition has it that a return trip usually follows within five years. But rather salaciously, the heir to the House of Borbón, the Infante Felipe, was knocking off a Norwegian model called Eva Sannum (he has since married a Spanish TV journalist) and the visit was postponed. Officially, it was said Juan Carlos was too busy, but privately it was understood no one fancied more of the tabloid headlines young Felipe's relationship was attracting. If only they had known then who the Norwegian crown prince would marry – but more of that later.

So Oslo is in party mode. The entire length of Karl Johans Gate from the parliament building to the royal palace is decked with pennants in the Spanish colours of red and gold and, opposite where I am sitting, the crowd is photographing anything that moves. There is no sign of the royals, so dozens of Oslonians (I have no idea if that's really what they're called – I just made it up) end up instead with photos of a pale-faced, unshaven Irishman slumping forward and clutching his chest as he is handed a bar tab.

The walking tour is wonderful. The guides are local volunteers and ours is a woman in her sixties called Lise. She starts by telling us how a Danish princess, Margrethe, married Norway's King Haakon. Her father died, she became queen, and being the one with the more prosperous country, she got her mitts on the neighbouring one too. And, as wedding presents go, Norway certainly beats a Breville sandwich toaster. Margrethe's bold move paved the way for Denmark to rule for four centuries, a period known in Norway as the Four-Hundred-Year Night. Danish rule continued until 1814 – or yesterday, as far as the locals are concerned. 'It was not a good time for Norway,' says Lise, a worrying glint entering her eye. She definitely takes it personally, and it is nice to know the Irish are not the only nationality for whom ancient history feels more like current affairs (we gleefully even made Tony Blair apologise for the Great Famine, which ended 100 years before he was born, as if he personally had adulterated every blighted potato).

We pass City Hall, built in a part of town that was once the red-light district. Rather than ignoring this, the city fathers incorporated into the wall a sculpture of a hooker, her pimp and a customer, though they have been sweetened up to look like three actors auditioning for parts in *Mary Poppins*. It is, nonetheless, as unexpected as passing the Beverly Hills telephone exchange and seeing a mural of Charlie Sheen, Heidi Fleiss and a surgically enhanced blonde called Tiffani.

Lise's English is perfect, as it has to be, since on a list of languages you might ever want to study, Norwegian is unlikely to leapfrog any other, with the possible exception of Flemish. Doubly so given that they can't even agree on a written form, so they have two – *bokmål* and *nynorsk*. The key difference appears to be whether you spell a word with two *A*s or the single *Å* character. Frankly, I would have thought the only living creature to give a shit would be the årdvark at Oslo Zoo, but every country is entitled to its little obsessions.

Oslo is squeaky clean, possibly because it is so wealthy. With a 2005 GDP equivalent to US$64,286 per head, it is second in the world only to Luxembourg and way ahead of Ireland (fifth with $48,531) and the UK (thirteenth with $36,599). It tops the UN Human Development Index, a comparative measure of poverty, literacy, education, life expectancy, childbirth and other factors (in this respect, Ireland is eighth, the UK fifteenth). But no country that levies such high taxes on alcohol knows anything about human development, in my book – if I were in charge of the index, I would boot them out of it and tell them not to return until a bottle of Hansa was two quid, tops.

As I walk back to the Hotel Bonderheimen (just 200 metres from Karl Johans Gate yet only €104 a night), I see a bit of a kerfuffle and here, from the side door of the Grand Hotel, emerge not just the King and Queen of Spain but Harald and Sonja too, with their son, Crown Prince Haakon, and his rather tasty missus, Princess Mette-Marit, every tabloid editor's dream. She was a single mother when she met Haakon, and her son's father was once convicted of buying cocaine. Foreign newspapers dined out on every morsel of the tale for weeks, but the sensible Norwegians – for most of the year far too chilly to be prurient – took it all in their jaunty stride and she is now a much-loved member of the family, certainly if the cheers from the crowd are anything to go by.

But as a resolute republican (with a small '*r*', an important distinction in Ireland), I find the whole scene completely pitiful. Imagine if Europe's top companies – Nokia, Royal Dutch Shell, Vodafone, BMW, Philips and so forth – were all run by chief executive officers thus anointed at birth. Shareholders would desert them in droves. Yet modern European countries still select their leaders from a gene pool so shallow that Prince Haakon, first in line to his own country's throne, is also sixty-first in line to the *British* one. I find it unfathomably stupid, but the people surrounding me clearly adore them and, as monarchies go, Norway's is progressive, so I dismount my high horse and decide to leave them all to it.

It is now 11.18 p.m., the temperature still reads 16 degrees and it is as bright as the afternoon, giving a slight lie to the claim that Norway ever had a Four-Hundred-Year Night. I can't sleep unless it is dark outside so, like Dracula in reverse, I roam the streets until night finally falls. I pop in to the Eilefs Landhandleri, Spiseri, Pub Og Dansesalong, which, despite the long and funky title, is just a bar with a dance floor, currently being hogged by one couple who are gifted at remembering precise mathematical patterns of movement and think this means they can dance. They can't, because if the DJ was playing Rolf Harris or Radiohead, they would not vary the routine by a single backhand clasp – and they are as distracting as grit in my eye, so I move on.

Ett Glass, which translates as 'a glass', is to be my last stop. I order a pint of Ringnes and am no longer shocked when asked for the kroner equivalent of €9. The barman, who is not wearing a balaclava and brandishing a musket, has the good grace to be borderline embarrassed – so much so that after I order a second, he throws in a third for free, bringing down the average cost to €6. I ask if it ever gets dark. 'Oh, yes,' he smiles. 'In winter, it doesn't get bright until eleven and it's dark again by three.'

I'm amazed the Norwegians are not more morose; they must have body clocks so adept at bending to circumstance they could have been painted by Salvador Dalí. I end up liking them and their capital city, and put it down to some sort of stored genetic empathy; it would, after all, be hard to come from Dublin, a city founded by the Vikings, and not be a little Norse myself. I like the way they're resolute, the way they face up to nature head-on. Even when snow blankets the country, they have a rhyming proverb that translates as: 'There's no such thing as bad weather – only bad clothes.'

Advice worth remembering as I am to depart the next day for Scotland, the birthplace of golf, which has given us more bad clothes than any sport in history.

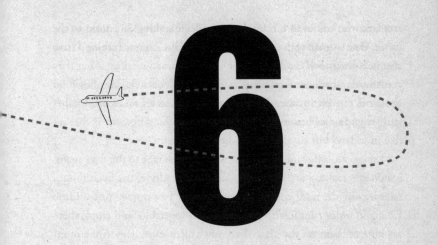

GLASGOW PRESTWICK

FR7803

Oslo Torp (TRF) to Glasgow Prestwick (PIK)

977 km

€55.64

My plan was to hire a car and drive to Glasgow – but when I arrive, western Scotland is ablaze with June sunshine and once I discover that Loch Lomond is only a ninety-minute drive away, I decide that is where I will head. I have, after all, been to Glasgow before, most recently last year for a riotous christening party that threatened to run all the way to the child's first birthday.

But first I need to urgently check some e-mails, so I take a detour to Kilmarnock, where I ask half a dozen people if they know anywhere that offers wireless broadband access. They look at me as if I'm the stranger who comes to a Transylvanian village seeking directions to the castle. One woman stares and actually says, 'Oh, I'm not sure we'd have *that* in Kilmarnock', as if wi-fi were virginal human sacrifice – but they actually do, because I eventually find a McDonald's. The fast-food chain has proven a godsend many times before, as it has one of Britain's and Ireland's most extensive wi-fi networks – the difference is that it's free in Ireland but costs a fiver an hour in Britain.

I stagger a coffee until my work is done, then take to the road again. I suddenly realise I am starving, which is a bit silly of me five minutes after leaving the motherlode of comfort food. I eventually find a Little Chef and order panini with Mediterranean vegetables and chips; there are nine of them on the plate. Two other silent diners are in the room and three equally silent staff are watching us all eat. It is definitely a meal for fuel and not fun for, if you had the choice, you would linger longer at a leprosy mission.

When I reach the shores of the loch, the dying sun has painted the water a mauve-tinged silver. There are pine-covered islets dotted throughout and midges everywhere. It is as quintessentially Scottish as Irn-Bru and it is, in a word, lovely.

At Luss, I find the Lodge on Loch Lomond, a three-star hotel. A room, I am told, is £140, or €203, which is a bit ripe when you consider I paid just half that last night for a room in Oslo, capital of the dearest country in Europe. Hotel accommodation in these islands is wildly overpriced, and I decide to take a stand and press on to find a cheaper berth. Sense prevails. Seeing that business is about to walk out the door and taking account of my protest that I am on my own, the duty manager magically drops the rate to £80, a 42 per cent saving on the original price. So, no matter where you are, haggle.

My room turns out to be well worth it. It is in a new wing and has a balcony looking out across the loch and I sit there until it gets dark,

quietly seduced by some of the most magical scenery you will find anywhere. And, perhaps because I seem to have spent the whole week
drinking and am now pickled in alcohol, even the midges decide to
leave me alone.

Next morning, after a massive fried breakfast that leaves me wondering
if I will fit behind the wheel of my hired Kia Picanto, I wander around
Ayr, a handsome town with attractive cut-stone houses, before
descending into the hell of Prestwick. My flight is delayed an hour, the
first hiccup on my travels – whatever else you say about Ryanair service,
its punctuality is seldom in question. Today marks the start of the World
Cup in Germany and the airport is full of Scots wearing Trinidad and
Tobago shirts, heading off to support that team. Six of its members
play for local sides, one of them is actually called Scotland (Jason
Scotland of St Johnstone) and, crucially, they are in England's group. If
Scotland can't be there to thrash the Auld Enemy, perhaps the Soca
Warriors will do so by proxy.

On the flight, I meet a couple who are flying to Dublin to see
Robbie Williams later tonight at Croke Park, then flying home tomorrow.
Ryanair makes such frivolous jaunts possible, and it seems many people
have had the same idea. It's not just Robbie who is playing this weekend,
though – Eagles, Metallica, Guns N' Roses, Mark Knopfler and Emmylou
Harris are all drawing the crowds too. A total of 235,000 tickets have
been sold for the weekend's gigs and it seems like every last ticketholder
is in Dublin Airport. One man tells me later that he enquired after hotel
accommodation at the tourist office and was asked if he would consider
Galway, 225 kilometres away.

This is also my first exposure to the airport's new temporary departure
gates. Thanks largely to Ryanair, Dublin Airport has seen passenger
numbers grow to 20 million a year, five times the population of the
republic. Trouble is, it was designed to cater for about two-thirds that

number, so it has grown in a higgledy-piggledy fashion that defies logic. The new additions may not exactly be Hell, but they make a bloody good Purgatory. So far from the arrivals hall they are virtually in another county, they are an insult to foreign visitors and I find it hard to believe that anyone in authority here has ever flown at all.

Cursing, I take my place in a taxi queue that looks like the evacuation of Saigon. I think it is nice to be home, but I can't be sure.

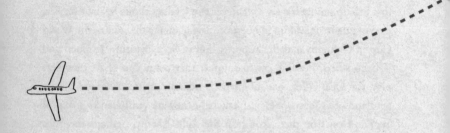

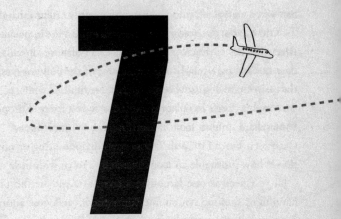

SALZBURG

It is 250 years since the birth of Mozart and Salzburg is squeezing the anniversary for all it is worth. Indeed, if a cow were milked this incessantly, it would have udders like Cheestrings. Mozart is everywhere – on banners, on flags, on wimples, in shop windows. You can buy chocolate pianos and liqueurs with his face on the labels, and, of course, you can line up with half the population of Japan as they take photos of each other queuing to get into the Mozart Gerburtshaus, where the child prodigy was born.

Just a heartbeat away from this singularly unprepossessing shrine to the greatest musical genius in history is an alley called Schmuckspassage, and I am inclined to think this a rather appropriate name for rip-off Salzburg itself (which, incidentally, becomes the rather more prosaic Fortress of

Salt when translated into English – there are ancient mines nearby).

Old Salzburg viewed from the new town on the opposite side of the River Salzach is much prettier than Old Salzburg up close, where it does not feel particularly old at all. Most of the buildings, especially on the main Getreidegasse shopping street, are finished with a plaster render that makes them look not unlike post-war eastern Europe; it's how Fantasyland might look if it had been commissioned by Nicolae Ceausescu instead of Walt Disney. Yet, disappointing or not, Salzburg proves how profitable an icon can be for a town with little else to offer – all you need is one famous son with a talent for the piano and a handful of sublime symphonies in his back catalogue, and you have a must-visit stopover on the musical map of Europe.

Of course, for everyone who comes to listen to the Piano Concerto No. 21 on his iPod as he soaks up what little atmosphere is going a-begging, another is humming 'I Am Sixteen, Going On Seventeen' as she ticks off the locations used in *The Sound of Music*. Salzburg has long been a favourite with set-jetters, people who fly all over the world to see where their favourite movies were made. Once the current Mozart hoopla dies down, the Salzburghers will no doubt remember that that 2015 sees the fiftieth anniversary of the release of the sickliest movie ever made and melt down all the unsold chocolate Wolfgangs to be remoulded in the image of Julie Andrews.

I am staying at the Hotel Altstadt, which is within walking distance of all the attractions I have suddenly lost interest in. (I do this some-times, and take against a town, just as I champion others that everyone else hates.) One of Salzburg's oldest inns, the Altstadt dates from 1377 – and I fear the curtains may be original. The bar is tiny, and that puts me off, but so too does the scattergun effect of décor that appears to have been assembled during an episode of *Changing Rooms* that was recorded as a politically correct sop to the blind.

As it happens, I am here for professional reasons – among other things, I write about cars, and the European launch of the new Audi TT takes place tomorrow. My attempts to fly here with Ryanair came to naught when the flight schedule didn't suit so, quite frankly, I have cheated, and come with Lufthansa and Austrian Arrows instead. I join colleagues for a splendid dinner at Der Goldener Hirsch, the golden reindeer. If I ever return to Salzburg, it will be for the angelic elixir that is the restaurant's asparagus soup, and Austrian sauvignon blanc that would have you rethink any understandable aversion to white wine.

Next morning, we return to the airport – which, imaginatively, is called the Wolfgang Amadeus Mozart Airport. We are, however, on the opposite side of the runway to the main terminal, at Hangar-7, to pick up our TTs for the drive to our next hotel at Zell-am-See. Hangar-7 was built by Dietrich Mateschitz, the enigmatic entrepreneur behind Red Bull, who turned his caffeine-and-taurine power drink into a €2 billion personal fortune. Whatever about those who drink it, Red Bull has certainly given Dietrich wings – and this is the hangar he houses them in. The Flying Bulls is his pet project, and he and his team number among their many aircraft the Douglas DC-6B that served as Yugoslav despot Marshal Tito's private plane. There are three Alpha Jets bought from the German military, the first to make their way into civilian hands. And there is a B25 Second World War bomber, a Corsair, a Cessna Amphibian seaplane and a handful of helicopters too.

This impressive collection of toys dominates the hangar, a vast steel and glass structure 100 metres long, 67 metres wide and 14.5 metres high. There are 1,754 glass panes held in place by 12,800 pivots and sealed with 16 kilometres of silicone in the joints (if you're trying to figure out just how much silicone that is, let's just say even Jordan is jealous). There is an award-winning restaurant called Ikarus, and for those who truly do want to fly closer to the sun, a bar called Threesixty suspended just below the hangar roof. Accessed via a glass bridge, it also has a glass floor to allow you view the planes from above. As someone who suffers from mild vertigo, the thought of going anywhere near it has me as jangly as a night on the vodka and Red Bulls.

Looking around, I have the vague feeling I've been here before – and then I realise that's only because the whole edifice looks like the baddie's lair in just about every James Bond movie ever made. Throw in the fact that the staff are all as beautiful as Heidi Klum, are dressed in unstructured suits that come in seven shades of grey, and speak in English that is so carefully clipped they seem to be avoiding some mysterious tax on extraneous syllables, and the fantasy is complete.

Fortunately, we are not strapped to tables while lasers take aim at our groins. Instead, we get the keys to our TTs and roar off into neighbouring Germany. I love press launches in Germany, because you can drive like a lunatic and it's still legal – and, at 230 kilometres per hour, I can feel the blood pooling at the base of my skull as I suppress my natural inclination to whoop like a baboon at an orgy.

Soon I have to ease off the TT's pedal because we are back on the chocolate-box Alpine roads of Austria en route to Zell-am-See. Our destination is the Mavida Balance Hotel and Spa, opened late in 2005. The Mavida is just one of hundreds of hotels in a spa archipelago that extends from southwestern Portugal to the Urals; middle-class Europe can think of nothing better to do with its time than be pampered. Sadly, while all of these palaces may appear different, they dispiritingly are all the same, dispensing white fluffy or waffle robes, peddling the rival charms of Carita and Biosel, Dr Hauschka and ESPA, and resting hot stones on the continent's weary spine before kneading and brushing its weary limbs.

Massage is still something of a mystery to me, which is why I mostly avoid it. The first time I had one, at the Breakers Hotel in Florida, I practically glued the elasticated band of my jocks to my waist and practised exercises to stop my heart pumping blood to, well, any part of my body, actually – if necessary, I was prepared to bring gaffer tape to avoid any embarrassment. I was admonished by the masseuse, Claudia ('my friends call me Clouds'), who said I needn't have bothered as she was an expert in wrapping and, frankly, she could have FedExed me from Palm Beach back to Dublin without a square millimetre of flesh on view.

The second time, in the Givenchy Spa at the One&Only St Géran in Mauritius, I was handed what was called a modesty panty, though I remain convinced it was just a sweet wrapper attached to an elastic band. I'm not boasting when I say it wouldn't fit – there are perhaps only half a dozen men on earth with packages so modest that this panty would have conferred immunity from public scorn. Manoeuvring the panty was like playing with an eel. To borrow a metaphor from *There's Something About Mary*, I could just about cover the frankfurter and one bean with it, but if I attempted to shoo the second bean in, the frank fell out. When I had a brainwave and arranged the frank verticaly, flat against my stomach, both beans dropped to opposite sides, leaving the modesty panty looking like a pygmy Wonderbra.

So next time, in the Italian spa town of Fiuggi, I thought to myself, well, these people are Europeans, they're all used to nudity, so I wore nothing under my robe. On command, I dropped it to climb up on the table – and the masseuse started blessing herself and ran from the room throwing a towel at me. I'm going to start a campaign for spa undress codes to be hung above the reception desk, just as soon as I can figure out some appropriate symbols.

So, at Mavida, I decide to forego massage. Instead, I intend to try the flotation tank to see if it can cope with all ninety-five of my kilograms but, alas, it's broken.

'But you can do the Blue Box,' the receptionist says.

'What's that?' I ask.

'It channels your alpha waves,' she says.

'What are they?' I ask.

'They're, um, your alpha waves,' she says, slightly tetchily, in a manner that suggests the German-speaking peoples of the world learn about this sort of thing in kindergarten.

So we make for the Blue Box and find a sculpted, contoured chaise longue. She twiddles a few knobs and blue lights illuminate a circular space hung with shiny net curtains that twitch psychedelically. As she leaves the room, she says, 'You will get more from this without the robe.'

So, having established that every Italian masseuse is indeed on the opposite side of the Alps, I slip it off and lie on my back, naked again, as the lights start to change colour and the chair heats, then cools, then heats again. Suddenly, we are in James Bond territory once more, this time the brainwashing bit in *On Her Majesty's Secret Service*, where Blofeld is attempting to cure an heiress of her aversion to chickens (a small stopover on the road to world domination, obviously, but then even psychopathic megalomaniacs need to chill occasionally).

Two speakers built into the chair's headrest pump out natural sounds I vaguely recognise – water running, whales birthing, a zephyr kissing corn ears and, a wild guess here, calves farting. The chair gets warmer and warmer, and now occasionally vibrates too, which just reminds me how much weight I need to lose as my stomach wobbles like Mariah Carey's tonsils when she hits a high note.

Instead of drifting off to a higher plane, I fumble around in the foothills of the mundane, thinking about the gas bill, my niece's imminent birthday, why no one ever tells Anne Robinson to fuck off on *The Weakest Link*, and how grey my body hair is becoming. Much later, I learn that alpha waves are sounds in the eight-to-twelve decibel range that mimic the electromagnetic pattern of the brain in high creativity mode, promoting mental resourcefulness, boosting the ability to co-ordinate and enhancing the overall sense of relaxation. To be honest, I think I would have performed just as resourcefully after a cup of decent espresso, and I could have kept my clothes on too.

Modestly reinvigorated, I go to bed early to the sound of a massive thunderstorm (delta waves, probably) so I open the curtains and watch for an hour as, one by one, lightning brings the jagged peaks of the Alps into stark relief before they disappear again. It is a thrilling spectacle and might even lay claim to the title of the greatest show on earth were it not for the fact that, for this month anyway, that's actually taking place elsewhere. Yes, tomorrow I'm returning to Germany to join fans from Holland and Argentina as their teams meet in the World Cup.

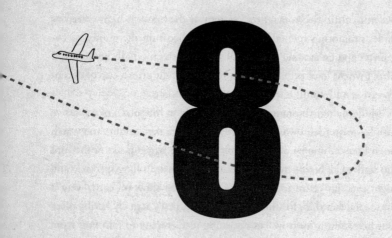

FRANKFURT-HAHN

I have done something very stupid. I've arrived in Frankfurt International Airport with no hotel booked and now find myself competing with every Japp and Jorge for what little cupboard space is left. I start to wander around the terminal to see if there is a World Cup tourist office helping people find beds, and quickly become intrigued by the airport itself, a Kafkaesque warren of tunnels, walkways and escalators heaving with people who, unlike me, appear to know where they're going.

I've transited here many times but never actually ventured forth. Now, I find that the airport, Europe's third busiest after London Heathrow and Charles de Gaulle in Paris, is in fact a medium-sized town with a life all of its own. In a subterranean passage, there is a Chinese restaurant, then an Irish bar, which I find quirky but not totally surprising. No, the surprise comes in the form of a sex shop in the arrivals area.

I know continental Europeans are open about this stuff, but at what point do you ever actually need to use a sex shop in an airport? Do you get a call from a business colleague and hear he's delayed half an hour, or does the monitor alert you to the fact that your parents' holiday charter is running over schedule, and you think to yourself, oh, I know, I'll just kill the time cracking one off in Toss'R'Us? Mesmerised, I amble in and find all the usual stuff – DVDs, toys, magazines, underwear. There are even private video booths, so if you're ever on a delayed flight to Frankfurt and are being met by one of those men who holds a placard bearing your name, for your own sake, don't shake his hand.

Eventually, I find a number and call the local Mercure Hotel, where rooms usually cost around €80 a night. With the football match just hours away and people desperate for accommodation, I expect to pay a premium – but when the reservations clerk asks for an utterly ridiculous €291 for the night, I long to say, 'Look, I only want to sleep in the bed, love, not take it home with me.' In truth, I am too afraid to, in case she tells me to piss off and I have to sleep in a gutter.

After settling in, I take a taxi back to the terminal and from there take a train to the city. I love Germany, because they still make things there, unlike Britain and Ireland, where half of us spend our working days cold-calling the other half, trying to sell ephemeral services none of us needs. Manufacturing industry that produces an end product is all but dead in Ireland – if you want an Intel chip, some Microsoft software or a packet of smoked salmon, we can help, but if you want something with real value, forget it.

It's all so different in Frankfurt. The cars are Audis, Beemers, Volkswagens and Mercs. They build their own trains and buses. The lifts are made by ThyssenKrupp. The bathroom fittings are all Grohe. More to the point, everything works.

I take the S-Bahn train to town. The airport appears to be rather cunningly hidden in the middle of a gloomy forest and the first few stops are obviously for elves and trolls who live there, since doors open and close but no one appears to get on or off. Eventually, we pull to a halt at the station beside the stadium where the match will kick off in two hours (the Commerzbank-Arena has been renamed the FIFA World Cup Stadium Frankfurt for the duration, so as not to offend top-tier sponsors of the overall tournament). Already, it is thronged with fans and I toy with the idea of trying to buy a ticket from a tout, but on the basis of what I've paid for a hotel room, I decide that I cannot afford the hike in my mortgage.

This turns out to be a blessing. The minute I arrive in Hauptwache underground station downtown, I discover an unfamiliar Germany, one with a permanent smile plastered to its face. There are pensioners wearing World Cup tabards, all of them volunteers helping strangers to find their way around, and they do so with patience and an entreaty that you enjoy yourself. On the streets, Argentinians tango, Mexicans salsa, and even the Dutch are singing and dancing along.

In this most beautiful of summers, the sun is shining, the air is crackling with bonhomie and Germany, I think, is having a moment like Ireland had at the Italia '90 World Cup. For different reasons – two lost wars for them, the IRA terror campaign for us – we had each been nervous about celebrating our national identities. The Irish and Germans were not flag-wavers in the way of the French or the English, who even stick the Union Jack on their boxer shorts, then wear them at half mast.

Now, this World Cup is running with predictable precision, Jürgen Klinsmann's home team is having a good run, the football has been of an unusually high standard and the innovation of the Fan Fest in special areas dedicated to feeding and watering those who couldn't get tickets has drawn global praise for its responsible and mature treatment of people who want a few beers and a laugh, two ambitions that don't always have to be confronted by riot police and tear gas.

As I reach the Frankfurt fanzone, I actually get goosebumps. I did my backpacking in my teens and twenties. Later, I did the package stuff (the Costas, the Canaries, the nooks and crannies of the Med) and started to venture further afield, to the States, South America, the Far East, the Indian Ocean, South Africa, Australia. Now, looking at the beer-and-bratwurst tents arranged in an endless ribbon along the River Main against a backdrop of medieval spires and flamboyant skyscrapers behind, watching the barges plying the waterway, hearing the local oompah bands competing with the *bateria* of the Argentinian drums, marvelling at a cliff face of orange shirts where the Dutch have congregated on temporary bleachers, I feel elated in a way I haven't done for thirty years. Europe has me in thrall just as surely as it did in the fiercely hot June of 1976, thirty years ago last week, when I stepped off a ferry in Ostend at the age of thirteen and clapped eyes on it for the very first time.

A huge TV screen has been set up in the middle of the river, and fans in the makeshift grandstands on both banks have gathered in their thousands. The atmosphere is edgy, in a good way. On the screen, a special TV service is playing hits for everyone to sing along to – Queen's 'We Will Rock You' is just one hilarious highlight – and picking out clusters of fans who wave and mouth messages when they see themselves on camera. Suddenly, the screen is filled with an image of an Argentinian fan from neck to stomach only. She is dancing up and down and her unrestrained bosom is hopping around like the balls in a Lotto machine. To a man, the crowd rises to its feet and roars its approval. She jiggles more and the noise becomes deafening. At this stage, her tits

47

are, quite frankly, in a frenzy. People on either side of her are moving away and shielding their children from harm.

Slowly, the camera moves up to her face. I hear the rumble before it erupts and what follows makes me pretty ashamed to be a man. The woman may well be what a friend of mine calls a Bobfoc – Body Off Baywatch, Face Off Crimewatch – but there is still no justification for what happens next. Because the crowd, in unison, literally roars, 'Yuk!' The woman looks like she has been harpooned with a barrel of Botox. Her features freeze and, as the booing goes on, her lower lip wobbles and she seems close to tears. Her hurt is palpable and distressing, and the cameraman does the only thing he can think of to spare further blushes, and returns to her chest. But her breasts are now as deflated as she is, and this sets the tone for the night as a drab nil-all draw never once threatens to revive the brilliant spirit that just two hours earlier had made this most sober of German cities so endearingly giddy.

After attempting and failing to buy a souvenir shirt ('Ve only take MasterCard, zey are ze sponsor,' I am told, which is pretty useless when all I'm toting is Visa and AmEx). I take the train back to the airport and grab a taxi.

'The Mercure, please,' I say.

'In the city?'

'No, the one down the road, the airport one.'

The driver starts to hyperventilate. 'I have only ten minutes,' he says hysterically.

'What?'

'If I get back in ten minutes, I can go back to the top of the queue, but if I take longer, I'll have to join the end and I might not get another passenger all night,' he wails, in perfect English.

I am just about to point out that he appears to have confused me with someone who gives a fuck, but the sound is sucked from my mouth as he takes off with a screech and embeds me in the vinyl of the back seat. We break lights. We join an autobahn where streetlamps in my peripheral vision join up in a kaleidoscopic streak, like birthday candles on a camcorder video. The loose skin on my cheeks is spreading out in ripples as G forces play a tug-o-war on it. As we leave the motorway on a cloverleaf junction, I am thrown to the side of the car and clutch helplessly at the ceiling as he turns a 180 in the opposite direction for the hotel, where we screech to a halt, leaving trails of flame sizzling along the asphalt.

'That'll be €12,' he says through the torrent of sweat washing over his lips.

I hand him ten and start rooting for coins. 'That's OK!' he shrieks. 'That's OK! Ten is OK! I must go! I have to go! Goodnight!'

I am barely out of the cab when he roars off again. I have no doubt he made it, but wonder what happened if the next guy in the queue said, 'The Mercure, please … No, the one at the airport.'

Next morning, I take the hotel's courtesy bus back to the terminal, but I'm not getting a plane. I'm waiting for the bus to Frankfurt-Hahn. The two-hour journey takes me for the first time through the real Rhineland, where vineyards tumble down terraced slopes to the water, boats bob slowly around S-bend curves, pretty villages raise their lazy heads above hedgerows. It is a fairytale landscape, and a gentle counterpoint to last night's fun – and a useful bridge between football fanatics and pilgrims of a much different hue.

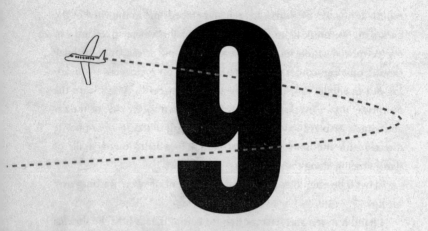

SANTIAGO DE COMPOSTELA–
SANTANDER

FR4477

Frankfurt-Hahn (HHN) to Santiago de Compostela (SCQ)

1,440 km • €49.93

I was determined to get to Santiago de Compostela before August, to avoid a month-long bash called Festiclown. I can't tell you how much I hate clowns. Far from finding them funny, I think they are sinister and repellent – largely because clowns were the next act to arrive in the ring after the biggest circus disappointment of my life, and I've been taking it out on them ever since.

This loathing started when I saw a circus poster that promised a woman swimming in a glass tank with crocodiles. I was beside myself with excitement and for weeks badgered my parents to bring us along. After tedious warm-up acts, such as Romanians standing on ponies and shooting at their wives and some old ex-Nazi cracking a whip at drugged-up tigers, an Asian woman (I can still see her – long, sleek, jet-black hair, a tight body stocking, a smile as wide as the Severn Crossing) stood on the platform beside the tank. The tank with no crocodiles in it.

A man arrived with another smaller tank and tipped its contents into the water. Twelve crocodiles, none longer than 50 centimetres, swam around, bumping into each other and into the walls. They were so young, I suspect their eyes were still closed. Then the woman jumped in, but instead of swimming a gentle breast-stroke, she just thrashed about. I'm not joking you, she kicked the living shit out of the poor little bastards. They tried to swim for their lives, but the whole scene was like a forerunner to *Kill Bill* – it was amazing she didn't produce numchucks. In panic, the croc-odiles raced for the bottom of the tank, so she churned them up with her feet and gave them another good pummelling. If they had been above the water, I'm not sure we could have sat through the shrieking. It was carnage.

Bitten? Listen, she had more chance of getting a nasty nick if she shaved her legs with a banana. She stood on the platform waiting for applause, but we were all so disappointed that she was still alive (and, let's be honest, every boy there came to see her get eaten) that there was just total silence.

And then the fucking clowns came on. A Freudian could work it out in seconds, but from then on, I would sooner have watched live operations than sit through Charlie Cairoli and the Blackpool Tower Circus. All that mugging. All those pratfalls. All the stupid routines with wooden cars and umbrellas. All that stomping around. It was about as funny as being on the Greek Islands in the 1980s without a toilet roll.

But even more than clowns, I hate other people's reactions to clowns, especially those who, like me, think that clowns are indeed vile but know that any public expression of hatred for an old man just trying to make kids laugh attracts vicious public opprobrium. So besides their real laugh, they have a Clown Laugh, one that sounds forced and hollow but they fake it because they think that if they don't, the clown might put on the sad face and direct the children to start kicking their shins.

So when I read about Festiclown, the prospect of hundreds of clowns wearing self-congratulatory smirks as thousands of Clown Laughs echoed around the cloisters of Santiago made my blood run arctic. I couldn't swear I wouldn't do time for one if he came within two metres of me. I might have yanked his smirking head off his little body and kicked it from there to Vigo in the driver's seat of his stupid wooden car. So I went in June to see the pilgrims instead.

The Camino de Santiago – the Way of St James – is one of Europe's oldest Christian pilgrimages and dates back over a thousand years. You can start it anywhere you like and so long as you walk the last 100 kilometres, or cycle the last 200, they will give you a certificate and call your name out at mass as an example to lazy Catholics like myself who have lapsed both from their religion and from doing anything that looks remotely strenuous. Personally, I believe that if God had wanted us to still walk the Camino instead of driving it, he would have sunk the ship that brought Henry Ford's father from County Cork to the United States. But our noughties obsession with spirituality, allied to the growing popularity of activity holidays, makes the Camino a one-stop shop for fitness freaks with voids in their lives, and they arrive in their thousands all summer long.

In a bar to watch that night's World Cup football, I meet Rik, a sixty-four-year-old Belgian who has just finished his fourth Camino. 'Are you a practising Catholic?' I ask.

'Well, you would have to be to do it more than once,' he smiles serenely. 'Though I think this is my last Camino.'

I can see why. He looks dusty and wizened. His spindly legs, his arms and his face are burnt umber, though when he lifts his T-shirt to scratch his stomach, the skin there is as milky as midsummer moonlight. I step back a bit – when anyone has spent forty-seven days walking 1,000 kilometres, as Rik has, and they can't seem to stop scratching themselves, keeping your distance is always a good idea. He explains how he set off from the Marian shrine at Lourdes in France and stayed along the way at €3-a-night *alberques*, or hostels, where you have to be in bed by 10.30 p.m. and no alcohol is tolerated. Tonight, he will make up for it, he says with a wicked laugh as I buy him a large Cruzcampo.

He raises a toast his newly svelte self. 'I lost four kilos,' he tells me. 'I'm so happy.'

Happy? I'm mute with shock. That means he lost just one kilogram for every 250 kilometres and a quick calculation reveals that if I were to set out from Lourdes and walk until I had arrived at my optimum weight, I would be in fucking Mumbai.

Dejected, I ask when he plans to return to Belgium. 'Well, my wife said to come either Friday or Sunday, because she's out Saturday,' he says ruefully. Imagine. The poor bastard has shed four kilos dragging his sparrow-like frame across Aquitaine and the País Vasco, Cantabria, Asturias and now Galicia, and she couldn't stay home just one day to welcome him back? It is uniquely monstrous behaviour, unless Mrs Armstrong has for four decades concealed the fact that the day Neil came home from the moon, it was to a note saying: 'I'm at the hairdresser's. Your dinner's in the oven. I'm sure you can manage another small step…'

I leave Rik to enjoy his achievement and walk in the still night to the façade of the Cathedral of St James, which is the repository for the relics that the pilgrims come to venerate. The cathedral is sombrely lit and covered in an orange-tinged algae that makes it look ghostly. You have seen the cathedral hundreds of times, if you have ever checked out the back of the Spanish copper euro coins, which feature the very view now sending a chill through my body.

A sound across the quadrangle draws me to a band of medieval-attired minstrels playing what I take to be Galician folk music and it sounds familiar in the way that most Celtic music does to those of us who carry that particular strand of DNA. Dozens of people are dancing and I am somehow dragged into the mêlée. Thankfully, all the childhood training in Irish dancing pays off – Santiago doesn't exactly rock to the news that St James has miraculously delivered a new Michael Flatley, but I have acquitted myself well and I'm not being interviewed in connection with the mysterious death of a clown and that's enough to send me into a contented sleep when I reach the hotel.

After a leisurely breakfast, I log on to the net. I am always astonished at the disparity in the cost of internet access in European hotels. In the really upmarket ones, it's prohibitive. At one five-star, all-villa resort near Cannes I stayed in on business last year, the rack rate is €800 a night for a villa in July, and another €25 a day for internet access. If you're staying for a month (and, remember, that would leave you with a room bill of €24,800), they offer a special internet deal of €595. After the dotcom collapse, you could have bought the whole internet for €595. It's outrageous.

Yet here I am in the Hesperia Peregrino in Santiago. It has cost just €75 for bed and breakfast and parking, it's clean, decorated in an attractive modern style and it offers Wi-Free, the chain's name for its always-on wireless broadband that doesn't cost a cent. Nada. I vow there and then that wherever I travel in Spain, I will be staying with Hesperia. Their slogan is catchy too. No 'where dreams come true' crap here, just 'Hesperia – We are hoteliers'. I always like anything that does what it says on the tin.

Anyway, once on the net, I go to viamichelin.com for a route map of my journey. I am flying out of Santander tomorrow night, which looks a stone's throw away from Santiago on the ryanair.com website. It, in turn, is near Bilbao, where I plan to visit the Guggenheim Museum, which has been on my wish list since it opened in 1997. Now Michelin is telling me that what I envisaged as a gentle mid-morning drive is actually 593 kilometres, only 403 kilometres of which is motorway, and it will take six hours and thirty-five minutes. Which might be amusing were it not for the fact that I hired an Opel Corsa.

The drive is endless. Northern Spain looks like West Cork looks like Devon looks like the Cotentin Peninsula in Basse-Normandie looks like oh, there's another cove, there's another hedge, anyone for tea, let's push on, Jesus, is this a maze or what? I'm sure it's captivating if you have a week to tootle along at your leisure. In a day, in a Corsa, it is exhausting, and I am a broken man by the time I reach Bilbao, or Bilbo in Basque.

There are so many names banging around in this part of the world, I'm not quite sure what is where. País Vasco, it transpires, is just the Spanish for Euskadi, the Basques' own name for this autonomous region. Bizkaia is the Basque name for the old Spanish province of Vizcaya (in France, it's more familiar as Biscay). The street signs are pregnant with *K*s and they make the words look harsh and guttural. I'm way out of my comfort zone because the language does not have a Latin root (it apparently resembles Chechen) and I can't even make a good guess.

So I head for the place with most *K*s in it and eventually cross a bridge where, from the side of my eye, I catch my first fleeting glimpse of the Guggenheim, which has a twizzled turret that looks like a filo pastry hors d'oeuvre at a chi-chi cocktail party. At I get closer, I see Jeff Koons' giant floral puppy, which has become something of a symbol for the city; it doesn't exactly thrill me as art, but it does make me smile. I learn from a policeman that my hotel is on the opposite bank of the river, but get tied up in the one-way system and keep arriving back at a pet shop with a large banner announcing that it sells Eukanuba dog food. This will become sadly relevant later on.

Finally, I check in to the Hesperia – a cheery, modern building with coloured glass panels for windows, making it look like the TV test card. For €15, I upgrade to a superior river-view room, and from the chaise longue in the bay window, I can see the inevitable bridge designed by architect Santiago Calatrava (every city in Europe has one now, I think – bling, new-money Dublin is about to build its second) and the aluminium shell of the museum further downstream on the Nervión.

Crossing Calatrava's footbridge (boring as ever – a big steel arc, lots of suspension cables, glass walkways, long approaches, steep steps and so many more familiar design tics you have to rub your temples to ease the throbbing déjà vu), I am boyishly enthralled by the light-rail system, which runs on tracks embedded in a strip of manicured riverbank grass that makes each of the trams look like it is levitating on baize.

It is now so late the gallery has closed, so I walk around the old quarter of town, where I eat an iffy meal, watch another World Cup game, drink a bottle of wine and ask the café owner where I might go to hear some authentic Eukanuba folk music. He looks at me as if I have stepped off the first shuttle from Endor. 'What is Eukanuba folk music?' he asks.

'You know,' I say, 'local music. Basque music. We have Irish music, you have Eukanuba music.'

'No, mister,' he says tartly, 'we have Euskadi music.'

I can feel the colour rise from my feet and by the time it reaches my face it is giving off heat like Jeff Koons' puppy in season. I have mixed up the name of this man's country and its traditions with the name of a dog food and all because I drove past a pet shop three times two hours ago. Mortified, I blurt an apology and race for the door.

On the street, I see a young couple and ask, 'Do you speak English?'

Even as he is saying yes, she looks at me sarcastically and says, 'No, we speak Basque', and she literally frog-marches him away.

And I think to myself, well, good for you, love, but no one else does, and with all those *K*s, the only reason anyone might want to is to win Scrabble, or perform a little better on *Countdown* ('I'll have an obscure consonant please, Carol'). I always make an effort to address people in their own language, but there's a limit. I don't expect someone from Dagenham to come to Dublin and say 'Dia dhuit' instead of 'hello', and I'm quite sure the Dutch all have perfect English because they have long since accepted that the rest of Europe doesn't fancy speaking as if it is rolling snot around the back of its throat.

But her response is typical of regions where long terrorist wars have given them a disproportionate prominence and, therefore, a deluded self-importance (and ETA, or Euskadi Ta Askatasuna, the Basque Homeland and Freedom Movement, has murdered so many people and broken so many ceasefires, it's in the news more often than Brad and Angelina). You also see a lot of this nonsense in Northern Ireland, where staunch loyalists and nationalists have been dug in for so long in their respective trenches they have lost all perspective on the fact that the six counties they're fighting over are smaller than the Paris commuter belt and the rest of us, even in Ireland, are just a tad more preoccupied with Manchester United, getting laid and figuring out ways to buy a 50-inch plasma telly.

I was, I suppose, very peripherally interested in what the Basques are fighting for, but I have now decided to be as simplistic and blinkered as my little friend was (and if the boyfriend has any sense, she's already toast). So, here is a rough translation of the Basque constitution: 1. We demand the right to call Vizcaya 'Bizkaia' and to restore the letter *K* to its rightful prominence. 2. Though we understand that English is the lingua franca of the entire world, the most widely spoken second language on the planet and therefore a useful bridge between people who speak pointless regional languages, we reserve the right to insult tourists who ask the simple question 'Do you speak English?', even when it is in an effort to establish if there is somewhere worth going to so they can put a little more money in our economy.

Next morning, I finally get to the Guggenheim. It is wondrous, audacious and everything else that has been said about it. The exhibition of Russian art is mesmerising – I had no idea that all the major movements in Western art were shadowed all the way through the Soviet era by gifted painters behind the Iron Curtain, or that, even earlier, Russian Impressionists were painting to a standard just as seductive as the celebrated French pioneers.

On the outside, superstar architect Frank Gehry's building is softly burnished and beautiful. I love the way it is integrated into the city, the way a busy traffic bridge has been incorporated into the site, the interplay between aluminium and stone and water. It is genius, yet flashy in a way that still speaks in the American vernacular rather than the European and engages intellectually without plugging into my emotions. I have left myself too little time to see Santander itself, but as I drive the 100-odd kilometres to the airport there and replay the past few days in my head, I am surprised to find that the building that haunts my thoughts and has stolen my heart is not the Guggenheim but a centuries-old cathedral, covered in algae and looking out over a timeless quadrangle.

I'm not sure I'll ever walk there, but I definitely want to go back to Santiago. As for Bilbao – sorry, Bilbo – well, Bilbo is just one iconic building and a bridge that everyone else has too. Oh, and a great name for a clown.

STANSTED–GATWICK

FR2613

Santander (SDR) to London Stanstead (STN)

990 km • €70.19

FR119

London Gatwick (LGW) to Dublin (DUB)

484 km • €26.05

I have flown through Stansted twelve times before today but this is the first time I've ever been fingerprinted. And it's by Hertz. Yes, a civilian company has been asked by the British government to ink its customers. I have lived in Ireland for all but six months of my forty-two years and I have never, ever been fingerprinted for any reason whatever. En route to the States, since 11 September 2001, I have stuck an index finger on a light box and smiled for a camera, but the immigration service is an arm of government and, however reluctantly I may accede to the demand, at least I know my prints are safe in the hands of a government agency.

But to be fingerprinted by Hertz is the end of a wedge so thin it can now be seen only with an electron microscope. We are always told that 9/11 changed our world but, in truth, it didn't. If the deaths of 3,000 in a day could actually change our world, how come Rwanda didn't change it? Or Darfur? Or the tsunami?

Like all but the perpetrators and their sympathisers, when I watched those unforgettable World Trade Center images unfold, I was shocked, appalled and rendered mute with sadness, but attacks on buildings in New York and Washington and the loss of all those lives, no matter how dreadful, simply did not change my world. No, what changed my world was the hysterical response of two governments to 9/11 – namely the Americans and the British. The nineteen hijackers came from Saudi Arabia, Lebanon, the United Arab Emirates and Egypt, all Middle Eastern countries with one other thing in common – not one of them has since been invaded or attacked by the US or the UK. A smoke-screen stretching from Afghanistan to Iraq has hidden the fact that this really is all about oil, not justice. And you and I are caught in the middle. In airports.

'Why do I have to have my prints taken?' I ask.

'The government has asked us to,' the clerk tells me. 'It's a pilot programme at Stansted. All the other companies are insisting on it but it's voluntary with us.'

'You didn't ask me if I wanted to skip it,' I say.

'Um, no, but you don't mind, do you?'

'Well, yes, I bloody do, to be honest. I'm not sure it's even constitutional.'

'Well,' he says, a smirk spreading across his face, 'you're in Britain now and we don't have a constitution.'

'I know that,' I say and then, bluffing like mad, add, 'But under the Treaty of Rome, and also of the treaties of Maastricht and Nice, as a citizen of the European Union I have the right to travel unimpeded within the union, and I'm quite sure I could take this to the European Court of Human Rights if I chose to. I mean, come on – you're a civilian fingerprinting me to hire a bloody car!'

He looks ashen, but I decide not to waste any more time on a man who thinks not having a constitution is something to smirk about, instead of being appalled that his rights can be manipulated on the whim of a government minister or a judge. Why would anyone be proud of having no constitutional rights? Why would anyone smirk? Of course, I can't understand why anyone would prefer to be a subject rather than a citizen, though if Britain wants its monarchy, that's Britain's business. But the nonchalance with which the English in particular greet infringements of their rights to go about their business unhindered (Celts tend to be a little more truculent) is utterly shocking – and how sad it is that in allegedly defending the freedoms we enjoyed before 2001, the English have sacrificed so many of them.

I get out of Stansted eventually and into my little Hertz Ford Fiesta. There are fingerprints on the windscreen but I resist the urge to call the cops. Instead, I head onto the M11 for the M25 and my sister's house (she has long since left Watford and now lives in Epsom, in leafy Surrey). I have never driven this road before (I usually fly to Gatwick or Heathrow, which are nearer to Annie's) and, without warning, I look ahead and see the top of Canary Wharf Tower in the far distance, peeping above the horizon with its sister skyscrapers raising their hands and saying 'look at me too'. It is a dazzlingly sunny evening and the City and the buildings to the east of it look as mythically gilded as Tintagel.

I love London beyond measure – alongside New York, it is the world's greatest city and it is the nearest place I can hop to when Ireland gets a little claustrophobic, as it tends to. Like most Paddies, I even lived here for a time in the mid-1980s, when Ireland was writhing in vicious recession but Thatcherite London was booming (and I say London deliberately, for these were also the years when the coal and steel industries in the north of England began their cataclysmic decline, and the traditional manufacturing industries disappeared offshore, leaving a vast call centre in their place).

It is nine o'clock on Saturday night when I arrive at Annie's, but it is still over 20 degrees, so we sit in the garden until it gets dark, and a day that began in Bilbao finally begins to catch up with me. I awake on Sunday to another scorcher. We're in the middle of a mini heatwave and the combination of the weather and a good run in the World Cup has England in carnival mood. Today, the team takes on Ecuador in the Group of 16 and we're all off to – where else? – the pub to watch the action.

There are many in Ireland and, indeed, in Scotland and Wales, who will cheer the South Americans to win, but I have no time for this petty aspiration to see England exit a tournament as quickly as possible. No, I'd much rather they went all the way to the final, and then got beaten. So I cheer myself hoarse with everyone else, and though England remain as unconvincing as ever, they eventually win thanks to a glorious David Beckham free kick in the sixtieth minute, his first goal for his country in three years.

On the Sunday, we have a barbecue that has been planned for two months now. I envy Londoners that. They can actually plan barbecues, unlike Dubliners who, on a given Sunday, stick a head out the window, detect mild heat and no moisture, and phone all their pals to say 'get round here quickly' – though, by the time the burgers are being flipped, your have to take out the tarpaulin as the women head inside and the men stand outdoors, soaked and frozen but convinced they're having a good time.

Eventually, the time comes to leave and I drive to nearby Gatwick for my flight home. I used to love Gatwick but age has caught up with it (the main structure is nearly forty years old now) and it looks worn and shabby. I arrived in England to fingerprinting and leave to having my photograph taken and matched to my boarding pass so that when I get to the gate and the security officer swipes it, I see my own picture staring up at him and get the nod to go through.

The South Terminal wasn't designed for heatwaves, and by the time the gate lounge fills up, the sheer mass of humanity has ramped up the temperature by about 10 degrees. Rivulets of sweat run down my back and I decide that while the small airports of Ryanland may be well out of town and short on facilities, they usually are more comfortable than the bigger airports because they are not so congested. Eventually, we are released from the Black Hole of West Sussex and, after another week of travelling and another 4,812 kilometres flown, I'm back to Dublin, where my next trip is altogether less complicated. It's time to go to Cork.

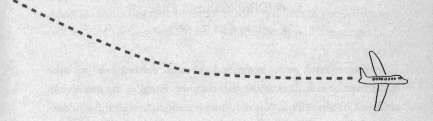

CORK

FR9845

Dublin (DUB) to Cork (ORK)

FR9844

Cork (ORK) to Dublin (DUB)

232 km • €54.34 (Return)

From time to time, I work as a consultant to the *Evening Echo* in Cork, and I have been invited to the staff summer outing at the greyhound track at Curraheen Park. Not only does this sound like great fun, it also means I can use Ryanair's relatively new service between the two cities. Normally, I would either drive or take CityGold, Irish Rail's excellent first-class service, which employs the best staff on the railway, serves one of the best cooked breakfasts in Ireland and is possibly the single most civilised mode of transport in the entire country. Today, by the time I get from my home in south Dublin to the airport on the northside, leave the car at the long-term, check in, clear security, fly to Cork, wait for a cab and reach the hotel, the thirty-five-minute flight has become an almost four-hour journey, or half an hour more than it would have taken to drive.

At least Cork Airport is open. Built on top of a hill on the outskirts of town, it is frequently closed by fog. If you ever want to go to Shannon but all the flights are full, book one to Cork and you have a very good chance of being diverted there anyway.

Once I'm checked in to the Clarion Hotel, which has become my home from home in the city, I seek out a TV to watch the England–Portugal World Cup quarter-final, which ends with a penalty shoot-out and the only result England ever seems to get from such a scenario, which is a respite from the overseas spending and drinking of the players' wives and girlfriends. I feel sorry for the few English lads in the bar who are over for a stag weekend, but they are more sanguine than I expect. 'We build ourselves up every time, but we know we're crap,' one says, and orders a round of compensatory sambucas.

I wander out onto Patrick Street, the city's main thoroughfare (mysteriously called Pana by most of the residents, though none could tell me why – or, more likely, they knew exactly why but couldn't be arsed sharing the info with a Dub). It used to be a chaotic traffic artery with an almost perpetual clamour and bustle. Then Cork was anointed a European City of Culture for 2005 and the council decided that Patrick Street's organic hurly-burly, the very thing that made it uniquely Irish, should be replaced with something more continental. Catalan architect Beth Galí was invited to turn it into another Rambla, the celebrated road that runs between Barcelona's Plaza Catalunya and the port, though we'll leave aside for a moment the fact that, at night, the nearer you get to the port, the friendlier the girls get too.

So Beth went off and spent millions on Spanish granite and French brick, and reconfigured the pavement to be wider in some places than others, and installed new street lighting that looks like docking stations on *Battlestar Galactica*. But she forgot the one thing above all others that she should have remembered – the weather. The reason the Rambla is the Rambla is because people ramble there, and the reason they ramble is because they like to get out in the heat. But unless the weather is perfect, Patrick Street is just wide and inhospitable. Rain, on the bad days, comes in horizontally like a squadron of bombers bearing down on Pearl Harbour, and the busiest man in Cork is the one selling new umbrellas to the people whose old ones are now somewhere over Cornwall. So while the new grid and all the marble and brick inlays probably work from above and exhibit the geometrical precision of a Busby Berkeley musical shot from a crane, at street level, the main difference you notice is that the chewing gum is stuck to classier stone.

One thing they haven't tampered with, but rather restored to its pristine glory, is the English Market, the finest food hall in Ireland and alone well worth a trip to the city. And they still talk, as always, in a sing-song accent dripping with words unique to the area, my favourites of which are 'lasher', which is an attractive woman, and 'langer', which is, basically, someone who's a bit of a prick. That takes no account of the vocal inflection, though – if a Corkman looks at you and says, 'Ya langer', the contempt is in the voice, not the word.

Anyway, spruced up for my night at the dogs, I get into my taxi and the driver asks where I'm off to.

'Curraheen Park,' I say.

There is a silence, and she turns round to me and asks, 'And how would you get there?'

'Well, I don't know,' I reply truthfully. 'I rather expected you to know.'

'I think I do,' she says. 'I think it's out the Link.'

So we drive for a while until we pull up beside another cab. She winds down the window and has a little chat with the other driver, who confirms that the Link is indeed the way to go.

Then comes the expected grilling. 'What's on out there?'

'Well, an ancient sexual initiation ritual, actually – sure what the fuck else would be on at a dog track?'

Actually, I don't say that, I just want to. In fact, I tell the truth.

'And are ya going by yourself?'

'No, there's a party on.'

'Who's having it?'

Oh, sweet Jesus.

'The *Evening Echo*.'

'D'*Echo*!' She practically crashes the car with excitement. 'Are you a reporter?'

I always find it easier to say no to this question because otherwise I will be bored to constipation by the ins and outs of some endless problem with the local council, or getting told off because newspapers failed to prevent the war in Iraq/starvation in Africa/abuse by priests or, even worse, being urged to share gossip about a politician or actor. So I say I work in newspaper design.

'Do you think I could be a reporter?' she asks.

'I have no idea, because I don't know you. Have you ever written? I'd say you might be a bit old to be starting out and you'd probably need to have an arts degree.'

'Art? Art? I love art. Maybe I should do that. Do you think I could be a painter? Or a sculptor, maybe?'

I'm now looking around for hidden cameras. 'Look, ma'am, I don't mean to be rude but I have no idea if you have any talent in that department. I don't know you. And an arts degree is not art, as in painting, it's philosophy, English literature, the humanities, stuff like that.'

'Hmmm,' she sighs, looking out the side windows. 'I wonder if I'm going the right way here.'

'Don't know that either,' I volunteer.

'Well, this is the Link, so I think I need to take the next roundabout. C'mere, if I went to college to study art, would I make money from it?'

'Unlikely. Very few artists make really good money.'

'But maybe I'd get good rental for the taxi plate, would I?'

I'm at the end of my rope and can barely suppress the urge to shout. 'Look, I truthfully don't know – but if I were you, I'd definitely lease it to someone from eastern Europe, because they're really hungry to do well and they work every hour of the day.'

'Oh, I couldn't do that,' she says.

'Why not?'

'Sure they wouldn't know where anywhere is.'

I swear to Christ, she says it without missing a heartbeat. 'Now,' she continues, 'this is the roundabout. Which exit do you think I should take?'

Wearily, I slump back in the seat. 'Let's do something really mad and follow the one with the huge pictogram of a dog on it, shall we?'

And finally she delivers me into the welcome embrace of my friends, with whom I have a terrific night that ends with us all roaring our heads off for a hound called Doggie's Tile which, when said quickly, is rather rude – but he gets a bad start and fails to live up to his potential to come from behind.

I hardly seem to have got to bed before I'm up again and off to the airport for the return flight, which leaves three hours late. From now on, it's back to the car for this particular journey. No hassle at the airport – and no need for a taxi either.

ABERDEEN–EDINBURGH

FR182
Dublin (DUB) to Aberdeen (ABZ)
491 km • €29.63

FR182
Edinburgh (EDI) to Dublin (DUB)
335 km • €21.72

Disaster has struck. It started on the morning of 10 August, when I turned on *Sky News* to find a British Home Office minister, Douglas Alexander (a quiet-spoken Scot who, because of that, sounded utterly terrifying), outlining an alleged al-Qaeda plot to kill us all with Lucozade. The police staged dawn arrests in London, Birmingham and High Wycombe, where men of mostly Pakistani ethnicity were lifted. It is said (and, as with anything the British government announces, I take this with a Siberia of salt, never mind a pinch), they were plotting to detonate explosives on as many as twelve transatlantic flights, an act of terror that might conceivably have killed as many people as died on 9/11. As explosives are the easiest component of bombs to spot during security screening, the twist in this particular tale is that the perpetrators would instead improvise them on the planes by combining everyday liquids and chemicals disguised as them (and some explosive gels look just like Lucozade, it seems).

So everyone passing through British airport security has to carry liquids separately in Ziploc bags and there has been chaos for a full week by the time I travel to Aberdeen. Of course, it's not only me who is sceptical that the plot existed at all, many commentators have pointed out how it has rather conveniently distracted attention from Israel's ill-fated invasion of Lebanon. And, you know, the cynics may not be wrong, since among the two dozen arrested, few are in possession of plane tickets, and many don't even have passports.

The new security measures are playing havoc with the schedules of the budget airlines in particular, which operate to very tight twenty-minute turnarounds that have become impossible under the new regime. Once baggage is loaded, an aircraft may not depart until the person who owns the bag is also on board. Since half the passengers are still in the queue having their weapons of mass destruction (water, deodorant, orange-and-mango smoothies) confiscated, Ryanair alone has already cancelled 500 flights and British Airways estimates it has lost £40 million. Never one to miss a PR opportunity, Ryanair boss Michael O'Leary (who, to be fair, is talking common sense for once) is threatening to sue the British Airport Authority and the government itself for the lost revenue.

The whole sorry episode points up the fact that it is time we had a mature debate on security issues. There is little doubt that another atrocity is due – as the IRA always said, a guerrilla army only has to get lucky once, but the police have to get lucky every time. Even if another plane is to be blown from the sky, or hijacked and flown into a building, and if another 3,000 die as a consequence, is that still not better than all this cowering in terror? Is it not preferable to the television images I've watched all this week of people queuing to drink formula from their babies' bottles to prove to the police that SMA isn't triacetone triperoxide? Personally, I'll take my chances and hang the consequences if it means I can live a normal life. Maybe I'm wrong on this, as out of step as a bachelor uncle at the 'New York, New York' stage of a country wedding. I just don't understand why, when the London Underground was bombed, everyone went back to using it again the very next day, in defiance of the extremists and in solidarity with the dead and the bereaved – yet when planes are *not* bombed, the response is hysteria. At this stage, paranoid New Labour Britain might as well raise a white flag and turn the BT Tower into a minaret.

Things get no better when I arrive at the Travelodge in downtown Aberdeen at 10 a.m. and am told that the police will not allow the porter to hold my bags – and, since my room will not be ready until 3 p.m., I have to walk around town for five hours dragging my wheelie Samsonite case, and with my laptop-bag slung over my shoulder. Surely the receptionist can identify an Irish accent? Surely she knows I'm a little unlikely to fit the profile of someone wishing to start a solo jihad against a minor Scottish city? No matter – rules are rules, and I'm sent on my way.

I'm afraid it rather negatively colours my opinion of Aberdeen, which, in the gunmetal grey Union Street, boasts one of the longest main thoroughfares in Europe, not the greatest attraction to happen upon with 10 kilos of Sony Vaio and accessories tearing the ligaments from your neck, and a bag with a mind of its own trailing behind. It also means that every time I'm spotted by department-store security, they too get the jitters ('Finlay, there's a man out there carrying a bottle of *water*…'), so I end up having a three-hour lunch in the Monkey House café before finally getting my hands on a £60 room that, ironically, doesn't have shampoo in the bathroom (not because it could blow the hotel from here to Inverness, but because, Travelodge explains, it helps keep costs down, an argument that would be more convincing if the accommodation was even worth sixty quid in the first place).

Later, I venture out to the Stadia Sports Bar to watch Ireland being thrashed 4–0 at Lansdowne Road by the Netherlands. I wasn't sure the match would be shown in eastern Scotland, traditionally the more Protestant side of the country, until I remembered the opposition were the original Orangemen and, indeed, there are some here revelling in the Republic's embarrassment. I finish with a beer in Soul, a church converted to a lively nightclub, at number 333 Union Street, though given the amount of drink going down, it would have been altogether more appropriate at number 666.

Next morning, I take the train to Edinburgh. The rail line mostly hugs the wild east coast and it's the type of scenery that appeals to me, rugged rather than pretty, tough not twee. After Dundee, we pass over the Tay Bridge, opened in 1887 as a replacement for the earlier one that collapsed in a storm just eighteen months after being inaugurated by Queen Victoria on 1 June 1878. That Christmas week tragedy killed seventy-five, and sent William McGonagall, the pathologically abysmal poet, to pen a piece of doggerel called 'The Tay Bridge Disaster', which ends with the memorable lines:

It must have been an awful sight,
To witness in the dusky moonlight,
While the Storm Fiend did laugh, and angry did bray,
Along the Railway Bridge of the Silv'ry Tay,

Oh! Ill-fated Bridge of the Silv'ry Tay,
I must now conclude my lay,
By telling the world fearlessly without the least dismay,
That your central girders would not have given way,
At least many sensible men do say,
Had they been supported on each side with buttresses,
At least many sensible men confesses,
For the stronger we our houses do build,
The less chance we have of being killed.

I love that line: 'Had they been supported on each side with buttresses', which is as refreshingly candid as Robert De Niro's ode to his mother in *Meet the Parents* ('I selfishly tried to hold on to you, / While the cancer ate away at your organs'), prompting the squirmingly brilliant response from Ben Stiller: 'That's amazing. So much love – and also so much information.' The memory of it makes me chuckle out loud.

An hour or so later, we round a gentle bend and line up to cross the Forth Rail Bridge. It's the first time I've seen it for myself, and no picture or video gives any realistic impression of the sheer size of it – or, indeed, the vibrancy of its Irn-Bru redness. I'm so overwhelmed by it I temporarily forget my fear of heights as we pass along its approaches and canti-levered sections for 2,528.7 metres of silent exultation, 50 metres above the firth. The bridge is 116 years old and, surely, represents the apogee of engineering achievement in Victorian Britain. It has been to the fore of my thoughts for months now, because I have been telling people that attempting to cover all of Ryanair's routes would be akin to painting the bridge I'm now crossing – every time you'd think you had Europe covered, Ryanair would announce ten new routes.

I arrive into an Edinburgh thronged for the annual festivals (there are about half a dozen running side by side, covering television, books, theatre, comedy and so forth, though most people call the whole extravaganza by the simple name of the Edinburgh Festival). I walk to the festival hub at Pleasance to book tickets for an afternoon show, but the queue is so long I miss the start of the one I wanted to see, and instead take an open-top bus tour of the city, which proves to be just as entertaining.

My first stop is the Scottish Parliament, a new addition to the landscape – and it is the Punch to the Forth Bridge's Judy, the most expensive eyesore in these islands. Designed by the late Enric Miralles, yet another Catalan architect-du-jour whose capriciousness is mistaken for genius by far too many commentators, it looks like a wild Scottish meadow out front and a Chinese prison behind, thanks to windows with bars of what seems to be cast-iron bamboo (I later learn it is supposed to be oak). The budget for construction was originally forecast at £40 million, but it eventually cost a fraction under eleven times that sum, a hideous overrun that left Scots reeling as charges of ineptitude and mismanagement eventually ended up with a tribunal that chastised everyone but punished no one – an outcome which is, of course, the purpose of tribunals everywhere. Classical Edinburgh, with its Athenian influences, is much prettier.

I beat my way on foot to the Royal Mile, the thoroughfare that runs from Edinburgh Castle, high on its volcanic plug, down to the Palace of Holyroodhouse, and it is thronged with people watching street theatre, the most democratic of all the attractions at the festival. Four Italian mimes are performing a synchronised swimming show that is full of delightful surprises (not the least of which is my own enjoyment of it, since mimes are dangerously close to clowns on the list of people I would like to physically harm). An irritating juggler is all patter and no balls, two children with guitars singing Beatles songs clearly are chancing their arms, but the day is saved by a teenage string quartet sending a sublime Mozart concerto heavenward. It is completely captivating, and I stay so long I nearly miss my flight home.

At airport security, a huge bin is filled with bottles of confiscated water. I knock back my own drink, even though I long to brazen it out and say, look, sorry, officer, the water may be guilty but my smoothie is Innocent. Sadly, a joke can get you arrested these days, so I keep humming Mozart and lament the fact that I have left the sublime far behind and entered the realm of the ridiculous. The world, officially, has gone mad.

CARCASSONNE–MARSEILLE

FR1984

Dublin (DUB) to Carcassonne (CCF)

1,300 km • €70.46

FR1989

Marseille Provence (MRS) to Dublin (DUB)

1,400 km • €73.00

For some time now, Ryanair has operated a system where boarding passes have a sequence number. Passengers carrying 1–90 get to board the plane first, followed by those between 91 and 189. The problem is that this is seldom explained on the public-address system at Dublin Airport departure gates, so first-time fliers haven't a clue what's going on and just join whatever queue they are nearest to. When they get to the top of that queue, hardly anyone bothers to look at the number, which

76

completely undermines the entire process. Today, after months of this nonsense, I finally challenge it and ask why dozens of people in the bottom half of the draw have been boarded before me, even though I am first in the 91–189 queue. The check-in clerk denies this has happened, until I point out that the top pass on his pile is number 126, yet the holder has gone through in the 1–90 queue. Far from apologising, his face flashes red with anger and he leans closer to me, asking menacingly, 'Do you want to get on the aircraft, *bud*?'

Bud, short for buddy, is one of those Dublin words that often means exactly the opposite of what you might think. When someone says 'bud' to you, it is very likely you're not their buddy. At all. His response is typical of Ryanair, though, because Michael O'Leary seems not to care what he says or who he insults, and sometimes this cavalier behaviour seems to filter down through all levels of the company. So I shut up, because you have absolutely no rights in an airport, and even invoking legitimate consumer legislation can be interpreted as obstreperousness and it can see you bumped off a flight. All airline staff now conveniently label any complaint as threatening behaviour, a practice made possible by the scandalous capitulation of airport authorities and governments alike, who live in fear of the power of budget airlines because of their landing charges they pass on from the passengers who pay them, and the tourism boost they bring to the cities they fly into.

It's an early-morning flight, so I immediately fall asleep only to be woken minutes later by the child in the row in front, who has crawled up the back of his own seat, leaned so close to my face I can smell his breath and roared at the top of his voice, 'WAKE UP!' To be honest, I nearly shit myself – in the current heightened security atmosphere, anyone shouting at you on a flight could be the last sound you ever hear. When I see it is just a vexatious little boy, I glower at him in an unhealthy manner. Wondering what his son is at, the father looks backwards and, seeing me glowering, just glowers back without chastising his ignorant little brat at all. The child is lucky he hasn't left the plane by the emergency door. The father's attitude reeks of, oh, it's OK, he's only a kid and I think to myself, that's right, he is only a kid. No one will miss him if I wind my seatbelt as tightly as a tourniquet, smash the window and cheer as he is sucked into the troposphere. 'Wake up, yourself, you little bollix!' I smirk, and the thought consoles me all the way to Carcassonne.

I like Salvaza – it's the quintessential Ryanland regional airport, with one baggage belt, a gate-to-pavement walk of about 30 metres, a fabulous restaurant, and just enough staff to have you on your way in minutes. But the last time I was here, early last year, was a catastrophe – and a salutary lesson in what happens when the slightest thing goes wrong with your travel plans when you fly with a low-fare, couldn't-care airline.

I had taken a figary to fly there and drive to see the Viaduc de Millau, the world's highest bridge, which soars over the Tarn Valley in Languedoc-Roussillon. I was flying via Stansted, out early on Tuesday morning, back late on Wednesday evening. I would grab a car, drive to the Viaduc de Millau – the central pillar of which is taller than the Eiffel Tower – and see if its British architect, Norman Foster, had achieved his ambition of making all who crossed it feel like they were 'flying' their cars.

I mentioned it to a friend and discovered he too was a closet bridge fancier, and he volunteered to join me. Within hours, we were booked, for €90.22 each, return. Better still, I shamelessly used my position as a motoring writer to blag a car that suited the occasion. BMW Ireland phoned BMW France, which arranged for a local dealership in Carcassonne to line up a Z4, the sporty little roadster that gets through the kilometres like a termite on steroids.

I was beyond excited. I had driven much of the same route two years ago and cursed the 40-kilometre gap in the Clermont-Ferrand to Béziers A75 autoroute, which necessitated wending my way through the notorious Millau bottleneck. For Parisians heading to the beaches between Agde and Collioure in the southwest, this could add four hours to a July or August drive. I had also seen hope that day, for, in the distance, the seven pillars of the viaduct – all 205,000 tonnes of meticulously poured concrete – were already rising from the valley floor. Via webcam, I occasionally checked in on progress. I saw the topping out of the central pillar at a world-record 343 metres. I saw the steel deck of the bridge eased into position – at 36,000 tonnes, it weighs as much as five Eiffel Towers. And I gasped when I realised that this deck was 270 metres above the river – in old money, that's 886 feet.

All of this was going through my head when I got onto the plane at Dublin Airport – just as it started to snow. I became mildly uneasy when what began as a flurry stuck to the windows, though the pilot was reassuring – we would be de-iced and on our way forthwith. But when we got to the runway, the plane developed a technical fault and we returned to the gate. And there we sat, and sat, and sat a little more. With the clock approaching 10 a.m., I began to fear for the connecting Stansted flight at 12.10 p.m. So did the two guys across the aisle who were booked to fly to Biarritz ten minutes earlier, but the steward told them we would be underway in minutes.

'Could you organise boarding passes for the onward flight at the other end?' they asked.

'No,' he told them. 'Ryanair is a point-to-point airline and does not guarantee connections, nor compensate when people miss them.'

But he did return with a Bisc&Twix for each of them, with his compliments, for the inconvenience. I had the strong feeling the men were torn between thanking him and kicking him to death.

By the time we got to the gate at Stansted, it was 11.20 a.m. Lungs bursting, Eamonn and I got to check-in to find the desk for Carcassonne closed. At information, we begged to be allowed make a dash for it – after all, we had only hand luggage. The Spanish clerk began her spiel. 'Ryanair is a point-to-point airline,' she began, 'and does not guarantee…'

'I know all that,' I barked. 'All I'm asking is for you to be a human and not a robot.'

Her lip quivered. She had, I suspected, been here before. 'I am not … a robot,' she asserted in an eerily similar way to the Elephant Man declaiming: 'I am not an an-i-mal…'

A nice older gent from Ryanair tried to help. He wasn't sure if he could radio the gate but he would try. After a crackle, a voice said, 'Hello.' Success!

'Could you take two more passengers?' he asked.

'You're talking to me,' a voice came back.

'Who are you?' he asked.

'Me,' came the voice, louder now. From behind me. From the robot, who was looking at me with a defiant smirk. The gate staff, unfortunately, could not be raised, and the game was lost.

This is where Ryanair gets silly. For £40, we could avail of a 'missed flight' concession on tickets to Montpellier at 3 p.m. – or we could fly back to Dublin for £155. With images of the world's tallest bridge sustaining me in my trials, I committed to the former option, which is how we found ourselves, six hours later, on the platform at Montpellier TGV station waiting for the train to Carcassonne.

The taxi from the airport had cost €20, and the train tickets another €22.50 each – the price of our cheap trip was beginning to mount. In Carcassonne, we found a reasonably priced three-star hotel (the third of them awarded by an idiot on crack, I suspect) and an Irish bar called O'Sheridans. Things were looking up – up to about 2.30 a.m., actually. Another mistake.

At 8.30 on the Wednesday morning, Eamonn and I were at the showrooms of Passion Automobiles, the biggest BMW dealership in the region. We nosed the Z4 out onto the motorway and started the 430 kilometres that we had to complete by 2 p.m. if we were to make the 3.35 p.m. return flight. Five and a half hours to cover the equivalent of Dublin to Galway, return.

The journey up was uneventful, as the A75 climbs to the plateau of the Massif Central. It is a feat of not inconsiderable engineering, clinging to mountainsides that would induce vertigo in a cocksure goat. But it was also 4 degrees Celsius outside and the road was icy, which kept the speedometer in check. Time was ticking on and a little warning bell had just started ringing at the back of my mind when, suddenly, we rounded a bend.

There, in front of us, was the deck of the Viaduc de Millau, its seven sets of cable stays ranged in perfect symmetry. As we launched ourselves across the Tarn Valley, I looked sideways and saw nothing but sky. I had to stifle a cheer – the most ambitious piece of bridge engineering ever conceived is also, rather roguishly, a work of art, maybe the most beautiful man-made thing I have ever seen.

The return trip from north to south was even better. You see more of the bridge, with its gentle eastward and upward curve. For 2,460 glorious metres, I was practically punching the air. I was soaring, scorching across the deck and, yes, flying. It was a moment of complete and deeply satisfying epiphany.

And so, energised, I nosed the car back in the direction of Carcassonne – and missed the flight home.

How? Well, we knew the Passion BMW garage was beside the Géant hypermarket with the McDonald's in the car park. What we didn't know that Carcassonne had two of each and they looked identical. After half an hour of fruitless searching, I rang the dealership.

'Ou êtes vous?' the receptionist asked.

'A coté de Conforama,' I replied, identifying the furniture warehouse to my right.

There was a pause. 'You are 10 kilometres away in Carcassonne Ouest, Monsieur,' she told me, 'and late for your flight.' She was right. By the time we found her, in Carcassonne Est, and got back to the airport, it was 2.55 p.m. Check-in had closed twenty minutes before and even though the plane was sitting there, 50 metres away, the airport lady was not for turning. At 3.25 p.m., ten minutes ahead of schedule, a roar of engines heralded the departure of Ryanair flight 075 to Stansted. Without us.

I looked at Eamonn, who seemed a little ill.

'What?' I asked.

'I've never missed a flight,' he said. 'Ever. Now I've missed two in two days.'

Things went from bad to worse. Creative thought was needed – Toulouse was 80 kilometres away and Aer Lingus flew direct the next morning. So we hired a car (€191, for a day!) and returned to the autoroute under a thunderous sky. The Ford Fiesta was a bit of a comedown from the Z4, but I let it pass. When we arrived, we found an internet café and printed off our reservations (another €71 each for the flights and €3.10 for the printing), then headed for the airport twelve hours early. Just in case.

There was no accommodation there, though – thousands of people were in town for the debut of the Airbus A380, the double-deck plane. So we found a Formule 1, the most basic accommodation in France, in the middle of an industrial estate on the outskirts of town, and paid €29 each for rooms with a sink but no shower or toilet. I blanched at using the sink at all, because I know what men are like with a few pints on board, and in any room with a sink and no loo, well, I wouldn't be too trustful that propriety was observed.

We were first at check-in the next morning, where the bad news was delivered. 'Your flight, it is delayed,' the woman told us, adding that most French of all excuses, 'There is an air-traffic control strike.' Three hours later, we finally escaped our Purgatory, each of us about €400 poorer, and all because of a snow flurry in Dublin that triggered the chain reaction. From that day on, I always try to leave about four hours for any Ryanair connection in Stansted.

What was most annoying, though, was that Ryanair later inaugurated a direct flight to Carcassonne from Dublin – and when I arrive off it today, the sun is high and ferocious. I am joined by my old school-friend, Jonathan Nolan, and his partner, Stephen Brown, on holiday from their home in Australia. We skirt Perpignan, another Ryanland outpost, and make for Collioure, a beautiful village near the Spanish border that for many years was home to Patrick O'Brian, the old fraud who wrote *Master and Commander* and twenty other Aubrey/Maturin seafaring novels – he pretended to be Irish but was actually Anglo-German.

I would love to explore this intriguing little port but the nearest available parking space appears to be in Calais (this is southern France in August after all), so we move on to Argèles-sur-Mer and have a dip in the Med before returning to the medieval citadel of Carcassonne, one-time fortress of the mysterious Cathars. The name comes from the Greek for 'to cleanse', and other words that derive from the same root include 'catharsis' and 'catheter'.

From afar, the citadel is the most perfect physical manifestation of what a fairytale castle should look like, with a hilltop setting, turreted sentry towers and thick, crenellated walls. It looks authentic, but was actually saved from demolition and restored in the mid-nineteenth century.

We are staying at Les Remparts, an outlying wing of the Donjon Hotel within the old city walls (a *donjon* was the fortified keep of a castle), which is a bargain at €105 per room per night. Once the day-tripping crowds disappear, *la Cité* takes on a completely different aura, lulled to sleepiness and sunburnt by the dying rays. We have a drink at the pavement tables of Les Grands Puits before dinner at La Feu d'Or. It has been a long day and we finish with a *digestif* in the main square, which is crisscrossed by magical hanging lights.

Next morning, after breakfast in the Donjon garden, which is as cute and appealing as a three-legged spaniel, we make for the Camargue. The swampy delta of the River Rhône, it is home to flamingos, Camaguais horses, fearsome bulls and, we have been warned, mosquitoes the size of sparrows, though my early-morning bath in Deet has clearly had the desired repellent effect. I have wanted to see the national park ever since I read Alistair MacLean's *Caravan to Vaccarès* as a child (and, of course, in his eyes, it was full of swarthy gypsies, all up to no good), and it doesn't disappoint. On the western fringe, in the Petite Camargue, we lunch in the fortified medieval city of Aigues-Mortes. The main pedestrian avenue that leads to the square is hung with the red and yellow pennants of the region and, with the strong sunlight and the cobalt sky, the view is a visual endorphin that lifts the spirit.

Aigues-Mortes was the embarkation point for the Seventh and Eighth Crusades, waged by Christendom against Muslims in 1248 and 1270 respectively. Be warned, though, that crusade history is tricky. Some scholars take the Sixth Crusade as merely the second wave of the Fifth, which makes the Seventh the Sixth and the Eighth the Seventh. As for the Ninth, well, that is often classed as part of the Eighth, unless you believe the Eighth was the Seventh, in which case it was part of that. Hope that's cleared everything up.

Later, we arrive in Arles, the capital of the Camargue, and check into the Best Western Atrium Hotel because something urgent has come up at home and I need internet access. Once we have completed registration and paid for our stay, I ask what I need to do to get on the wi-fi system and am told it is out of order, which is a bit of a shame since it genuinely is the only reason I'm staying here. There is, I am told, an internet PC for guests in the lobby, so I wander over and sit there waiting for half an hour, watching a man looking at aerial pictures on Google Earth. Pictures, I might add, of Arles, which is just outside the fucking door.

Arles turns out to be a wonderful walking city with delights around every corner – views familiar from paintings by Vincent Van Gogh, a well-preserved Roman amphitheatre, narrow cobbled streets, cheerful cafés and warm, good-natured inhabitants who rather overdo things by greeting each other with four kisses, two on each cheek. In a salsa bar (I know – Europe is *weird*) on the Rue Georges Clemenceau, I watch two large groups meet up and the kissing lasts a good nine minutes, which seems to me a rather silly waste of valuable drinking time.

I mooch over to the Théâtre Antique, another Roman ruin built in the classical proscenium style, where an open-air film festival is in full swing, showing the Technicolor Cinerama sword-and-sandals Roman epics of the 1950s in the most perfect setting imaginable. Through the flickering rails, I can see a woman about 20 metres high, dressed in an aquamarine satin dress (a compulsory uniform for every woman in gladiator-movie history), her face dominated by a slash of red lipstick that makes her mouth look like a burst slipper.

On our final morning, we drive to Marseille, mouths agape at the yachts in the harbour (a quick check on *Power and Motoryacht* magazine's list of the World's Top 100 shows the 241-foot *Ilona*, owned by Australian real-estate mogul Frank Lowry, at number thirty-nine and the 229-foot *Reverie* at number fifty-two). The port area itself is attractive, but Marseille feels big and bustling, cramped and loud, and an unwelcome sensory assault after the timeless calm of the past three days. We decide to push on to Salon-de-Provence, home of the medieval seer, Nostradamus, who is said to have predicted the rise of Hitler, the assassination attempt on Pope John Paul II and the events of 9/11 in rhyming quatrains almost as crap as William McGonagall's. But by the time we arrive, the museum dedicated to his life is closed for the day. Wish we'd seen that one coming.

Finally, after four days covering over 900 years of history in 900 kilometres, we make for Marseille-Provence Airport, which is huge but almost deserted and probably the best Ryanland airport yet for ease of access, facilities and, yes, calm. They even board us in sequence so, you see, it's not that difficult. *Bud.*

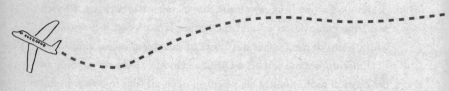

LÜBECK

FR7075

Lübeck (LBC) to Dublin (DUB)

1,120 km

€45.73

For the first time in my life, I am completely naked in front of strange women in public (that's 'strange' as in women unknown to me personally – I have, on occasion, been naked in front of genuinely *strange* women, but always one at a time). Today I am starkers and surprisingly detached, seeing myself from afar, like in one of those dreams where you find yourself without clothes in the middle of a busy street and everyone is staring at you. Except, of course, they're not, because this is Germany and Germans just don't care how they, or you, look in the nude. In fact, in certain parts of Bavaria, they don't seem overly fussy about how they look clothed either.

I am in Travemünde, on the Baltic coast, staying at the A-ROSA, the new name for the renovated Kurhaus Hotel which dates from 1802 (its claim to literary fame derives from the fact that local boy Thomas Mann used it as a setting for *Buddenbrooks*). The revamp has delivered a huge new spa featuring saunas (all with names new to me, such as 'laconium', 'tepidarium' and 'caldarium', the difference between them measured in fractions of degrees and minor variations in humidity), ice grottoes, steam rooms, *rasul* baths and the like. I sign in to kill an hour before dinner and find men, women, children, many generations of the same families, wandering around in their pelts.

There is something refreshingly uninhibited about Germans, and it is contagious. I leave the changing rooms with a towel around my waist and walk to the shower, where I immediately am joined by two mature naked women who stand alongside and wash themselves from top to bottom (one of them literally – from the side of my eye, I catch sight of a hand dripping liquid soap disappearing rather alarmingly between the fleshy folds of a fairly enormous pair of venous buttocks). So, when the shower stops, I take a deep breath and, emboldened, decide to walk to the sauna with my towel in my hand. No one looks. No one laughs. No one swoons either, but you can't have everything. After four decades of bottling it, I finally have overcome the fact that I used to empathise with Woody Allen when he said he was one of the few men who suffered from penis envy.

And then I see it...

A man of about eighty is shuffling, deep in thought, in a long, lazy circle around a foot-spa pool. His skin has been burnt to parchment by years of exposure to the sun and, at the back of his arms and his knees, it is striated like pastry. Bones threaten to push through at about eight pressure points – elbows, knees, hips, shoulders. I am feeling sorry for him until, slowly, he moves around and is facing me. I'm glad there is no likelihood of my ever having to identify his face in a police line-up because his face is not what catches my eye. He has not been deep in thought at all, just dragged forward by the weight of an appendage that looks like a toddler's forearm with a plum in its fist. If someone declared an instant fancy-dress party, he could just stick it in his ear and come as a petrol pump. If a plate of buns was anywhere nearby, he could use it to snaffle them like an elephant. I know it's rude to stare, but it is like trying to look away from a bad toupée. I slowly return the towel to my waist and walk away – I would happily engage in conversation with a man twice my age, but I draw the line at twice my length.

Deflated, I get ready for dinner in nearby Lübeck, where we are celebrating the launch of the new Kia Carens MPV. We are deep in Schleswig-Holstein, one of those European provinces like Alsace-Lorraine that for years seemed to belong to a different country every time it woke up – Germany today, Denmark tomorrow, bratwurst for breakfast, lamb for lunch, and hold the butter cookies until we see how the day pans out. Lübeck itself has a distinguished place at the heart of European history, the founding city and long the focal point of the Hanseatic League, a trading association that stretched across the Baltic and central Europe and trickled down the great cities of the North Sea, including Antwerp, Brugge and, er, Great Yarmouth. Effectively a forerunner of the European Economic Community, it resisted the urge to morph into a full European Union, thus delaying by centuries the introduction of an acceptable angle of curvature in the average banana and the imprisonment of grocers who wished to use pounds and ounces instead of kilograms.

The Hanseatic League, possibly the last European league for which Sky Sports failed to secure the broadcast rights, largely fizzled out in the sixteenth century, though Hamburg, Bremen and trusty Lübeck ignored this until 1862, when it finally dawned on them that they were the last three contestants in the *Big Brother* house and they closed the curtains for ever. Today, Lübeck remains a handsome town in that no-nonsense German way, though teeming rain gives it a bedraggled air. I'd like to explore it fully some day, but make a mental note not to bother until the ten-day forecast on weather.com promises an unbroken string of smiley sunshine faces.

Our drive also takes us to Hamburg, and I cannot resist the urge to take a look at the Reeperbahn, the legendary thoroughfare of sex shops that is the city's most famous attraction. Maybe I'm getting old, but I just find it tired and seedy, as each shop out-boasts the other – fifty private DVD-viewing cabins here, seventy-five there – and features window displays of sex toys that leave little to imagination and, in one or two cases, actually challenge it. Well, mine anyway.

And, you know, it's all very well for the Germans to be open about public nudity and not to be hung up on body shape or size (though the latter, clearly, is easier when you've reached eighty and still have a schlong like an aubergine). It's right that if someone wants to buy a jazz mag, or a vibrating egg, or the scrotum ring I'm looking at in the window (it has little spikes and reminds me of Silas the monk's cilice in *The Da Vinci Code*), that he or she is able to. But the Reeperbahn is just too unabashed, too brazen, too over-the-top for comfort. Here, sexuality is just another commodity, piled high and sold cheap like autoparts in an out-of-town motor mart. There is a lot about European life I wish Ireland and Britain would embrace – artisan cider-making, smellier cheese and some French pop music – but I'm glad we never allowed unregulated proliferation of brash sex shops on boulevards as fine as the Reeperbahn, Hamburg's oversexed and unromantic heart.

REUS SALOU

R1972

Dublin (DUB) to Reus Salou (REU)

1,470 km

€33.43

I arrive at Dublin airport with time to kill at the hellish temporary departure gates on Pier D and start surfing the net aimlessly. Yahoo! has launched a new service called Yahoo! Answers and, as an example of the sort of question that might be answered, it offers: 'What is déjà vu?' This has been the sample question for months now and has, therefore, also become its own answer.

I board the flight and listen yet again to the taped messages that now haunt my dreams – ads for Ryanair's new callcard from Starfish Telecom and for Bullseye Baggies, which are double measures of spirits served in sachets; a safety spiel delivered by a man with perfect English who displays what I think may be a Dutch inflection only when he asks us not to 'remyoove' our safety belts until the captain switches the sign off; and a woman with an Irish accent who says, 'The use of laptop computers is prohibited during take-off but can be used once airborne.' So, can you use a use? I think I'm getting laughably pedantic and going just a little mad.

I'm also getting pissed off at the fact that despite buying the equivalent of three trolley-loads of food and drink since launching myself into Ryanland, I still haven't won the onboard competition for a free flight. You get double tickets for the draw with some items (it's Red Bull today, and I've drunk so many my heart is ricocheting off my rib cage) but, yet again, when they announce the winning number, the cheer comes from ten rows away. Once we land, the passage through Reus, as with all these smaller airports, is problem-free, and soon I am at the Hotel PortAventura on the edge of the theme park of the same name. It used to be jointly owned by Universal Studios and was known for a time as Universal Mediterranea, but la Caixa, the Spanish banking giant, now owns it outright.

Salou in Catalunya turns out to be a perfect place to site a theme park. Though I'm fond of Disneyland Paris, I always believed it was built in the wrong place. I once went there under the grey blanket of an October Île-de-France sky and found myself hurtling backwards on the Indiana Jones et le Temple du Péril rollercoaster while my head was pelted by hailstones the size of Cadbury's Crème Eggs. No, Spain is where you want to see a theme park and, at PortAventura, deliciously warm sunshine dries me off when the first adventure of the day, the Tutuki Splash, lives up to its name and drowns me.

I stare for about an hour at the Hurakan Condor, a wicked ride in which you are strapped to a chair, run swiftly to the top of a 100-metre flagpole, tilted forward so that you are looking straight down at the ground, then dropped in an 86-metre freefall that takes about four seconds and, I imagine, four years off your life. The fear-of-heights issue proves insurmountable, though, and I wander away defeated. Fortunately, I am not so lily-livered about rollercoasters. Though I'm not wild about the slow climb up the first hill and close my eyes for the duration, I love the exhilaration of being turned upside down, and Dragon Khan was a world-beater in its day with eight full inversions (Colossus, in London's Thorpe Park, beat that in 2002 with ten inversions). I learn from the Rollercoaster Database (log on to rcdb.com and wave the day goodbye) that the elements are a loop, a dive loop, a zero-G roll, a cobra roll (which turns you upside down twice), another loop and two interlocking corkscrews. The track is 1,270 metres long, the biggest drop is 50 metres, and, at 105 kilometres an hour, the ride will take one minute and forty-five seconds. And it is just as billed, punch-the-air liberating and the acceptable way to stare imminent death in the face.

Later, I wander down to Salou, a seaside resort I last visited almost twenty years ago. I remember it as lazy and authentically Spanish but, tonight, a built-up area full of lively bars and clubs is hopping, even though peak season ended last week. One tout is doggedly trying to get me to go to a club and, from his accent, I deduce he is Russian – in fact, he is from the West of Ireland. He looks about fourteen but confides that he has had sex three times this week, adding proudly 'and with three different women'.

I go to the club he has recommended, and near the end of the night, I buy a bottle of water. As I leave, the barman accuses me of stealing it, and this attracts the attention of a bouncer, who demands I give it back. I refuse and the bouncer lunges for me, delivering a sledgehammer punch to my shoulder, then throws me down a flight of stairs, where three surprised and refreshingly plump English girls mercifully break my fall – if they had been stick insects from Russia, we'd all be dead. Enraged, I go outside and stop a police car, but the 'cops' turn out to be a private security firm paid for by the clubs, so they refuse point blank to come with me to log a formal complaint. When I insist they have to, one of them leaves his SUV and draws a truncheon on me, making it clear that he too will assault me first and face the consequences later.

This all leaves a very sour taste in my mouth. I know they have to deal nightly with drunks and louts – and, yes, I have a few beers onboard tonight, though the last time I looked, that is not a crime – but the way they treat me is disgraceful and I vow to make a formal complaint at the Spanish embassy when I get home. Of course, I never get around to it.

Another day in civilised PortAventura heals the hurt, though the rattling wooden coaster, Stampida, is probably best not ridden when you are nursing a bruise that looks like the mauve-to-purple palette in the Dulux catalogue. After a few hours at the Caribe Aquatic Park and dinner at the new Beach Club, set among the pines nearby, it is time to move on again. I have business in Austria, so I stay the night in Castelldefels, near Barcelona's El Prat Airport (named, one presumes, after my favourite nightclub bouncer). I'm at another Hesperia hotel, now my favourite chain in Spain, in a bijou property that has separate accommodation blocks ranged around a small central pool and it reminds me of the apartments on that 1980s TV show, *Melrose Place*. Only €69.95 for a room, too.

As I fly early next morning to Innsbruck, via Vienna, I am reminded of why we love Ryanair, even when we occasionally hate them. The only flight I could get on this route was a one-way business class with Austrian, and it cost €600.90. And, you know, that's what we would all still be paying if it wasn't for Michael O'Leary, and Stelios Haji-Ioannou of easyJet, and the people behind Sky Europe, Germanwings, Air Berlin, Vueling, Wizzair and all the other low-fare carriers who have brought air travel to the masses and who forced legacy carriers like Aer Lingus and British Airways to introduce sensible fares we could actually afford. The thought lasts, I would say, about halfway through the hot cooked breakfast served at my reclining seat as I slowly sip my champagne and wash the rigours of the morning away with a hot towel.

Hmmm, maybe 600 quid's not so bad after all.

16

BIARRITZ–PAU

FR1982 • Dublin (DUB) to Biarritz (BIQ)
1,160 km • £104.02

FR2357 • Pau (PUF) to Stansted (STN)
953 km • €54.92

FR293 • Stansted (STN) to Dublin (DUB)
472 km • £20.82

Thanks to a monumental booking cock-up in which I was supposed to fly to Biarritz from London but then had to change back to a Dublin departure, I have somehow managed to spend £104.02 on a one-way flight with Ryanair, a fare more reminiscent of the flag-carrier airlines in the bad old days, especially when expressed as €157. While much is made of Ryanair's one-cent special offers, they are like Christmas lights in the otherwise drab window of a provincial department store. If you're happy to wait for a sale and let Ryanair tell you where to go, it is a wonderful airline. If you know, three months out, that you want to travel on a certain date to a specified destination, you will get a bargain. If you book just a week ahead, a cheap fare is less likely but not impossible. But if you need to reorganise a flight at short notice, you not only must pay the difference between the old and new prices of the individual sectors, you must pay an administration fee of €25 per sector too. In many instances, it is cheaper to start the whole booking procedure from scratch and just take the financial hit.

I can't tell you how many Ryanair flights I've booked over the years and not used. Not only does the airline get to keep the fare I paid, it does not have to pass on the passenger charges to the relevant airport either. Yes, I could apply for a refund, but the 'administration' fee is actually more than the sum I would recover, a classic Catch-22. No matter which way you turn, Michael O'Leary has thought of it first and unravelled barbed wire around the brick wall at the end of the cul-de-sac. It is not illegal, and since we flock to fly with the airline no matter how badly it treats us, nothing will ever change. When it comes to Ryanair, all of Europe suffers from that emotional dependence on a captor known as Stockholm syndrome – though given the airline's fondness for playing fast and loose with geography, Skavsta syndrome might be more apposite in this particular instance.

So I sulk all the way to Biarritz-Anglet-Bayonne Airport (so good they named it three times), which is, refreshingly, just 4 kilometres from town, a Ryanland record. This means that even though I have to grab a taxi, dump my bag at the Radisson and walk to the Grande Plage, I am still in time for breakfast on the promenade outside the casino. It is Sunday and Biarritz is mobbed. Along the prom, a 100-metre-long barre has been erected and about 200 people, women and men alike, are performing ballet steps to classical music under the tutelage of a man with a megaphone. I order strong coffee and a croissant with jam and sit back to watch. Of all the entertainment disciplines, I loathe ballet more than any other, because it is so prissy and narcissistic – yet, on this warm September morning, when viewed as a communal exercise session rather than an elitist performance, it is entrancingly graceful and soothing.

And it becomes a motif for Biarritz, because this turns out to be one of my favourite stops on this whirlwind tour of Europe, a resort with innate style and vast reserves of allure. In European holiday-resort terms, it might be the oldest courtesan on the block, but it still knows the best tricks.

A home from home for almost two centuries to the cream of European royalty, it was put on the map by the Empress Eugénie of France, wife of Napoleon III. She introduced him to the beaches where she had played as a child, and he was so taken with Biarritz that he ordered the construction of a royal palace, La Villa Eugénie, which later became the Hôtel du Palais. With the Napoleons in residence almost every summer for sixteen years from 1854 onwards, it was inevitable that Europe's incestuous monarchies would follow. As the years passed, visitors included Leopold II of Belgium; Bismarck, the Iron Chancellor of Prussia; Queen Victoria and her son, Edward VII; the Empress of Austria and, later, the new aristocracy of Charlie Chaplin, Sarah Bernhardt, Igor Stravinsky, Gary Cooper, Frank Sinatra and Jayne Mansfield. It also became a second home, from their exile in Paris, for the Duke and Duchess of Windsor, Edward and Mrs Simpson, the couple whose love affair led to an abdication and set in train the process by which the reigning Queen of England found herself on the throne.

Biarritz became famous because of the beach – doctors insisted the sea had healing properties for rheumatic ailments. I dip a toe in but it is far too cold for me, so instead I make for a café and have a superb *salade du berger*, which is topped with goat's cheese in filo pastry, then *moules marinières* and *crêpes suzettes*, washed down with a pichet of white wine, a beer and a *café irlandais*. I note, looking back over my travels, that I appear to do nothing but eat and drink, but when you travel alone, that really is all you can do. Certainly, the only place you have any likelihood of chatting to anyone is in a bar, and chatting is what I enjoy most. Tonight is no exception and I talk for an hour to a German couple who are as taken with Biarritz as I am, though when you come from the Ruhr, as they do, I suspect you would be taken with Ellesmere Port.

As the sun starts to set, the horizon disappears and sea and sky become one in a washed-out, brilliant-white, Persil-commercial kind of way. Shadowy stick figures wander along the beach, gulls wheel in torpid arcs, the tang of ozone is like a Spangle on the end of my tongue and the wind is starting to whip up, gently warming the promenade. I notice a crowd gathered in front of the casino and, from a parapet above, watch the most extraordinary dance performance I've ever seen.

When I tell people this, they think I had more than one *café irlandais*, but the dancers are, in short order, a man and a mechanical digger. Their elegant minuet is not only wildly inventive, it transcends scepticism to become deeply moving (and, in this respect, I sometimes wonder if I had more than one Irish coffee myself).

I'm truncating a ten-minute routine here but, basically, the man dances and turns his back to the digger. The digger playfully taps him on the shoulder. The man lies down, the digger scoops him up. The man hangs upside-down from the bucket by the back of his knees and the digger twirls him around; then he stands and the music builds and he and the digger go into a kind of rapture as he is framed against the last rays of the dying sun before slowly being rolled gently to the ground again as the music finally comes to a halt. I am so engrossed I haven't noticed how the crowd has swelled to fill every available vantage point, and when the last note dies, the parapet, the promenade and the adjoining cliff face erupt in cries of 'encore' and 'bravo'.

And in that moment, I am once again reminded why I love Europe, for the precocity of anyone who would choreograph a love story between a man and a machine, and bring it to such sinuous and compelling life that maybe a thousand people could suspend disbelief and see the romance in it. I play and replay it in my head as I have a nightcap on the roof terrace of the Radisson, looking over the town to my right and across the bay to San Sebastian, 40 kilometres away in Spain, to my left. She may be an old-age pensioner, but bewitching Biarritz is as sexy as Lauren Bacall.

Next morning, I leave for Pau, an Impressionist painting posing as a Pyrenean town, for yet another car launch, this time the new BMW 3 Series coupe. It's a useful way to combine a bit of real, paid-for work with the whimsical decision to abandon Ireland for months to wander around Ryanland. The car is a belter, needless to say, and we have an enjoyable day throwing it around the back roads in this sleepy corner of France. Next morning, my colleagues depart, but I borrow a Beemer and drive to Lourdes, the most famous shrine dedicated to the Virgin Mary, who is said to have appeared to a young shepherd girl, Bernadette Soubirous, in 1858.

During the ninth of eighteen apparitions at the grotto of Massabielle, the 'lady', as the young visionary described her, asked Bernadette, 'Would you mind going down on your knees … kissing the ground … and eating the grass that is there … for sinners? Go drink at the spring and wash yourself there.' In front of scandalised onlookers, Bernadette did so, lapping up water that had been fouled by animals. But next day, a new spring burst forth, and people who drank from it started to report cures for ailments. The legend of Lourdes was born.

Visitor numbers have risen to over 5 million a year, yet in the almost 150 years of the shrine's operation, only sixty-eight 'cures' have been verified by Church investigations. The triumph of Lourdes, then, is faith over logic, never more evident than when I enter a public car park with more spaces reserved for the disabled than any equivalent facility on earth. The main street, the Boulevard de la Grotte, is to Catholicism what the Reeperbahn is to sexuality, a tawdry row of Marian hyper-markets selling dime-a-dozen holy-water bottles, rosary beads to accessorise with just about any outfit ever made, candles, candle-holders, fridge magnets with prayers printed on them and, in one shop, rubber dinosaurs. I clearly missed out on the best part of Leviticus: 'And Jonah, son of Jor-El, went unto the desert and smited the velociraptor...'

But once you reach the sanctuaries, as the greater shrine is known (and it is huge, a series of outbuildings topped in splendour by the basilica built over the grotto itself), a sort of peace descends. Though I have long since lapsed, I know that leaving the faith is a great deal easier than ensuring it leaves you, so I am the ultimate à la carte Catholic. That's why, in a time-honoured ritual, my mother shakes holy water in my general direction around the time of every take-off – if I'm delayed more than an hour, I phone her to make sure she shakes it again. Nor have I ever hurtled down a runway without blessing myself, which seems especially terrifying to the British, who assume all public displays of piety to be the precursor to some suicidal act and who watch in ill-concealed panic as I playfully tease out a two-second act into some-thing bordering on two minutes.

Walking up the main avenue of the sanctuaries, I recall the old joke that tells of the Irish boy in a wheelchair who goes through the baths in Lourdes and comes out as unable to walk as he went in. His disap-pointment is brought to a rapid end by his mother, who roars, 'You ungrateful little bastard – look, there's a new set of tyres on the chair.' Only someone with an Irish mother would truly get that joke; all our lives, Irish mammies have taught us to look for the good in everything and to be grateful for what little we get. There is no point in dreaming big when life is just a series of knocks – expectation is the root of all sorrow.

Most of the people here must also know that; after all, that batting average of less than one cure every two years, those odds of 10-million-to-one against leaving here in better health than you arrived, would not encourage a non-believer to get out of bed to buy a lottery scratchcard, never mind travel here to have his hopes dashed. I decide to go to the baths anyway. I had always assumed, ignorantly, that Lourdes had a large pool where you went for a dip, maybe even a proper swim, and felt your muscles loosen, the extra fat roll off you in a sort of spiritual liposuction, your jug ears correcting themselves, and other parts of your body realising their full potential and measuring up to the proportions of a German octogenarian.

What I find instead is something much different. I join a queue on a bench outside the baths, and we shove along it until we are invited indoors. Everyone is praying, and even I start to pray too, recalling the chants of my youth. It would be a lie to say that I feel any more religious than usual, but a strange peace descends on me, perhaps because so many in this queue look so much more in need of this than I do, especially a man yellowed by cancer. I suddenly remember that my own grand-mother, Annie Kavanagh Nolan, came here in 1938 by boat and train from Dún Laoghaire in a last attempt to beat the ravages of tuberculosis, which had already claimed her daughter and husband and which, sadly, returned to claim her too, leaving my late father the sole survivor of his immediate family and an orphan at nine years old.

I think of her as I am called into a small, tented vestibule along with five others, where we are invited to strip to our underwear. There are three men in their thirties whom I take to be from the Indian subcontinent, the fourth clearly is a native Central American and the last is an Italian man of around seventy with a stomach slashed by angry scars and depressed like that of a dog insufficiently stuffed by an inept taxidermist. He is called first and disappears behind a curtain for about four minutes. Then, it is my turn.

An American man – he may be a priest, I'm not sure – tells me to go to the corner, turn my back and remove my boxers. As soon as I am naked, a state I appear to have spent the entire summer in, he wraps a linen towel around my waist and ties it at the side. I register that there is just the one towel and realise with a slight start that everyone who has been here before me has been wrapped in the same one. This leaves me unsure as to whether the aim is to be cured of something or to catch it.

In the middle of the room is a stone trough filled with water which, I later discover, is changed just twice a day, and I am at the tail end of the morning session. I am told to stand on the steps above it, to look straight ahead at a statue of the Virgin while saying a prayer and to think carefully of my intentions. There is no need to hurry, the American man says. He wants this to be a meaningful pilgrimage and I am to take as much time as I need.

I say a prayer for a sick relative and then hold out my arms to indicate that I am ready for the bath. I walk down the steps and two aides take an arm each and lower me gently until I am waist-deep in the freezing water. They then throw me backwards quite quickly, and I am aware the towel has flipped up to my waist, so they are getting a view I wouldn't wish on anyone.

When I stand up, something strange happens. My eyes are actually stinging with tears. I don't know why – maybe it was thinking of the grandmother I never knew and the desperate hope she invested in her trip here, a trip which to me seems futile but to her may have brought comfort, even in the face of certain death from the disease ravaging her body. Maybe it was because thinking of her made me think of my dad, who I still miss terribly. Whatever, the American man sees what has happened and he smiles gently and with so much kindness he practically glows like a Ready Brek kid. I shake his hand and mutter an embarrassed 'thank you', completely thrown by my own reaction to this traditional ritual.

I slip back outside and dress again; there are no towels, because the Catholic belief is that this water is not 'wet' in the conventional sense. On the avenue, I phone my mother, just to tell her that I feel light-headed and dizzy and 100 per cent more alive than I did when I arrived here. And it strikes me that maybe I feel this way because you always feel like that if you have to get dressed straight after a swim in cold water. Maybe I'm just caught up in the spirit that keeps Lourdes alive, the sense of camaraderie that is all around me, the selfless dedication of the helpers pushing wheelchairs, the tangible scent of hope that gives the place its energy. I'm a sceptical bastard at the best of times but, today, I just feel like being nice. That's a miracle that will never be documented, but it sure feels like one to me.

I drive back to Pau-Pyrenees Airport in a warm trance (well, mostly – I still make time to wonder what happens if someone is clocked by a cop hopping into a car in a disabled parking space, and who protests 'but I was cured', to which the inevitable response would be, 'oui, Monsieur, they all fucking say that, but you're still nicked'). My reverie comes to an end when, as we queue for the Ryanair flight, a troop transport flies overhead and disgorges about a hundred parachute trainees, prompting one Englishman to shout, 'Jesus, I knew they were a no-frills airline but this is ridiculous.' Everyone on the plane is still laughing when it takes off. This has been a good day.

And then I get to Stansted, where the new security measures have caused unmitigated havoc. It takes a full ninety minutes to clear security and I finally get home physically exhausted, but refreshed in ways I would not have believed possible this morning. Weird. Unexpected. And lovely too.

17

KNOCK IRELAND WEST–LONDON LUTON

FR8143
Knock (NOC) to London Luton (LTN)

FR8142
London Luton (LTN) to Knock (NOC)
608 km • €16.54 return

Since my last Ryanland trip, three weeks ago, I've been busy with work, most of which has involved me flying around Europe – clearly, someone is taking the piss. I've been back to Barcelona (and a sensational hotel, La Florida, which looks out over the whole city from Tibidabo Mountain and has a stainless-steel horizon pool to enjoy the view from) and put a new diesel V8 Range Rover through its paces off-road. Then I flew to Grosseto in Italy, via Zurich, and drove to Siena for the launch of the

Ford Focus cabriolet, this time staying at the Borgo Scopeto, a stunning, converted Tuscan estate owned by the seemingly 'illustrious' Sozzini family – and, thanks to a raid on the wine cellar, I managed to get fairly Sozzinied myself. From there, I dashed back to Dublin to see Pete Doherty and Babyshambles play live, had about four hours sleep (I was in bed for eight, but you don't get the sight of Kate Moss in a denim miniskirt out of your mind that quickly), then went back to Dublin Airport for a Ryanair flight to Beauvais and two days at the Paris Motor Show.

Unusually for Ryanair, the flight was four hours late. A group of Derry City fans heading to the French capital for their team's clash with Paris St Germain in the Uefa Cup used the opportunity to seize control of the PA system at the gate and spent about two hours making stupid, bogus announcements that drove me to distraction. ('Would the owner of car registration number DEZ 123 please remove it from the runway where it is causing an obstruction?' was representative of the general level of wit – and these people still cling to the fallacy that citizens of the Republic of Ireland are bereft at having artificially been parted from them in 1921. Yeah, right.)

After a welcome lull, a deep, vaguely Anglo voice crackled over the loudspeaker and asked, 'Ladies and gentlemen, could I have your attention please?' There was a ripple of 'ssshhhhs' before the voice continued, 'Would the real Slim Shady please stand up? I repeat, would the real Slim Shady please stand up, please stand up?' And, despite my better judgement, I and about 200 others fell around laughing.

Once in Paris, I made my way to *Le Paquebot*, a *bateau mouche* moored at the Quai Henri IV, where Toyota treated the world's media to a cruise on the Seine. It was a warm night, and I spent most of the trip on deck, eating canapés, drinking wine and watching the magnificent light show as the thousands of popping bulbs on the Eiffel Tower turned it into an exploding torch. I know Paris well and, through over-familiarity, went through a phase of being slightly jaded with it. Tonight, the city has cloaked itself in magic again and I feel like I am seeing it all for the first time, even though I've been coming here for twenty-seven years.

Eventually, I am called downstairs on the boat to meet Katsuaki Watanabe, president of Toyota Motor Corporation and one of the world's most powerful businessmen. I make a pathetic attempt at bowing, and am invited to ask him a question. I resist the temptation to open with 'Is that guy Ken Watanabe in *Letters from Iwo Jima* any relation?' and instead ask an inane question about the company's business plan. This is translated, then he talks. The translator looks at me and delivers an answer shorter by about three-quarters than his, then everyone bows again and Watanabe-san is whisked off to be translated into German. I feel like I've had an audience with the Pope.

With a couple of colleagues, I end the night in the bar of the Hôtel Costes on the rue Saint-Honoré. Famous as the haunt of supermodels during Paris Fashion Week, it also boasts a seriously cutting-edge DJ in Stéphane Pompougnac, whose jazzy lounge compilation CDs, nine of them to date, have put Costes on the map. The hotel is decorated in sumptuous deep reds and the floor staff themselves look like supermodels resting between ramp jobs. It is stylish in a way only the French can pull off, and just a single fringed cushion short of camp. It also makes even Oslo look cheap – a bottle of beer here is €10 and a gin and tonic is €17, but the weapons-grade chic makes it all worthwhile.

My flight home is with Aer Lingus and, as usual, I get lost in Terminal 1 at Charles de Gaulle, mainly because check-in is so subterranean, you virtually have to swim there through the sewers – then you must make your way to the gate via escalators that crisscross the central atrium like the cocktail sticks in a game of KerPlunk.

Two nights later, I am in the Welcome Inn Hotel in Castlebar, County

Mayo, 1,000 kilometres and a million chilled beats from the Hôtel Costes. I have driven from Dublin and used the opportunity to road test the Chrysler 300C, the big sedan with a Mercedes engine and a front grille like the gate on Skull Island that keeps King Kong from molesting the natives. En route, I stop off at Strokestown House in County Roscommon to see the Famine Museum and am delighted to discover that the menu in the café does not depend entirely on the potato. Who says we never learn from history?

I have never been to Castlebar, and I retire to bed early after deciding a Monday night in October probably doesn't show it off at its best. Nor, indeed, does the Welcome Inn, where attempts to draw hot water from the shower meet with no success. After breakfast, I point out the problem at reception and am asked how long I left it running for.

'A good ten minutes,' I say.

'Ah, it'll need a bit longer than that,' the girl tells me. That's all very well, but at the rate it's going, I'll have to pay for a second night's accommodation. Eventually, the trickle warms to tepid, just enough to get me washed and underway.

I'm off to Knock Airport, but decide to first stop in Knock itself, a Marian shrine that is a sort of Lourdes Lite. The basilica is also, unquestionably, the ugliest church in all of Ireland. The Virgin Mary is said to have appeared to a group of townspeople here in 1879, though it must have been a bit rougher than Lourdes, because she brought St Joseph and John the Evangelist with her and, having spent two hours hanging around the gable wall of the old parish church, she never came back.

The grandly titled Knock Ireland West Airport was the pet project of Monsignor James Horan, parish priest of Knock, who in the 1980s raised funds to build a runway on top of a bog then badgered the government into funding the rest of it. At one point, in a money-making scheme aimed at lowering the debt, you could show up here in your car, pay a quid and race down the runway at whatever speed took your fancy. It was always wise, however, to bear in mind that at the end of it was a ledge which effectively performed the same function as the lip on an aircraft carrier that helps jets become airborne and, as a consequence, it wasn't necessarily the best thing in the world to approach at 160 kilometres an hour in a Datsun Cherry with dodgy brakes.

After a coffee in the sunny airport café, I make for the departure lounge, where a woman approaches me.

'Could I have your €10 departure fee, please?' she asks.

'I beg your pardon.'

'€10,' she says again. 'You have to pay €10 to leave.'

I am utterly gobsmacked. It never said so on the Ryanair website, I point out.

'No, we've asked them to put up a note about it but they haven't done so,' she says.

'And what if I choose not to pay?' I ask.

'Then I'm afraid you won't be flying today,' comes the answer.

So I do pay, and take the explanatory leaflet, which tells me the fee goes to 'providing passenger and airline services and the ongoing maintenance and operation of the airport. The services include terminal facilities, car parking, safety and security, and airline services such as navigational aids, runway systems, aircraft parking and fire services.' Everything, in other words, that every airport in the world provides without the need for a supplementary development fee on top of the €6 passenger service charge that already appears on my Ryanair ticket.

I think briefly of brokering a deal – they can have the cash in exchange for giving me ten minutes on the runway in the Chrysler, just to see what the 218 horsepower engine feels like at full throttle. Instead, as I root around for my wallet, I ponder the fact that there never was a justifiable commercial demand for an airport in Knock. It has too small a hinterland and serves too few destinations to attract the number of passengers it needs to survive in the real world, and an island the size of Ireland, already served by international gateways at Shannon, Cork and Dublin and with existing regional feeder airports in Galway and Sligo, simply doesn't need Knock Ireland West. If the 'development' fee is a valid charge, then management should insist that airlines add it to the price of an online ticket, so I can make a decision to proceed with the booking, or not, at the time of purchase. But hitting me at departures for a tenner is cheap and grubby; I have no choice but to hand it over, but I would sooner fly into the Cliffs of Moher than ever use Knock again.

I used regularly to fly to Luton when my sister lived in nearby Watford, but given that it's yet another airport on top of a hill, I quickly discovered that this was a great way to see Birmingham. One memorable foggy night, the pilot tried to land three times before finally diverting, and the woman beside me actually handed over her vodka and Coke and said, 'Look, love, I think you need this more than I do' – perhaps because I actually roared out, 'Jesus, Mary and Joseph!' as we shot back up for the last time in a wail of thrust and hope.

So, despite the fact that I've flown to Luton Airport maybe a dozen times, I've never actually been to Luton. I look for tourist information at the airport and find leaflets on neighbouring Buckinghamshire, Hertfordshire and Essex, but nothing on the municipality or its surrounding county, Bedfordshire, which sets a few alarm bells ringing – and, yes, the town centre turns out to be emblematic of a malaise that has swept Britain, and England in particular. I love England, always have done, but it seems to me now to be a country in crisis, cowed and beaten and overwhelmed by bad architecture, poor planning and out-of-town shopping malls that have sucked the marrow from the cities they encircle. In most countries, pub happy hours straddle that 5–7 p.m. period between the end of the working day and the time people

CITY OF DERRY–EAST MIDLANDS

FR1676

City of Derry (LDY) to East Midlands (EMA)

FR1675

East Midlands (EMA) to City of Derry (LDY)

454 km • £26.18 return

I am back in Knock, and I scurry through arrivals and exit the car park in record time, lest a wretch in a shawl, with naked children chewing at her shins, hops from a bush and begs, 'Arrah, sure go on there, mishter, and givvus another tenner to keep the ould airport going for another few hours.' It's just past 11 a.m. and I have seven leisurely hours to cover 205 kilometres before flying from Derry to East Midlands on this ping-pong match over and back across the Irish Sea. I drive through Sligo town and am delighted to find that it is still lined with family-owned drapers' shops, and pubs that have real people's names over the doors, not Frog and Firkin, or Rose and Crown, or Blū with a macron over the '*u*' or, dear Jesus, a Yates's Wine Bar.

That thought reminds me that I am not far from the final resting place of William Butler Yeats, Ireland's greatest poet and winner of the Nobel Prize for Literature in 1923. Personally, I always thought the greater talent in the family was his younger brother, the Expressionist painter Jack. This view was shared by John Butler Yeats Senior, also a painter, who said, 'Some day, I will be remembered as the father of a great poet, and the poet is Jack.'

But old WB is an icon revered all over the world (his verse even turned up once in *Seinfeld*), and, as always, there is a mix of languages and accents in the air when I call by his grave at the old church at Drumcliffe. The simple headstone carries the epitaph: 'Cast a cold eye on life, on death; Horseman, pass by!', taken from his poem, 'Under Ben Bulben', the mountain which rises dramatically behind this very spot. When I drive on, I round a corner and face a view of stirring loveliness, the shore of south Donegal, lolling in autumn sunshine as the deep-blue Atlantic waves crash onto the shore. I always forget how much I adore Ireland until I drive around it – then I let another year pass and say to myself, I always forget how much I adore Ireland until I drive around it.

I have only a couple of hours to spare in Derry, so I walk the old city walls before pausing at the plaque in Bishop Street that commemorates Mrs Cecil Frances Alexander (1818–95), wife of the Bishop of Armagh, who wrote two of my favourite hymns, 'All Things Bright and Beautiful' and 'Once in Royal David's City'. She is said to have hated flattery or praise of any kind – how wonderfully Protestant! – so let's oblige her posthumously by agreeing that the middle eight in the former needs a bit of work and the latter makes impossible demands on anyone whose voice has broken. Close, Mrs A, but no cigar.

Derry looks lively and energised, and I'm delighted to see that it is finally getting its share of the peace dividend. On previous visits, I felt that the Troubles, as we so euphemistically refer to almost four decades of strife and death, exerted an unbreakable stranglehold on this very Catholic city, just minutes from the now invisible border with the Republic. It's a shame, because the moment the ink dried on the Good Friday Agreement, Belfast effectively shed its cocoon of sorrow and fizzed forth as a cool, outward-looking city – but Derry, riven by a strain of sectarianism bordering on apartheid and nowhere near as prosperous as Belfast, took longer to find its groove. Today, the bustling Foyleside Shopping Centre and the busy cafés and bars on the hilly side streets testify to the fact that life has changed for the better. It is nice to browse and to realise that I really have entered free Derry, in every sense of that adjective.

All too soon, I am flying back to England from the petite City of Derry Airport, with its wonderful views over the Foyle estuary. I manage to park the car literally outside the terminal door – the last time that was possible in Dublin, Aer Lingus was still flying a single De Havilland Dragon to Bristol. I have not booked a hotel for tonight. In fact, I have decided to prostrate myself before providence and have not even decided which *city* to visit. The candidates are Nottingham, Coventry and Leicester, but when I land at East Midlands and check the information board, the first thing to hop out at me is a tourist leaflet for Lincoln. I have never been, and was intrigued by it when I saw footage of the filming of *The Da Vinci Code* there last year, so I decide that is where I will make for.

I nose the car onto the motorway and notice a sign for Luton. For the first time on my travels, I feel a little guilty about the emissions

I'm responsible for and make a mental note to donate money on carbonneutral.com as reparation for a carbon footprint which must by now be the size of Luxembourg. Today, I have flown and driven a combined total of 1,267 kilometres and the net result of my endeavours is that I am just 136 kilometres further up the M1 from where I started the day.

Lincoln is, allegedly, a seventy-minute drive but virtually none of it is on motorways, so I get hopelessly lost in the dark and find myself on a country road lined with huge, whooshing wind turbines, which is unnerving, then deep in Sherwood Forest, which is spooky, and even marooned in the car park of Tesco in Mansfield, which is frankly terrifying. It's even more annoying because I miss the handy presence of my wife to roar at for not reading the map properly and am left with no option but to go into a deep sulk after I round on myself.

By the time I arrive in Lincoln (fortunately, the illuminated cathedral on top of a hill is more help than any road sign), I search for a hotel and finally settle on the Duke William, a little pricey at £65, but it is getting late and beggars can't be choosers. The oldest parts of the building date from the 1680s and it was recorded as a hotel as long ago as 1777 – and this explains a lot of things. For starters, my room is so tiny the television completely fills the space between the far corner of the bed and the wall, so if my wife actually was with me, she would have to crawl across the bed to get under the covers. The confines I can live with, but less easy to comprehend is the fact that the table the TV sits on is too low, so when I lie on the bed, I cannot see the entire screen. I wanted to watch the second half of the *ITV News*, but now realise that watching the top half of it is the only option available.

The age of the hotel also appears to have necessitated the installation of a weird pumping system for the toilet, which gurgles like a dyspeptic stomach. Even worse, on the outflow pipe, there is a built-in macerator that makes waste smaller and less likely to block the pipes. You're going to have to do some of the work here for yourselves as I explain this delicately, but after a ten-minute, er, read of the paper, I flush the loo and hear gruesome grinding noises that remind me of the day I put cherries in the smoothie maker having forgotten to pit them first.

Re-running the previous twenty-four hours in my mind as I desperately try to remember what it was I ate, I wander down a steep hill called Steep Hill and stumble across a massive party consuming the town. Wednesday night, apparently, is student night, and every undergraduate of the nearby university seems to be on the piss. I'm too old for this and find a quiet bar where, as I have my first beer, a man strides in and orders a drink.

He turns out to be Irish and as we chat, an older man comes in, very well dressed in that sergeant-major way. He claims to be Irish too and tells an amazing tale of how his parents were murdered by the IRA in the 1950s, prompting him to leave for England, where he joined the British army and served as a marine on the Golan Heights. My new Irish mate is behind him making wind-up gestures and I'm starting to giggle, so to break the string of stories and regain my composure, I extend a hand and say, 'Philip Nolan, nice to meet you.'

'You too,' the elderly man says. 'My name is Fritz Heinrich von Walthausen, but you can call me Paddy. All my friends do.'

Sadly, I have taken a mouthful from the bottle as we shake hands, and the sheer implausibility of his name sends rivulets of a Brazilian beer called Brahma pouring from my nostrils like, rather fittingly, a rainforest waterfall after a sudden shower. (I google Fritz later and find no trace of him, nor of an IRA double murder in 1952, or indeed of the British army having been anywhere near the Golan Heights since Jesus was in a short tunic. There are, however, 13,500,000 hits for 'Paddy'.)

He has amused me so much, and the beer is going down so well, that I wander around Lincoln, as far as the Brayford Pool, an inland harbour surrounded by a hotel, a few pubs, restaurants and a multiplex. But I had earlier spotted an Australian bar on the main drag, and I pay two quid to get in and settle myself by the bar. It's past midnight and the place is hopping. There is a raised dance floor as well as a ground-level one, and with the drinks all discounted to suit student budgets, the place is heaving in a way that proves infectious. One group includes a young man in a wheelchair who clearly is paralysed completely from the waist down. If truth be told, my generation was brought up to be slightly fearful of disability and to treat the disabled as somehow different from everyone else. One bloke I know who was confined to a chair told me that everywhere he went, people would say to his mother, 'Would he like a sweet?', as if he was a child rather than an adult who simply couldn't walk.

Life couldn't be more different for the young man in front of me. He is at the centre of the conversation. When he wants to dance, someone – a man or woman, no one seems to care – takes him out and throws the chair around the floor while he waves his arms. They are plying him with as much drink as they are having themselves. It occurs to me, shamefully, that I am the only person here who even sees his disability – his friends certainly don't – and I think to myself that while students are the perennial butt of abuse for excessive drinking and drug-taking, this generation is a great deal less judgemental and a lot less scared of difference than mine was.

Further proof of this comes when I stand beside the dance floor, tapping a middle-aged foot to the music. Noticing me standing alone and clearly dying to join in, a girl on the podium shoots her arms forward and yells, 'Come on!', and she and her friend dance with me for half an hour even though I'm probably as embarrassing as her dad singing along to 'Agadoo' at a wedding. I fall into bed at three in the morning after eating a three-quid takeaway all the way back up Steep Hill and locking myself out of the hotel for an hour.

Next morning, I wake too late for breakfast, have a quick chat with the shredder ('fancy a kebab and chips...?') then pay four quid to savour the medieval hush of the cathedral and to mutter a prayer that my head will stop hurting. It is a humbling place, though I spend most of the time trying to find the exact spot where Tom Hanks looked quizzically at Audrey Tautou and – though allegedly wondering if she understood the message in the cryptogram – was, like me, probably just wondering if she had any plans to start acting before the movie ended.

As I drive back to East Midlands Airport, a sign for Grantham leaves me no option but to make a detour. I simply have to see for myself the town that could give birth to Margaret Thatcher, who allowed big business to take over the running of Britain, and who promoted the cult of the individual at the expense of society – society being a concept she famously said she didn't believe in. I'm no fool – I don't believe in endless handouts, or the pernicious hold the trade unions had over the Labour government that preceded her first term in office, or the untrammelled power of Europe to override the basics of national sovereignty. I admire the way she broke a culture of dependence by making it easier for people to buy out their council homes, but I hated her policies on Northern Ireland. Not because she stood up to the IRA, which was admirable, but because the way she did so, particularly during her cack-handed response to the 1981 hunger strikes, fuelled the Troubles for a decade longer than they needed to run.

The Grantham Museum is pleasant and engaging. It has a section on another of the town's famous children, Isaac Newton (and there are times I wish the apple had hit Thatcher on the head instead of him), and on the planning for the Dambusters raid, co-ordinated from an RAF base nearby. Then, in a cabinet, I see the blue Aquascutum suit most associated with Mrs Thatcher and presented by her to the museum. For some reason, it makes me shiver. The exhibit is no hagiography, though, for in another cabinet close by is her *Spitting Image* puppet and it almost snarls in caricatured nastiness.

Amused, I walk to see her childhood home, where she learned her brand of self-reliant Methodism in the small flat over the family grocery. The shop is now an alternative health centre and, if Margaret Hilda Roberts were to look from her old bedroom window, she would see why there was no longer any need for Daddy's grocery shop. Just 100 metres across the road is an Asda supermarket the size of a football field. The irony is so obvious it would look overcooked in a novel.

Minutes later, as I drive back to East Midlands, there comes a timely footnote. Thatcher's privatisation of national assets led many other governments to sell off their own family silver. Just last week, the Irish government dispensed with almost half of Aer Lingus. I am listening to the wonderful Jeremy Vine on BBC Radio 2, when the news comes on. 'The Irish budget airline, Ryanair, has launched a takeover bid for the recently privatised flag carrier, Aer Lingus...'

I swear to Christ I nearly crash the car. If Ryanair succeeds, then Ryanland will grow in size by a third. I could be doing this for the rest of my life. Once I get to Derry, I hop in the car and make for Dublin at speed. I need to lie down.

LEEDS-BRADFORD–BIRMINGHAM

FR152

Dublin (DUB) to Leeds-Bradford (LBA)

306 km • €17.49

FR8142

Birmingham (BHX) to Dublin (DUB)

320 km • £11.74

I first came to Leeds on holiday when I was a year old, and then every year until I was eighteen, often for three weeks at a time. Now I think of it, I have probably spent well over a year here if you add it all up. My father's Auntie Kit and her husband, Jack Taylor, lived on Intake Lane in Bramley, halfway between Leeds and Bradford, after following the emigration path well-worn by so many Irish in the past century.

Throughout the year, we would go on weekend trips to watch football matches, taking the overnight boat from Dún Laoghaire to Holyhead, then the train to Leeds, which almost always meant two hours on a freezing bench at Manchester Piccadilly waiting for the connection. Our spirits were always buoyed, though, by the prospect of bacon sarnies for breakfast in the cafeteria at Woolworth's, then a trip downstairs to scoop up all the sweets you couldn't buy in Ireland (Opal Fruits, Skittles, Curly-Wurlys). Then we would walk from the city centre to Elland Road to watch Norman Hunter feast on the femurs of some hapless opposition, in the days when visiting teams brought extra paramedics along for this much-feared fixture.

My father revered Leeds all his life, but never more so than in the Don Revie era. We would spend our holiday mornings at the training ground, running after the stars for autographs and pictures (my mother still has hundreds of photos of us with Allan Clarke, Eddie Gray, Peter Lorimer, Paul Madeley, Gary Sprake, Jack Charlton, and every other player of that golden era of First Division and FA Cup wins). One day, as we hung around the gates of Elland Road, Billy Bremner, the team's inspirational Scots captain, spotted us and got out of his car, chatted to my dad and posed for pictures with all of us. The man was a prince.

We got truly lucky, though, when we were approached by Louis Plowman, the stadium caretaker. When we told him we had come from Ireland, he manfully resisted the temptation to call the cops (this was the early 1970s, after all) and instead offered us a private tour of the stadium and showed us the trophy room where the Charity Shield took pride of place. He and his wife, Lewie, became firm friends and we used to visit them every time we went on holiday. One year, they even arranged for Don and Elsie Revie to send us a Christmas card, which took pride of place on the mantelpiece.

On match days, Louis would smuggle us into the players' lounge after the match, where Lewie worked the bar and passed bottles of pop to us to keep us happy. We overstayed our welcome one day when – with my brother, Mark, chasing me around the room – I wasn't minding where I was going and accidentally head-butted Joe Jordan. If you think for a moment about the relative heights of a striker and a nine-year-old boy, you will know exactly where I head-butted him, and my father, ashen-faced, sat me down and explained in words of one syllable that if I cost Leeds the league that year while Jordan recovered, there would be no more Spangles or Opal Fruits. Ever.

If there was a Mrs Jordan at the time, I don't suppose she was too happy either.

When the team was playing in a European tournament, we would go to the airport to wave them off. It was called Yeadon then, and it was just the most glamorous place imaginable to a boy who had never flown. The team all used to wear the same suits (not like nowadays, where flying footballers look like the cast of *Con Air*) and they would line up on the aircraft steps and wave to all of us cheering them from the balcony. Players made a lot less money back then, but they were a lot more considerate of the fans who paid their wages.

The first time I actually flew to Yeadon, by then renamed as Leeds-Bradford Airport, was in 1992, after my dad had a serious heart attack while he was on holiday.

'Is your visit for business or pleasure, Sir?' asked the police officer at the immigration desk.

'I'm on the way to see my father at the Infirmary – he's very sick,' I replied.

'So,' he asked, pulling himself up to full height, 'would you say that's business or pleasure, then?'

Contemptuously, I repeated the fact that my father was ill, and he let me pass. It is an exchange that has always sullied my memories of the airport.

Today, I make my way into the city centre, which is all shiny and pedestrianised. A branch of Harvey Nichols, the first outside London, opened in 1996 and it kick-started a fashion and style revival that has left much of the city unrecognisable from my young days of wandering around the Briggate, Vicar Lane and the Headrow. The covered market looks exactly the same as always, though, and I wander around it with a warm glow, with a pie, chips and mushy peas in my hand.

I forgot to pack spare socks for this trip, so I ask an Asian man at a clothing stall if he sells any and he hands me a pack of ten that costs three quid. I explain that I really need only one pair, and don't have space in my bag for any more, but the concept of selling anything in ones is obviously a first at Leeds market. Eventually, baffled as to why I would pass up a deal on bulk, he sells me a pair for 40p.

I see in the distance the new home of BBC Yorkshire, on the site of what used to be Quarry Hill Flats, then the biggest council-housing project in Europe. This reminds me that we were interviewed on BBC Radio Leeds once. My dad used to pick up the station on his old valve radio and he thought someone might like to know that the signal somehow wended its way to Dublin. A passing producer overheard the conversation with the receptionist and appeared so amused by the fact that anyone would holiday in Leeds year after year he asked us to come back next day and go live on air. I was asked a question but was so nervous my tongue grew to three times its usual size, so the answer that came out was a kind of gurgling and whistling noise that must have had half of the city twiddling the knobs to find out what had happened to the signal. It was excruciating. There is a reel-to-reel tape of it some-where in the attic but I have the feeling it was all so ghastly that no one has ever listened to it since the day it was broadcast.

I drive to Stanningley and call in on Auntie Kit's next-door neighbour, Mollie, still sprightly in her eighties, who makes tea and chats about the old days. And then I drive to Elland Road, the first time I've been back for, I guess, twenty years. There's a statue of Billy Bremner outside the ground, though it looks more like Bob Marley, and a bar called Billy's, named in tribute to the club's most famous son. Leeds have had ongoing financial difficulties and the training ground next to the stadium has been sold and lies undeveloped – but the grassy bank we used to sit on as kids, waiting for passing players to sign autographs, remains as it always was.

I rest against it and look around. My mind drifts, and suddenly the car park is filled once again with Ford Granadas and Capris and Jensen Interceptors. We are piling out of our two-tone Ford Anglia estate (as always, I'm in the boot). My mother has jet-black hair and is wearing a turquoise knitted suit with black and white piping on the lapels. My younger sister, Joyce, is beside her in a mustard trouser suit. Anne (she became Annie after she moved to London over twenty years ago) has a psychedelic tunic dress on, over purple bell-bottom trousers, and Mark and I are in striped brown, yellow and green polo shirts. And in the centre of it all is my dad, tall and strong and with his flyaway mop of hair slightly Brylcreemed to keep it in check. He had three passions in life – his wife, his kids and Leeds United, though we never asked him to rate them in order. When he died in 1998, we buried him in his Leeds United tie.

I sit for ages, looking at ghosts, of the living as well as the dead, and leave only when the grapefruit in my throat shrinks to a more manageable gobstopper size.

I fly home from Birmingham tomorrow, so I decide I will stay there, but when I see a sign for Stratford-upon-Avon, I carry on and book into a Holiday Inn. Again, I wonder how they can get away with charging £87 without breakfast – it came up as €131 on my Visa statement – for a room in October when, in Santiago de Compostela in June, I could walk up to a comparable Hesperia hotel and stay for €75, with a huge breakfast buffet thrown in.

Next morning, I wander up town but a travelling carnival has beaten me to it, so it's hard to get a historical perspective on the streets now hidden behind waltzers, dodgems and fun houses. I walk to the theatre where so many landmark performances have been showcased over the years and where, year in, year out, new stars are born. This year, the Royal Shakespeare Company is in the middle of a triumphant staging of the complete works of the Bard. I had hoped see the matinée performance of *Henry VI* but it runs to four hours and I have to skip it in case there is heavy traffic on the M40 when I make for the return flight. Instead, I call in to Birmingham for the first time since I was a kid and find a wonderful new Selfridges in the Bullring.

The shop looks like a whale studded with giant shiny discs and features a dramatic elevated glass walkway from the car park to the main shop (I inch my way across it, eyes fixed firmly ahead to thwart my vertigo, but it still feels spongy underfoot). Designed by the London architecture firm, Future Systems, Selfridges fulfils just about every criterion for quality modern architecture I can think of, pushing the limits of form while retaining function, playing with our expectations of what a shop should look like and also telling us that here is a store that is as much about showmanship as it is about shopping. It is a neat nod to H. Gordon Selfridge, the American who opened his flagship London store in 1909 and who was the P.T. Barnum of retailing (on the plus side, his mantra was that the customer is always right; on the downside, he pioneered that gauntlet of perfume sprayers that attacks you inside the front door of every department store in the world). But it's not just Selfridges that impresses – most of the Bullring redevelopment seems to have avoided the pitfalls that towns like Luton are almost hypnotically lured to.

The price of this success is traffic and Birmingham, at the epicentre of the entire British motorway network, lives up to past form. It takes me nearly an hour to drive to the airport and I am sure I'll miss my flight, but someone here has done his or her homework and opened more security channels. The crowds are effectively corralled and people are forewarned many times about what they must take off before passing through the scanner. It cuts the wait time to less than fifteen minutes, which is acceptable, and I make it to the gate with time to spare. If only all airports could be so well organised.

BLACKPOOL

FR924

Dublin (DUB) to Blackpool (BLK)

FR925

Blackpool (BLK) to Dublin (DUB)

214 km • €35.01 return

I'm in a shop on Blackpool seafront, near the Tower, and things have changed here since I were a lad. Blackpool shops used to sell Kiss Me Quick hats, saucy postcards and sticks of rock. Nowadays, they sell penis pumps, and the packaging on one of them, on open display where no child could miss it, features a picture of a man lying back in ecstasy with what looks like an upright Dyson clamped to his genitals. The suction cup is so massive I'll venture it could pull the duvet through his arse and out through the tip of his knob. I wouldn't be at all surprised if both man and machine were bagless by the end of the evening.

On a distant shelf, I can actually see sticks of rock for sale, but they are placed next to lurid pink dildos. This perilous situation raises the entertaining possibility that the tiniest scintilla of confusion could bring an unexpectedly abrupt end to a drunken hen night. ('Hello, yes, this is the ambulance service. Yes, yes, I see, yes. I beg your pardon, she's got rock stuck *where…?*')

The shop is full of Scots, who have taken over the town for the half-term holiday. It's England's turn next week and the Irish mid-term break comes the week after, a nice triple boost to the resort's coffers at the end of the season. The reason they all come is for the illuminations, a world-famous display of lights that stretches for 10 kilometres from Starr Gate to Bispham and features moving tableaux along the route. There are over a million bulbs used in the display, and even though all of them are low-voltage, Blackpool's carbon footprint must look like a yeti's next to mine. The electricity bill for the sixty-six nights of illuminations comes to £50,000, but tourists who come to see them spend a fortune, so the investment is a no-brainer.

In truth, though, this would all work a lot better in the Canaries or Florida. The problem with late season here is that the weather has turned (some time in mid-July, probably) and sheeting rain is coming in intermittently off an Irish Sea as grey as barbecue ash. When I hop on one of the famous trams, which are not air-conditioned, I can see nothing because the windows are smeared with condensation, and I pass the whole journey in a fog accentuated by the pungent smell of damp pensioner.

I walk to the Winter Gardens, a huge complex of entertainment venues dating from the late nineteenth and early twentieth centuries. It has a stellar history, but today it hosts an indoor market that looks like a jumble sale in Soviet-era Russia. Paint is peeling everywhere, and though this is allegedly the premier venue in the northwest, with a vast ballroom, an opera house and a wonderful art-deco room decorated as a mini Andalusia, there is an air of decline about the place that is fatally off-putting.

A roll of honour on the wall – in gilt letters on wood, like those golf club plaques that list the captains – pays tribute to the headline acts who have played here every year since it opened. Among them are Arthur Askey and Gracie Fields, venerable names from a proud past. Things go a little wibbly when we get to Cannon and Ball, but the level to which Blackpool has descended becomes almost pitiful when I note the only name that appears twice, the most popular man in 100 years of music-hall legend, is Darren Day, tabloid love rat and 'star' of the first series of *I'm a Celebrity, Get Me Out of Here!*

Next to the Winter Gardens is a huge construction site where a shopping centre is taking shape. The tenant list includes all the usual High Street suspects, and it strikes me as odd that anyone coming here from Glasgow or Manchester or Hull would want to do on holiday exactly what he or she could do at home. Stylised billboards suggest this development will spearhead a regeneration of the town, but they have their work cut out for them.

I walk past Coral Island, which echoes to the sound of one-armed bandits chewing up and spewing out cash, though it is not yet lunch-time. The complex has a pirate theme that is rather subverted by the modern doors – somehow, 'shiver me PVC, lads' doesn't have the requisite ring to it. And this, in a nutshell, is Blackpool's problem – it has big ideas but no attention to detail. If an imagineer at Disney put aluminium doors on Pirates of the Caribbean, the attraction would pretty soon feature a live version of walking the plank. In Blackpool, there were so many years of plenty they have left a residual attitude of 'oh, it'll do'. After years of neglect, the Tower looks tatty, the Golden Mile between the North and Central piers has turned brassy, and the warren of bed and breakfasts in the back streets no longer caters for the needs of the next generation. I'm staying at a hotel where, once again, I would have caused less bafflement by asking for a char-broiled chihuahua instead of wi-fi.

I decide to take a wander around Louis Tussaud's Waxworks, founded by the great-grandson of the famous Madame Tussaud, and it soon becomes clear that the string of DNA containing the talent gene must have melted in a kiln somewhere along the way. The waxworks here are so risible it's often hard to stifle open laughter. David Beckham looks like Phil Mitchell from *EastEnders*. Michael Jackson looks like Teri Hatcher with a moustache. Robbie Williams looks like William H. Macy. Stars no one cares about anymore are still here – Pierce Brosnan as Bond; Gianfranco Zola, who was never that pivotal a figure in British football to start with; the late Les Dawson, dead for thirteen years, and depicted here in character with Roy Barraclough as northern matrons Cissie Braithwaite and Ada Shufflebotham.

In the colonnaded Regal Room, featuring the British royals and Pope John Paul II, Tony Blair is credited with being prime minister of Great Britain and Ireland, which will come as something of a shock to Bertie Ahern. It's all so depressing – the explanatory cards look like they were run up by a child on a PC with clip art and are about as sophisticated as the menus in a roadside caff. I've paid £8.95 for this and it is probably the greatest waste of money on my travels so far.

There is a break in the showers, so I walk the prom to the Pleasure Beach, the huge amusement park that features the Pepsi Max Big One, Britain's tallest and fastest rollercoaster. A crowd has gathered by the rail at the beach and when I join them I find they are watching JCB diggers at work on a coastal-erosion prevention scheme. I quickly scan the tourist leaflet which offers a six-day holiday planner, but since the erosion scheme is not included, I'm guessing some people are dashing back to their hotels to book a seventh night.

The longer I walk, the more depressed I get. When I was a kid, this was a magical place, but now it's just cheap and nasty. The Sandcastle, a big swimming pool with water slides, looks jaded and old fashioned, and the hotels on the prom, most of them glorified boarding houses, are about as welcoming as Abu Ghraib. Everyone I talk to agrees that Blackpool needs a miracle, and all of them are pinning their hopes on securing a licence for a new super casino to give the town an injection of adrenaline in its flagging heart. But they don't need a casino — they just need to get the bulldozers off the beach and set them to work on the prom. Or forget about the protection scheme altogether and let coastal erosion have its fun.

Alderman William Bean founded the Pleasure Beach in 1896, and it was later run by his daughter, Doris, and her husband, Leonard Thompson. Doris was a sprightly old woman who was still trying out the new rides almost until she died. I remember her sharing the PlayStation free-fall ride with Boyzone on its launch (it's now called the Ice Blast), and laughed myself sick when she shot upwards leaving her shoes behind. It was like one of those cartoons where only smoking soles are left when someone is hit by lightning. In 2002, the last new ride she graced with her indomitable presence was the Spin Doctor, which turns riders upside down at 60 mph. She was ninety-nine and still as fearless as the day she was born.

Doris' son, Geoffrey, in turn took over the business and developed many of the white-knuckle classics there today. He personally designed the Avalanche, a free-running rollercoaster with no rails except for the lift hill and the return to the station. For the ride proper, it follows a high-banked metal mesh track just like a bobsled, so no consecutive rides are exactly alike. Geoffrey also commissioned the Pepsi Max Big One, which on opening in 1994 was the tallest (215 feet) and fastest (87 mph) rollercoaster in the world (and, no, I just couldn't put myself through the slow climb up that first hill). He died, suddenly, after taking ill at a function in the park in June 2004 and, in one of those sad coincidences, his mother, by then 101, died just hours after his funeral.

Now the park is run by Amanda Thompson, Geoffrey's daughter, who was the real star of a 1998 BBC fly-on-the-wall documentary, *Pleasure Beach*. Then only in charge of the ice and circus shows, she was seen as a tough taskmistress. Now, running the whole enterprise, she is investing in new rides, painting and preserving the old ones (and the fabulous Grand National rollercoaster, where two trains race each other, badly needs a lick of paint, while the almost 100-year-old River Caves need the algae cleaned out), and bringing some real showbiz pep to Blackpool.

I buy a ticket for an acrobatic musical called *Eclipse*, and while it isn't quite on the scale of Cirque du Soleil in its staging, for quality and precision it need doff its cap to no one. Amanda, you see, has an eye for detail. Blackpool needs a despot, not a council, and who better than a fourth-generation impresario with the Pleasure Beach in her blood to oversee its restoration? I'd give her the job tomorrow.

I finish the day on Valhalla. Voted the best water ride in the world, it has a Viking theme, and features a hypnotic Norse song sung over and over again as I hand over six quid (six quid, for one ride – I knew I should have bought an all-day wristband) and queue for twenty minutes. The rain is back, so I buy a plastic poncho for £1.50 and eventually make it to one of the 'longboats'. The effects are wonderful – from blasts of icy arctic air to scorching belches of flame – but the drops leave me soaked to the bone. I pay another quid to stand in a booth to be irradiated with infra-red heat, but that just leaves me feeling like a kipper in a microwave, and tees me up to blend in with the pensioners on the tram.

My jeans are now cold and still plastered to me, so I stop off at the indoor market and buy the cheapest alternative I can see, a seven-quid pair of tracksuit bottoms with a desert camouflage pattern. I hang my jeans on the radiator in the hotel for an hour, but they're not exactly gifted in the plumbing department in Lancashire, and my guess is that it's set at around 15 degrees. If I'm lucky, the jeans might be dry by Saturday.

So I arrive to dinner in camouflage trousers and a white T-shirt, looking like a squaddie suffering from a rare form of Gulf War Syndrome that makes him believe, like many Japanese in another war long ago, that the conflict is still on. Dinner is massive, and included in my £49 room rate. There's a prawn-cocktail starter (and not an ironic one either, just prawns in a sauce made from one part ketchup to one part mayonnaise). It takes three staff to serve the components of the main course, which is chicken in onion and asparagus sauce with croquettes, garlic potatoes, carrots, green beans, baby corn and cauliflower cheese. It's like eating an allotment.

A young woman arrives and tells me what's for pudding – 'Chocolate Buccaneer, Strawberry Russe, Frangipane Flan' and dozens of other names that mean nothing to me, since they probably haven't appeared on a dessert trolley outside of Blackpool since Doris Thompson opened the Big Dipper. I go for the strawberry and ask for a sliver, but value for money is clearly what brings them back here year after year because the wedge she arrives with looks like the chocks that steady a 747 on the airport apron. I'm delighted the combat trousers have an elasticated waist.

I pull on a jacket and struggle outside. It's raining again, so I search for a cab, my eyes darting from side to side, the outfit making look like a fat mutant meerkat. I do a deal with a taxi driver to see half the illuminations for a tenner. The lights are as they always were, and the tableaux that rely on the switching off of some bulbs and the switching on of others, to give the impression that a character is moving, are particularly clever. But I'm sad because the driver tells me that Blackpool is on its last legs; without the casino, the decline will not be stemmed. Property prices are falling because so many jobs are seasonal, there's already a surfeit of rental property, and people who buy would rather buy new than convert an ex-B&B with creepy built-in hand basins in every room back into a family home.

I wander back to the hotel. My jeans are actually dry, but I go to bed – a mean little single with flannelette sheets and a nylon spread that crackles with so much static I look like the hero of *Eraserhead* – and I watch TV. Not for long, though, because it is a 14-inch portable on a bracket mounted about two metres from the ground and my neck can no longer take the strain.

Sleep comes slowly. My room is over the bar and a singer wails on until midnight. The last sound I hear before I fall asleep is a group of pensioners, high after supping crates of ale, doing what generations have done in Blackpool and ending the night with a sing-song.

As it happens, I don't actually know the way to Amarillo, but Blackpool has made me want to find out.

BRNO

FR8403

London Stansted (STN) to Brno (BRQ)

FR8404

Brno (BRQ) to London Stansted (STN)

1,200 km • £47.16 return

A chill has descended on Ryanland. As we line up for our descent into Brno, second city of the Czech Republic and a destination irksomely devoid of a second vowel that might offer a clue as to how to pronounce it, I can see trees denuded of leaves, cold furrows in fields and a leaden greyness to the skies that heralds sleet or snow. This is my first time in the country and I have decided to stay in Brno itself, rather than taking a bus to Prague.

The two cities do, however, seem to have at least one thing in common, as the first billboard I see on leaving the airport is for a lap-dancing club. The second billboard is for Tesco, and I am astonished to learn that there are thirty-five stores in the country, with a turnover of around £500 million a year. So that's what the fall of communism was all about. Instead of queuing for food, as the Czechs did in the bad old days, they can now buy cheese at four in the morning – all hail the Velveeta Revolution. Of course, the supermarket giant is not the only retailing superpower that set its sights on the emerging markets of the east, and all the usual US, Spanish and Swedish suspects sit cheek-by-jowl in town – KFC, McDonald's, Zara, H&M – while IKEA hovers on the fringes, making sure that Czechs too can sit back on their sofas while their wives or girlfriends ask, 'What's that spare screw on the floor for?'

One of the huge differences between travelling now and even a decade ago is the overwhelming volume of material available on the internet. As a child, I used to write to tourist boards to request brochures and information, which would arrive maybe a month later, often long after the holiday had ended. Now, not only does every city have its own website, there are thousands of blogs and advisories to steer you in the right direction. On virtualtourist.com, my favourite Brno post was under the heading of Tourist Traps, where one contributor wrote simply: 'No tourists, no traps.' Certainly, as I drive to town, I realise fairly promptly that the threat from Brno is unlikely to deprive the city fathers of Prague of an afternoon nap, never mind a night's sleep.

Another post warns 'be carful [sic], when meeting gypsies', but this is not a problem. Despite leaving several messages announcing my impending arrival, none of the gypsies has got back to me. They can be like that, you know – always somewhere else when you want one.

The taxi driver speaks good English and tells me the correct pronunciation of the city name is Brunno, and not Birno as I had volunteered.

I'm staying at the Grandhotel (and, on the evidence, spaces between words clearly are hoarded as covetously as vowels), which was built in the 1870s and seems to have had its last refit during the communist era. I'm told Emperor Franz Josef I of Austro-Hungary stayed here once. I'm not sure if the 'once' means 'in a bygone era' or, literally, 'once', though I have my suspicions. It is not really grand at all, but then if they'd called it the Dowdyhotel, it most likely would have diverted me from the opportunity of finding this out for myself. My bedroom is predominantly green, matched with dark wood; I feel like I'm staying on a snooker table. The hotel's own website says it is still one of the most famous places in Brno, which doesn't exactly make me optimistic that I will be able to fill two days here.

A quick walk around the city centre serves only to amplify my trepidation. Svobody Námestí, the main square, could have been built from a template (European Plaza No. 47 – Ersatz Medieval With A Couple Of Ugly Modern Boxy Structures) and while there is nothing exactly wrong with Brno, there just isn't enough of it to detain you for long. The Spilberk Castle, high on a hill overlooking the centre, was an infamous prison in the age of the Austro-Hungarian Empire, and no less intimidating as a Gestapo detention centre during the Second World War, when it was used as a staging post for the concentration camps. It's now a so-so museum that would appeal if you were particularly interested in Czech and Moravian history but, you know, I'm really not bothered.

As I get older, I find I'm truly interested only in the history of countries that directly influence my own way of life – Greece and Rome, which gave us theatre, democracy and religion; England, which bestowed on the Irish the language we speak, our literature, our legal system, and our most enjoyable and lingering grudge; Germany, which twice tried and failed to reshape Europe; and France, Portugal, Spain, America,

Russia and China, which carved up the wider world, or gave it the key ideologies that made the twentieth century such a volatile one.

Czechoslovakia's component republics were just like Ireland, always the colonised, and often fighting someone else to be free – and the history of such countries, sadly, tends to be a litany of failed revolutions and failed revolutionaries. If I want to get depressed, I can always find a wall in an Irish prison against which patriots were executed at dawn, without travelling 1,000 kilometres to find out why unsmiling young men shown in profile feature on the back of banknotes.

The most interesting building in Brno is the Villa Tugendhat, designed in 1930 by the celebrated German architect, Ludwig Mies van der Rohe. One of the leading lights of the Bauhaus movement, which promoted clean lines over architectural embellishment, Mies is the man who pioneered the use of construction with steel frames that allowed for lighter, often completely glazed, exterior walls and unimpeded interior space. As the 1930s progressed, Mies was ignored by the Nazis, who considered his unadorned work to be too socialist in tone, so he moved to the States, where he designed some of the most influential buildings of the modern era in his adopted city of Chicago. A friend lives in one of his landmark apartments on Lakeshore Drive and they are possibly the only monolithic structures I'm actually enraptured with and, despite Mies's nationality, they are buildings that speak with an American accent as broad as the prairies.

The Tugendhats, who commissioned the villa, were Jewish and fled in the late 1930s, for obvious reasons, never to return. Their name survives in the Tugendhat chair, a variation of Mies' earlier Barcelona and Brno chairs. You know them well – they're the ones that have a cantilevered C-shaped tubular steel frame and no back legs, and they look as contemporary now as they did eighty years ago. Part of the great joy of travelling around Europe is suddenly finding yourself at the birthplace of an everyday object you take utterly for granted, an item you have always assumed simply invented itself.

But the downside is that when you go to see a work of art such as the Villa Tugendhat, the fact that it was so influential also means you have seen literally thousands of copycats, and they deprive the original of its power to surprise. You can't undo your subsequent knowledge, so the unfortunate net effect is that you often come away with a 'so what?' feeling. In recent memory, I think only Oak Park in Illinois, where Frank Lloyd Wright designed over twenty houses in close proximity, retained the power to thrill me with the genuine shock of the new.

So I wander the streets and stop at a traditional restaurant for dinner, where I have the Old Bohemian pork chop, only because it conjures up a bizarre image of a very louche pig living in a commune and reared on absinthe and roll-ups instead of beets and meal. The food here is more Germanic than Mediterranean – all leaden dumplings and tangy sauerkraut – and I genuinely empathise with any woman in the late stages of pregnancy, because my dinner is so heavy I can actually feel it kicking. I make for the bar at the hotel, where a very friendly prostitute is reading a paperback and smiling at everyone who comes in, the women included. I suppose on a slow Thursday in October, everyone is a potential john, even if she's a Jean. One man is more interested in her than most and when the deal finally goes down, it happens in a blink. He gives an almost imperceptible nod and leaves. Two minutes later, she closes her book and follows. It is the last I see of either of them, though I think I hear them later on and conclude that must be one helluva book.

Next morning, slightly brd with Brno (see – anyone who can send a text can speak Czech), I walk to the train station and, on a whim, spend €37 on a return ticket to Vienna. I've never been there, though it was probably the first European city to take my fancy, after it featured on a *Blue Peter* special-assignment programme in 1973. The trip through the Moravian landscape is a little dull (I prefer my countryside to rock rather than roll), but it is enlivened no end when a sullen man in a preposterously grand uniform knocks on the compartment door and asks to see my passport. Ten minutes later, another one asks for the passport again, and when I say I have already shown it, he says curtly (and, indeed, he may even have been called Curt), 'He vos Czech, I am Austrian and I still vish to see your passport.' It is a nice *Third Man* start to my day.

I take a tram to the centre of Vienna, which is deserted, and all the shops are closed. I always find this disconcerting, since shops at home are about as likely to close, ever, as I am to pay full price for a sofa at DFS. But it is All Saints Day today, and a public holiday, and the pesky shop workers seem to want it off too, so I walk Vienna for hours, and finally arrive at the Prater. It is one of the loveliest urban parks I've seen, with a long central avenue lined with chestnut trees, and busy today with cyclists, joggers and families out for a stroll in the crisp autumn air.

Peeping above the trees – actually, it's waving like the cast of *Lost* would if they saw their agents – is the Riesenrad, the huge Ferris wheel built in 1897, with wooden gondolas that look like garden sheds. It is stationary today, though, which is just as well, as it means I don't have to feel like a coward for not venturing aboard (I went on the London Eye once and spent the whole circuit whimpering like a puppy with a thorn in its paw and leaping 3 metres in the air when anyone so much as brushed against me; I thought it would never end). I am also intrigued, as a lifelong James Bond fan, to see the very café door that crushed a British agent to death in *The Living Daylights* before the message 'smiert spionen' – death to spies – drifted to Timothy Dalton on a balloon released by a clown. I logged it as yet another reason to be wary of the smiley bastards.

Though I had pork last night, I cannot resist the imperative to order Wiener schnitzel at a park café. This is pork fried in a light batter (veal is more traditional, but I'm always afraid to eat it in case an animal-rights campaigner is lurking and hits me with a can of mace) and served with a slice of lemon, matchstick chips and a krugel of beer, which is a 50cl glass, all for €8.95. Half an hour later, I pay just 15 cent less for a large espresso and a slice of cake – but, then, I am in the Hotel Sacher and the cake is the world-famous Sachertorte, invented in 1832 by Franz Sacher, who literally turned his confection into a fortune. There are different rooms in the Sacher where the torte is served, though for some reason, I end up on the pavement, shielded from the elements by a transparent plastic tent. There is a touch of the conveyor belt about the operation as we are all moved in and moved out with good grace but a slight hint of steeliness.

I long to ask for a slice of McVitie's Jamaica Ginger Cake, just to see what happens, but Sachertorte and coffee arrive practically unasked for, given that all but maybe one visitor a year place the same order. The torte is basically a chocolate sponge with a thin layer of apricot jam in the middle, chocolate icing and a chocolate 'coin' atop every slice. To my palate, it is too sweet and too dry, and I leave half of it on the plate before walking to the Hofburg, former residence of, in short order, the Holy Roman emperors of the German Nation, the emperors of Austria and, latterly, the presidents of the Austrian federation (who for years now have thankfully been far too young to have to pretend they were never Nazis).

The Hofburg is just overwhelming in scale, so vast it makes Buckingham Palace (which is where I think of when I think 'palace') look like a suburban semi. Every millimetre of my peripheral vision is being mugged by palaces, a whole complex of them in so many clashing styles – Gothic, Italianate, Germanic – they look like a sort of mad pop-up book. I want to check out the interiors but I have no clue where to even start (and, more pertinently, no skateboard) and, given that I have just an hour before the train leaves for Brno, I decide to put the Hofburg on the back burner for another day – or, perhaps, a quiet year in my retirement when I can tackle the first four palaces and see how I go.

In truth, I'm sorry to be leaving Vienna so soon. It has the grace of a dowager empress and feels very comfortable in its beautiful art-nouveau skin. Every corner in the city centre offers a view you could linger over for hours, yet I have barely scratched the epidermis.

The return journey to Brno is little different from this morning's, except that the whole passport-at-the-border business seems even more thrilling in darkness (literally – the couple in my compartment are tired and ask if I mind them switching off all the lights). I am vaguely disappointed that we don't shudder to a stop in the middle of nowhere to find ourselves confronted by troops bearing machine guns, bathed in carbon-arc light and restraining Dobermanns that yelp maniacally as the woman beside me quickly swallows a roll of microfilm, kisses the man passionately, promises to meet him later at a safe house in Ostrava and then shimmies out through a vent in the ceiling.

Back at the Grandhotel, I say goodnight to the hooker in the lobby and meet her suddenly expectant gaze with a smiling but unmistakeable rebuff, and she also smiles and returns to her book to await a trick. Next day, after a final wander around streets that have overnight been lightly dusted with snow, I leave for Brno-Turany Airport.

I'm in the first ninety to check in, so I sit back in the bar to read a book and make for the gate only when I see the inbound flight touch down. When I get there, the queue is as unruly as one of those Monday mornings at Lidl when they're selling satellite dishes for 100 quid. I ask why no one is observing the queuing system only to find that Ryanair has introduced a new one. There is no more 1–90, guys – from now on, if you want to board the plane first, you have to pay €3 for priority. During the flight, I go to the loo and take a 50-cent coin with me, just in case they've fitted slots to the doors. Well, you never know, do you?

22

BRISTOL–BOURNEMOUTH

FR502

Dublin (DUB) to Bristol (BRS)

332 km

€32.63

I have become pathetic in my obsession with beating Ryanair's baggage restrictions, and winter has brought with it new ways of adding kilos to my allowance in the form of a biker anorak given out as a corporate gift by BMW. The corporate-gift side of the motor industry must, I reckon, keep an entire province of China in gainful employment. Secreted around my house, and bearing the logos of every car maker on earth, I have baseball caps, wheelie suitcases, fold-out suit carriers, kitbags, key fobs, briefcases, memory sticks, MP3 players ranging in quality from nasty plastic tat to engraved 1-gig and 2-gig iPods, sweatshirts, DVD wallets, wicker baskets, mouse mats, leather blotters, keyboard wrist rests, pens, golf-ball markers, umbrellas, sun visors, and jackets to suit every climate from arctic to monsoon. One SUV test vehicle came with the gift of a two-man tent, which maybe wasn't the best signal to send out to motoring writers about to take the car off-road.

In fact, just about the only thing a car company has never given me for free is a car – which, when you think about it, is the only thing you might really want from them if you actually *were* corruptible. But when I was laying down the wine I bought during a trip last month to drive the new Citroen C4 Picasso through the Gorges de l'Aveyron in southern France (I slipped the trip in between Leeds and Blackpool and you never even noticed), I chanced upon the BMW jacket and thought, bingo!, you're going to need that for eastern Europe. It looks like something a security guard on the docks in Murmansk might wear. It has a high collar that conceals a lined hood, detachable fleece lining that could make Condoleezza Rice warm and cuddly and, best of all, more pockets than the Crucible during the finals of the World Snooker Championships.

Oh, the things it swallows up – paperback books, litre bottles of water, apple-flavoured Aqua Drops, sandwiches, my Ziploc bag full of travel-size bottles of Lynx, Tylenol and shaving foam, enough Zantac to quieten heartburn in an ox (a new addition to the roster since I ate the Old Bohemian pork chop), a 40-gig iPod, noise-cancelling headphones, the chargers for my phone and computer, a three-to-two pin adapter and a multi-socket adapter to go in it, JBL speakers and, most important of all, my portable DVD player. Of course, I should be able to watch movies on my laptop, but the seat pitch on Ryanair is too tight for me to fully open the 15-inch widescreen on the tray table, so to view the whole screen I would have to occupy a second seat and lie sideways. To stave off boredom on the flights, I usually burn a week's worth of my favourite recorded TV shows to DVD and catch up with them on my 8-inch screen as I travel, though there is a man from South Shields who sat beside me on the return drive from Oslo to Torp in June and still probably tells his mates about the gobshite who was watching the final of *Celebrity X Factor* on the bus. To be honest, even I think that was a bit sad.

I need all the space I can find this week as I fly from Dublin to Bristol, drive to Bournemouth, fly from there to Girona in Spain, then Alghero in Sardinia, jet north to Tampere in Finland via Frankfurt-Hahn, again (and I've booked myself on the same flight, two days in a row, in case I miss a tight connection), then down to Riga, back to Liverpool, overland to Manchester and home to Dublin. The combined distance is 7,030 kilometres, or 4,368 miles (the equivalent of London to Miami), yet the total price of these eight flights is an astonishingly miserly €237, or £159. This includes one checked-in bag at €3.50 per sector. The total is less than you would have paid a decade ago for a one-day return on the Manchester to Dublin leg alone.

The trouble is that one 10-kilogram carry-on bag and a 15-kilogram checked bag will not be enough for two weeks of travel that will take me from the Mediterranean to thermal-underwear territory, so the BMW jacket is also stuffed with swim trunks, two vests, thick socks and two pairs of long johns. Looking at myself waddling towards the full-length mirror of the airport toilet, it strikes me that if Santa went round the world every year on a 1,000cc bike instead of a sled, this is what he would look like.

The first flight lasts only forty minutes and we land at Bristol just before 10.30 a.m. I pick up the hire car and drive to the centre to find another British city rediscovering its waterfront and remodelling itself to face the historic docks that once hummed to the sounds of commerce and exploration.

John Cabot left here in 1497 to sail the North Atlantic and discovered the 'New Founde Landes', which he believed to be China – though the absence of anyone stitching jackets for BMW or engraving iPods for Audi should have rung a few alarm bells. No one is sure if the New Founde Landes were indeed Newfoundland or, the other likely candidate, Nova Scotia, but given the medieval fad for calling things as you saw them, then Shitty Canadian Island That's Cold Even In August would have been my vote. (I've transited misty, chilly Gander en route to Florida and Cuba three times over the years and here is all you need to know – if you're ever stuck for a bookshop that sells thousands of novels about fur trappers, then this corner of Newfoundland is your Vegas.)

John Cabot was born Giovanni Caboto in Gaeta in the Lazio province that surrounds Rome, but he hadn't a chance of retaining his name once he decided to move to England. The English are really funny about names and play with them right in front of your eyes. I've never introduced myself to an Englishman as Philip without him saying, 'Hello, Phil.' By the same token, when my sister, Anne, moved to England, she was Annie within days. The general rule seems to be that you reduce any name consisting of two or more syllables to just the one, but extend names with just one syllable to at least two. The first Englishmen who met Cabot must have practically vomited with excitement at the multiple possibilities opening up before their eyes – 'Giovanni Caboto? You must be fahking joking! At least three of those fahking syllables are history, mate…'

A replica of Cabot's ship, the *Matthew* (I know, it's not exactly heroic, is it – I don't suppose Nelson would have sailed for Trafalgar on the *Nigel*, would he?), is tied up at the Great Western Dockyard, but she is not the ship I have come to see. Instead, I want to tour Isambard Kingdom Brunel's *ss Great Britain*. Born in 1806, Brunel was probably the greatest engineer who ever lived. He built the Great Western Railway, planned the Clifton Suspension Bridge, helped his father complete London's Rotherhithe Tunnel under the Thames and designed the ship sitting in front of my eyes, the very first ocean-going, screw-propeller, wrought-iron vessel. Even writing the word 'ship' thrills me, because pretty much everything that predated the *ss Great Britain* was just a boat – what I'm about to board is a cusp in industrial history.

For such a maritime superstar, the *Great Britain* took a lot of knocks. Conceived as a luxury transatlantic liner, she was, at 332 feet, 100 feet longer than her nearest rival when launched in 1843. She could carry 252 first- and second-class passengers and 130 crew members, and she sailed to New York in fourteen days. Yet pickup for the service was slow and passenger numbers not as high as expected. Disaster struck in 1846, when she ran aground at Dundrum Bay in County Down, Northern Ireland, and there she languished for almost a year until salvaged in an operation that left her owners bankrupt. Brunel was appalled she had been left for so long, 'The finest ship in the world [has been] treated like a useless saucepan kicking about on the beach at Brighton,' he wrote in one despairing letter to a friend.

The 'saucepan' was sold, her accommodation was reconfigured and she was put into service as an emigrant ship which could carry 750 passengers to Australia. In fourteen years, she ferried over 15,000, so many that 250,000 Aussies can now trace their ancestry to this one ship; that's around one in eighty of the population. From the manifests, I note that eight Nolans from Ireland sailed on her. Her service on that route also made Europeans realise for the first time that if you were in the pub in Sydney or Melbourne, it was probably best not to give Aussies your home address, or they would arrive at your front door the following year and ask to stay for two months.

She also served as a troopship, bringing soldiers to the Crimea and to quell the Indian Mutiny – and, finally and ignominiously, she became a transport ship, bringing Welsh coal to San Francisco around Cape Horn. On her third such voyage, in 1886, she was battered by a storm and gutted by a fire, and sheltered in Port Stanley in the Falkland Islands, only to be abandoned there as a storage hulk. Her cargo hold fuelled Britain's First World War victory over the German naval fleet in the Battle of the Falklands, but she was scuttled in 1937. It was a tragic fate and possibly terminal until, in 1970, thanks to a grant from English philanthropist Sir Jack Hayward (now there's a man I'd buy a pint for), she was refloated on a pontoon and towed home to Bristol. The BBC footage of her sailing up the Avon under Brunel's Clifton Bridge is a more affecting reunion than the day Lassie finally arrived home to Roddy McDowall.

The *ss Great Britain* now sits once more in the dockyard where she was built, her hull sealed by a glass 'sea' fitted at the Plimsoll Line (and Samuel Plimsoll, who devised the marker which shows the maximum degree to which a ship may safely be loaded, was another son of Bristol). This 'sea' is effectively a glass cover that seals the hull below and has a few inches of water above it to give the impression that the *Great Britain* is floating. Underneath, vast dehumidifiers keep the atmosphere as arid as the Arizona desert and will preserve the ship in her current state for a century at least. You can venture down there to inspect the hull and the propeller and it is the sort of day out that makes boys' hearts swell and women's minds turn to shoes.

This magnificent effort to save a genuine treasure, allied to a simply dazzling visitor centre and a portable audio tour of the ship that evokes all the sights, sounds and smells of an antipodean voyage, has just won the 2006 Gulbenkian Prize for British Museum of the Year. I can't think of a more deserving winner because, to me, a really great museum is one which of itself alone would convince you to visit a city. And, trust me, this alone makes Bristol worth the trip.

But there is lots more to see and do here. The converted dock ware-houses that now house bars, cafés and restaurants radiate a cosmopolitan air, and the fact that this is another big university town means there's always someone up for a party. It is a fine city to wander around, and the narrow lanes and hilly streets, allied with that West Country burr, vaguely make you feel like an extra in a pirate movie. Lofty Clifton has some magnificent private homes and a stylish village centre that is literally and metaphorically set above the city below.

It is the starting point for the other essential part of my Brunel pilgrimage, a drive across the Clifton Suspension Bridge. Brunel designed it for a competition when he was twenty-three, an age at which most of us have just about learned to sign our names in joined-up writing. His original plan was rejected by the judge with the casting vote, Thomas Telford, who designed the elegant Menai Bridge between the isle of Anglesey and mainland Wales, generally considered the first modern suspension bridge. Telford was, one supposes, a bit jealous in that Salieri-vs-Mozart way because this young usurper had arrived into the engineering profession fully formed, and cast a very large shadow on Telford's patch. Certainly, having dismissed Brunel's design, and thirty others, Telford came to the rescue with one of his own, but the public cried 'fix!' and Brunel won in the second round.

The Clifton Bridge was not built in his lifetime, but it became Brunel's monument and one of the most recognisable bridges in the world. Driving over it scares me shitless but it has to be done – and the view across the mudflats of the Avon at low tide, bubbling in the sun-shine like the rivers of molten chocolate that run between the squares of a bar of Dairy Milk in the Cadbury's commercial, is exquisite.

I wanted to push on to Filton, home of Concorde 216, the last one to fly supersonic before the fleet was retired in 2003. The captain, Mike Bannister, delivered one of the all-time great quotes in response to the fact that, for the first time since the Industrial Revolution, we were watching a technological reversal. 'From today,' he said sadly, 'the world is a bigger place.'

Filton is a working Airbus UK facility, and when I phone to check the times, I am told that you have to book at least a day in advance to see the Concorde. 'Do you have to stay a Saturday night too?' I ask, to deathly silence, and it suddenly occurs to me that the person at the other end of the line may actually be so young he has never been confronted with the restrictive terms and conditions that used to apply to booking airline tickets.

Soon after I skirt Bath, a thick fog descends and for most of the drive, which seems to take for ever, I can see no farther than the back of the truck in front. At a roundabout, I take a wrong turn and get lost, so I look at a map, shout at myself for five minutes, look down again, look up to find the front bumper mere millimetres from a tractor, brake in a manner that threatens the cleanliness of my undergarments, turn around, sob, and eventually locate Dorset – which, in fairness, is a not inconsiderably large target.

The day brightens and the Dorset of sunny days, cream teas and ginger ale waves a brief hello before darkness again reclaims it. Night falls just as I arrive in Bournemouth to look for the Connaught Hotel in West Cliff. What I didn't know when I booked it is that West Cliff consists entirely of hotels, and I drive for another hour before I eventually find my hotel tucked away behind a roundabout I have circled seven times.

At least sense prevails here. Supply clearly exceeds demand, and my room has cost a realistic £45, though I think they may deliberately have put me next to the lift shaft. As with so many English hotels, where guest wings were added over the years, the lift never quite serves every floor, so even though I am next to it, I still have to carry luggage up half a flight of stairs. The décor in my room is unapologetic chintz and, when I sit down, the seat falls through the chair. There is no mistaking which country I am in.

I walk down the hill to town and somehow fail to avoid stepping on a dog turd the size of a baguette. I then have to walk around for twice as long as I had planned to before I find a helpful puddle. The shoe simply must be cleaned before I enter a restaurant and clear the place with the smell. To make sure all is well, I kill half an hour leafing through the books in Borders until it closes and I am convinced all odour is gone, then walk around the corner to the Slug and Lettuce for a chicken and chorizo skewer, a goat's cheese salad, chocolate mousse and a quarter bottle of Shiraz. It is a miracle I enjoyed them because I forgot my glasses and the Slug, one of a chain of gastropubs, was so dark I just pointed to the third starter, fourth main course and fifth dessert. To be honest, I was chuffed I ended up in a restaurant – once, when I forgot my glasses, I tried to order a takeaway in a bookie's.

Back at the hotel (and though it is only ten minutes walk away, I take a cab so I can actually find it *and* ensure I evade the extravagant gifts the dogs of Bournemouth so generously leave for visitors to town), I chat at the bar to a business traveller called Lenny who lives on a £25-a-day allowance. He doesn't get to keep what he doesn't spend, so he has the barman announce the running total every time he orders a beer and vows to go to bed the very minute the limit is exhausted. Personally, I would imagine this to be an activity best filed under the 'life is too short' category, but then he probably saw me earlier, running my foot through a puddle on the seafront while muttering 'fucking dogs', and came to roughly the same conclusion.

I arrive at a critical juncture in a conversation he is having with Marcin, the Polish barman. They are talking about the English language and while Lenny graciously concedes that Marcim may indeed have a better vocabulary than his own, he also contends that Marcin's syntax needs work.

I have heard enough to agree and say, 'He's right, you know.'

Marcin looks at me and asks, 'Why you say that?' and the three of us crack up at this instant confirmation of the obvious. Drinks are ordered, the twenty-five-quid-limit nonsense comes to an abrupt end and when three delegates to a prison officers' conference – a guy and two girls who I fondly imagine must have 'cuffs somewhere – arrive to the bar, the fate of the evening is sealed. This is one of the great joys of travelling, ending up on the piss with people you have never seen before and will never see again. You volunteer, and listen to, details of private behaviour you would not dream of sharing with a friend and it becomes a secular confessional.

When Marcin threatens to close the bar, we vow to trade one new everyday English phrase for each pint he pulls, and it buys us an extension until one o'clock, when we finally call it quits. Next morning, I drive to neighbouring Poole, which detains me for all of about four minutes, before heading to Sandbanks, a spit of a peninsula that, in 2000, was named the fourth most expensive place in the world to buy property, based on the price of each square foot of accommodation. Only Tokyo, Hong Kong and Central London were dearer than the £689 per square foot that homes in Sandbanks were selling for. Of course, in the years since, Dublin property prices have risen so much – one house sold two years ago for €56 million and an entire city developed arrhythmia – that the Tailor Made estate-agency window here holds little terror for me. I could buy on Shore Road for £2.5 million, or rent a four-bed on Panorama Road for £4,250 per month, and when I drive around and look at the houses I don't find the prices unreasonable, just entirely unaffordable.

This is a very different England, one masquerading as the South of

France. Most of the houses are white, everywhere is freshly painted, and the balconies are adorned with aquamarine glass that glints in the autumn sunshine. It's even warm enough to sit outdoors at a pavement café and it's November. Only a blind man in a fur coat could miss the attraction.

I make for the airport and stop at a very popular pub called the Curlew in West Parley, which offers exceptional comfort food and unusually attentive service. I read the local paper and find out to my shock that Paul Simon played a gig at the Bournemouth International Centre last night, yet the town seemed dead on its feet. Where were they all? Probably in the Slug and Lettuce, but I just couldn't see them.

At the airport, I pull into the Hertz lot and see a sign that says I should drop the keys in a bin in the terminal, but a man in an anorak appears from nowhere and says, 'Don't worry, I'll look after those.' For the rest of this trip, the moment will haunt me. He could have been anyone. I probably just gave a Fiat Grande Punto to some bloke who used it in a ram raid. It will be weeks before I stop looking at Visa statements to check if a €15,000 excess has been lodged against my card.

I watch the news on a TV in the airport and see that Ryanair has announced record profits. I buy a pint to celebrate. That's me, you know. It's all down to me.

GIRONA–ALGHERO

FR9912
Bournemouth (BOH) to Girona (GRO)
1,050 km • £17.22

FR9261
Girona (GRO) to Alghero (AHO)
483 km • €21.21

Less than 2 per cent of people who fly into Girona with Ryanair actually go to Girona. Most just hop straight onto a coach or into a cab and dash to Barcelona, 90 kilometres away. The capital of Catalunya is Spain's superstar destination, more popular than Madrid, in a reversal of the usual pattern that sees national capitals attract the bulk of tourists.

My own relationship with Barcelona has become a little fractured. It was the first European city I was allowed run wild in, on the school tour back in 1978 (with Jonathan Nolan, who you met a few chapters back in Carcassonne). Our teachers were unusually enlightened and let us off the leash to explore by ourselves, so we spent two weeks combing every shop and side street, every beach and amusement park, every bus route and metro line. For a kid from Ireland who was used to austere churches, the sight of Antoni Gaudí's surreal Sagrada Familia, the unfinished Cathedral of the Holy Family, was a revelation, a vision of a different relationship between architecture, man and God. When Gaudí was asked why building work was taking so long, he replied, 'My client is not in a hurry.' They're still working on it to this day.

In much the same way as Spain itself was beginning to stretch after four decades of dictatorship by Francisco Franco, who died three years earlier, I too found myself leaving a repressive cocoon. It was spun in tandem by the also not-long-dead president of Ireland, Eamon de Valera, and the late archbishop of Dublin, John Charles McQuaid, two men who I believe actually never smiled in public. Certainly, I have seen no record of it if they did.

I went to Barcelona Irish, but I've always felt I came home European. That feeling may also have been something to do with my age, and the adolescent need to escape the family unit and stake out my own place in wider society – it is not coincidence, I think, that I celebrated my fifteenth birthday in the middle of that trip, or that I read *The Catcher in the Rye* while I was there, or, indeed, that in Sant Sadurní d'Anoia I visited the Codorníu cava and drank alcohol, in the form of sparkling wine, for the first time. I'm not sure that it would entirely be wise to let today's fifteen-year-olds loose in such a big city, but the world was a pervert-free zone back then (or at least seemed it) and we spent a fortnight blissfully unmolested.

After I started writing about cars, it soon became obvious I could go to Barcelona about once a month if I chose to. Because of the 1992

Olympics, it has a vast bank of hotel rooms and wide avenues allowing for easy access in and out of town. It has direct air connections to every country in Europe and, beyond the city boundary, there is a wonderfully mountainous hinterland with testing inclines and chicanes. In short, it is the perfect place to launch a new car, and it is cheaper for the likes of Opel or SEAT (which is based at Martorell, up the road) to station 100 cars to one location, plan one test route, book the same restaurant every night for six weeks and fly every motoring writer in Europe down there, than it is to arrange separate events in each country.

Because of that, there was a period when I was in the city about six times in a year, and when the PR people for the car companies rang to ask if I was free for a launch, I began to blurt involuntarily, 'Yes, so long as it's not in Barcelona.' You know, in Ritz-Carlton's Hotel Arts down by the port, I would easily be able to eat breakfast, find a bucket of ice, polish my shoes, vacuum every landing and take a leisurely shower, all in the dark. When I drive up the Passeig de Gracia, pedestrians wave and say, 'Oh, look, Philip's back.' The woman in the La Perla shop at the airport shouts when I walk by, to remind me it's almost my wife's birthday. That's how often I'm in Barcelona.

On the few test drives from the city that head north (most go west to the hills around the Marian shrine at Montserrat), I have often said to myself, 'Hmmm, I must go to Girona some time', then never bothered. Now, here I am and, wouldn't you know it, it is entrancing from the off. I check into the Hotel Meliá Girona (€95 without breakfast – sadly, there's no Hesperia in town), dump my luggage and grab another cab to the Plaça de la Independéncia, a handsome square with cafés tucked away under long porticos.

In the far corner, I spot the welcoming Bar Boira, which serves wickedly moreish tapas, those little snack foods that the Spanish do so well. I eat goat's cheese with purée of apple and balsamic, *patates braves* (mildly spicy potatoes you could nibble on all night), skewers of lamb, and chicken with Maldon salt. It's a lot of food but, as always, it doesn't feel quite the same as a proper dinner.

Girona is warm in every way – the local stone, the temperature, the atmosphere – and though I'm tired, I make my way across the Pont Sant Agustí that spans the River Onyar to the old Jewish quarter of the city, the Call. It is almost perfectly preserved, a maze of small streets that head in every direction. The sense of authentic history is overpowering – and there is lots of history here. Turbulent Girona survived twenty-five sieges and fell many times because it sits in far too strategic a location, on the flat flank of the Pyrenees, not to have been occupied by everyone who invaded the Iberian Peninsula, from the south as well as the north.

The Romans were here (and the Romans went so many places, I often wonder who stayed home). They built a castle and called the city Gerunda, which sounds like a book on the finer points of English verb usage. Then the Visigoths came and hung around until the Moors whipped their asses. The north Africans ruled for two centuries until Charlemagne, in turn, ousted them in 785. The Moors came back for a while (there was probably a courtyard somewhere the tilers had to finish) but Girona eventually became a duchy, and the title of Prince of Girona is today held by Felipe, heir to the Spanish throne and the man we last thought of on a sunny day in June when we bumped into his parents in Oslo. I was just about to remark that European families are linked in a way you just wouldn't find in, say, Tennessee, before I realised how foolish such a claim would be.

Anyway, lots of Jews settled here too, but there was a pogrom in 1492 and they were all run out of the city. Actually, in Spain's case, the pogrom was on a national scale, and it is odd to think that in the year when Christians were celebrating Columbus's discovery of the New World, they were also doing what they would do for another 500 years (ultimately with the most obscene consequences), namely blaming the Jews for the Old World's ills.

With all the marauders who passed through, I never quite get around to finding out which *independéncia* the *plaça* was named for, but medieval Girona seems to have been very lucky indeed that all of its sieges and liberations left it remarkably unblemished. Next morning, I walk the eighty-six steps up to the main door of the cathedral, wander around the back of it and find a small walled garden high on the ramparts of the city. Save for a man playing medieval tunes on a flute, I am the only person here. Everything I can see is ancient. None of the houses below has a visible aerial or satellite dish and if my phone hadn't rung at precisely that moment, it could have been any time between about 1070 and the present.

Having admired the widest nave of any Gothic cathedral (and the second widest of any church in the world, after St Peter's in the Vatican City), I pass a couple of hours wandering around the side altars, using an audio guide and a clever system of switches that triggers lighting timed for just long enough to allow you see the treasures in each. The adjacent cathedral museum is home to the Tapestry of the Creation but it is the small cloister outside that makes the lasting impression, a space of unmistakeable spirituality where half an hour flies by in what seems like five minutes.

Rested, I make my way through the Call to the Carrer dels Ciutadans, once the home of Girona's wealthy and now a perfectly preserved street you could use as a film set for a medieval epic without changing a single brick. It turns out to be home to an unexpected treasure, a food shop called Colmado Moriscot, which looks as if it has been in these same premises forever. It reminds me of Findlater's in Dún Laoghaire, where I grew up, one those old-style groceries we used to shop at before supermarkets took over, a place where women would stand and point, and men with ladders would shoot up and down the shelves, climbing to perilous heights to fetch baking soda and golden syrup, Bovril and Lipton's tea. Colmado Moriscot sells everything – a great selection of wines, a seemingly limitless variety of spirits in single-serving bottles, cured hams, oriental spices, cheeses and goodies from England like Heinz Salad Cream. I want to buy everything here, but a Ryanair baggage allowance is an unforgiving adversary. More to the point – under pressure from England and America, that Axis of Paranoia – the EU has this very week extended the ban on liquids to all flights, not just those emanating from the UK and Italy, so now the entire world has to carry 100ml bottles of its favourite toiletries in see-through bags. I'm beginning to wonder if the so-called plot we heard about in August was concocted not by terrorists, but by someone with a large block of shares in the SC Johnson company that holds the patent on Ziploc bags.

With the lingering aromas of Colmado Moriscot still humming a symphony in my nostrils, I wander along the pedestrianised Rambla de la Llibertat, with yet more shops and pavement cafés, before retracing my steps and ending up at the Café Irlandes on Ciutadans. Popular with ex-pats and locals alike, it's one of those bars where striking up conversation is expected rather than rebuffed. I chat for ages to a Scottish bloke who used to own a rock club in Glasgow and he tells me tales I couldn't possibly break confidence on and shows me pictures of his kids when they were young, including one of them posing with Ozzy Osbourne. The only thing that slows the conversation down is that he replies 'what?' to everything I say. At first, I wonder if it's my accent, though a Dublin one is quite flat and short on timbre and not usually a problem for any other English-speaker (unless, that is, you are trying to keep up with a conversation between *two* Dubliners, as these tend to be conducted at the same speed and aggressive pitch as a rally between Rafael Nadal and Roger Federer). But I soon realise what the problem is and note that the best way to preserve your hearing probably does not involve years and years spent in a rock club.

Next day, I make my way back to the airport, which is large and modern, and buy priority boarding for the first time. This is the day I also begin my love affair with Row 16. Rows 15 and 16 are the emergency rows, and if you happen to be first onto a Ryanair aircraft, a member of the crew will always be standing in Row 16 because there is more leg room there and she can step in to let people pass. The object of the exercise is to get a seat by the window in 16, because that is the row where the trolley service will start for the rear half of the plane. No children are allowed in the emergency rows either, so if I get 16, there is no chance of a repeat performance by the brat in the row in front who yelled 'wake up!' at me on the way to Carcassonne.

So, you should sidle into 16 and immediately engage the flight attendant in mindless banter so she stays in the row after you have slipped past. This subliminally appoints her as a sort of sentinel, keeping anyone else from taking either of the two remaining seats. When the aircraft is sealed and Magda or Veruschka moves off to affect about as much interest in the safety demonstration as the passengers do (and if we're ever going down at 700 kilometres an hour, I don't really plan to invest all my hopes in strip lighting), you can stretch out across the three seats. Even if two others do join you, you still will have more leg room than anyone else on the plane and be first in line for a beer. For all of these reasons, paying three quid for priority boarding has revolutionised my life.

And, indeed, all goes to plan tonight and I wend my way across the Med in less than an hour, necking two quick Bavaria beers because, unlike Heineken, they come with double tickets for the raffle – but I fail, yet again, to win a free flight. It's annoying to be the age I am and still behave like a child at a wheel of fortune in a funfair, desperately hoping my number comes up.

We arrive at Alghero shortly after 9 p.m. Thee airport is called Fertilia and it makes me laugh, because it sounds like a character in a 1960s movie, the sort of nubile young virgin who would make Frankie Howerd go 'ooooh!' in *Up Pompeii!* Such thoughts are quickly banished when, after a ten-minute drive to my hotel, I am asked for €24. It astonishes me that the European Union has rules on everything from the size of an egg to the composition of halloumi cheese, yet can't seem to insist that Sardinian taxi drivers follow the example of the island's most famous twentieth-century bandit, Salvatore Giuliani, and at least carry a firearm before they pick your pockets.

I check into the Green Sporting Club Hotel on the outskirts of Alghero and, tired now, decide to have a beer at the bar before going to bed. When I get to the room, the stark fluorescent light, bare floors and basic décor depress me. Within seconds, I am terminally morose. I've been travelling on and off for months now, almost invariably alone, and I have become sick of airports and Ziploc bags and hotel managements who think anyone is fooled when they say that leaving no shampoo in the bathroom keeps the price of the room down. I'm fed up with Ryanair loop tapes asking me to buy callcards and bus tickets and bloody Bullseye Baggies again, those awful spirits sachets that come two for the price of one ('el segundo gratis' will be a Spanish phrase etched on my mind forever).

As I always do when I'm maudlin and a little bit pissed, I put on my iPod and listen to Frank Sinatra singing 'One For My Baby', the finest wee-small-hours-of-the-morning song ever recorded. It presages a damburst of tunes to slit your wrists to – 'Here's Where the Story Ends' by Tin Tin Out, 'Wake Me Up When September Ends' by Green Day, 'Yellow is the Colour' by Bugge Wesseltoft, the theme from *Jean de Florette* and – holy fuck! – 'Goodbye to Love' by The Carpenters. I'm still amazed I wrote all of these tracks down instead of just leaving a note and plugging myself into the shaving light.

Next morning, I arrive downstairs at ten, have a quick breakfast and ask the woman at the desk where the bus to town leaves from and what time it is due. 'Across the road and 100 metres to the left,' she says, 'and the next one is at ten thirty.'

I have five minutes and make it easily, but no bus comes until 10.50 a.m. When I get on, the driver looks at me and says, '*Biglietto*? Teeket?'

I take out my wallet.

'No money,' he says. 'Teeket.'

'Where do I buy teeket?' I ask.

'Green Hotel,' he replies.

Now forgive me for picking nits, but I just asked the woman at the desk where the bus stop was and what time the bus came at and, to be fair, she told me – but the crucial piece of information she withheld was the bit about the tickets on the desk in front of her. Without one, the bus might just as well have left from the foothills of the Andes in January, because I'd have as much chance of getting on it. Simmering, I return and ask her why she hadn't considered this little nugget of practicality worth sharing. 'I didn't think of it,' she says and then, looking me up, down and up again, she adds, 'You can walk – it will be good for you.'

I start out for Alghero and notice for the first time that the hotel is on Viale della Resistenza, which I take to have been named in honour of those who stood up to occupation. So if the ancestors preferred to die while hanging upside down by their toenails as boiling water was poured over their gonads, is it any wonder the locals still tell foreigners nothing?

Seething, I walk a kilometre in the wrong direction, retrace my steps and just miss the next bus. By the time I get to town, sweating in 25-degree heat, I should be fit to be tied – but the walk around the headlands that led to Alghero was pretty, the sun is beating down on an aquamarine sea, and when I come upon the Martello tower and the bastions marking the start of the fortifications, I am ready to cut the town some slack. I settle myself in at the Bar del Corso, finally finish *The Lincoln Lawyer* by Michael Connelly (it will free up a pocket in the BMW jacket), order a snack and a glass of wine and congratulate myself for being somewhere warm and sunny in November. After last night, this is what I needed to do, to just sit and relax and let a destination wash over me for a change, instead of dashing to see everything in it. Later, I take a walk around the marina and the old walls of the town, and I am struck by the fact that it all looks and feels quite like Girona. Alghero is the most Spanish town on this otherwise Italian isle of Sardinia, but when a quarter of the population still speaks a dialect of Catalan and calls the town Alguer, that is hardly surprising.

Later, I eat at Al Refettorio (yes, it was once the refectory of a convent), where there are a lot of women in black knee-length trousers with gold piping, worn over lace-up boots. It is like happening upon a convention of drag queens all pretending to be Donatella Versace. Behind me, two couples – one of them is from Huddersfield and the rest sound no more than a dale away – are asking about the cannelloni and are told there is spinach in it. 'We always forget in England that you can do cannelloni with all sorts,' the woman tells the waiter.

I'm baffled. I've never eaten cannelloni that *didn't* have spinach in it and now find myself in the ridiculous position of wanting to go to Huddersfield to find out how it is served locally (stuffed with Yorkshire puddings, maybe? Or After Eights – who knows?).

A dog wanders over to me and starts to lick my hand, and I get goosebumps. Two months ago, both our dogs died within two weeks of each other, one at fourteen, the other almost seventeen, and I've been fragile ever since. Looking at this little fella – I'd say a Jack Russell/dachshund cross, with a chocolate coat as sleek and shiny as an Easter egg – makes me feel like one of those women who prowl maternity wards looking for babies to spirit into the night. Sadly, Al Refettorio is in a busy alleyway and well lit by infra-lamps doubling as heaters, so dognapping is not an option. I order a breaded lamb cutlet and potatoes, but the meat is overcooked and chewy. When no one is looking, the dog gets what's left of it and I decide to call it quits on Alghero.

I'm on an early flight to Frankfurt-Hahn in the morning so I book a taxi. When it arrives, I hop in the back and am overpowered by the smell of Glade – and fart. I hate that smell. I would much rather smell fart alone than the hybrid whiff of guilt and concealment. Soon after we pull away, I unfortunately get my wish as the driver farts again, loudly and unapologetically and so pungently it makes me gag. I try to lower the window in protest but he has some sort of child lock on and I am forced to sit for ten minutes with my stomach heaving.

When we get to the airport, he asks for €30, and I pretend to root around for cash as he gets out to remove my bag from the boot. And then I do the most juvenile thing imaginable. I let rip. This is no ordinary fart; this is the Fart of Vengeance. It rumbles across the leather with a sound like the very fabric of the universe being rent asunder. The windows fog up and there is the unmistakable smell of gases so noxious they can only have been generated by a breaded cutlet. I have no idea where the lamb was reared but, given the amount of sulphur in the air, it would be unwise to rule out the slopes of Mount Etna. Internally, I am high-fiving. If this was the Olympics, I wouldn't necessarily win a medal, but with a box of matches and stilly weather, I could do a week's duty as the torch.

As I pay him, he smirks. I smirk back; you don't know this yet but two-thirds of that is going on Glade, mate.

Alghero has one last surprise – the airport is the queuing capital of the world. I queue for check-in. I queue for hold-baggage screening. I queue for a ticket for priority boarding. I am told I must pay the €3 by credit card – if I pay cash, there is a €5 surcharge for handling the €3. I queue for coffee only to be told that I must first queue to pay for the coffee, and then I have to return to the counter and queue for the coffee all over again. I queue for security and, since there are a couple of people with web check-in and others with priority boarding, I queue there to make sure I get Seat 16F.

And then the plane arrives and stops 300 metres from the gate, and a bus pulls up and, yes, my €3 gets me priority boarding *on the bus*… When it stops at the aircraft steps, there is another free-for-all. As we take off, I bless myself as always, but the great thing about flying from a Catholic country such as Italy is that when I do it, it starts a sort of Mexican wave and soon everyone is blessing themselves. My prayers have been answered anyway. I stretch out with a smile in Row 16, which I have all to myself, I put on the noise-cancelling headphones and give myself a blast of 'Mr Brightside' by The Killers. Now that's what I should have been listening to at the Green Sporting Club Hotel.

24

TAMPERE

FR4823

Alghero (AHO) to Frankfurt-Hahn (HHN)

1,040 km • €36.17

FR1921

Frankfurt-Hahn (HHN) to Tampere (TMP)

1,630 km • €29.93

You might as well try to teach a goldfish how to programme Sky+ as teach a Finn how to queue. I'm always astonished that the legendary, nine-times Olympic gold medallist, Paavo Nurmi – the Flying Finn himself – ever got a clean start when, genetically, he was programmed to be halfway round the track before the gun was fired.

As a nation, Finns just don't get it. Here at Frankfurt-Hahn, they sit around nonchalantly until the flight is called, then they rise as one and just barge through whoever is in their way, looking into the far distance to avoid eye contact with the person in front, beside or, as is often the case, underfoot. Today, I am gambling that none of them has yet heard of the newly introduced priority boarding, and it proves a good bet. When the check-in clerk asks passengers holding the yellow tickets to board first, I make my way through the throng, savouring every moment as the Finns realise in horror that someone else will be first to the plane. I board it in triumph and sit in 16A (I often sit on the left side of the aircraft when flying north in the late afternoon, as you get more sunshine that way) – and the two women who are next to board, despite having 188 remaining seats to choose from, sit down beside me. For beating them to the tape, clearly I must be punished by being hemmed in.

As we take off, the Rhineland looks very different from that lovely morning after the World Cup match in June. The trees are russet, orange and brown, and tumble down over gentle hills to winding waterways – I think I may have stumbled upon Europe's Vermont. This is my favourite hour to fly, as the light is starting to die in the west. On a cold, clear day like today, the sky is graduated from powder blue at the lower end to baby pink at the top, with squiggles of gold light fringing long wisps of cloud. You get a lot of this on late-evening flights from London to Dublin, and it always makes me wistful to see a day scurry off with some of its favours squirrelled away for others. From 35,000 feet, you can see for 369 kilometres (trust me – there's a formula involving height and the curvature of the Earth), and I'm jealous of those who still have daylight while darkness claims my own day. Beyond the horizon, there is someone getting out of bed, or making love, or having lunch, or taking a meeting that will change his life, and I wish that real life was just like *Superman Returns* so that, from this height, I could hear all their conversations.

Tampere Airport is tiny and has one very short baggage belt, which the Finns have now surrounded like platelets at a wound. I eventually battle through with some difficulty, grab my luggage, flag a taxi and check into the Scandic Hotel in town. It is minus four outside (that's 29 degrees colder than yesterday afternoon in Sardinia) so, after dumping my bags in the room, I elect to eat in. There are nine others coming down with me in the lift and when we reach the ground floor, two women try to enter, even though we are all about to exit. The gene that tells every Finn that queuing in an orderly fashion represents some sort of loss of face kicks in anyway – and so do the women, arms and legs flailing and defiance written on their faces. One by one, we pick our way past them silently, until it is my turn and I whisper from the side of my mouth, 'assholes'. And one of them looks at me. And she smiles…

None of this makes me dislike the Finns. In fact, they're among my favourite Europeans, friendly without being mindlessly effusive, with a deliciously black sense of humour and a capacity for alcohol even more prodigious than that of the Irish. I remember a hotel manager in Benalmadena on the Costa del Sol telling me he kept a lifeguard on duty all night because he was sick of coming down to the pool in the morning and fishing drunk Finns out of it, only very occasionally alive.

The Piazza Bar at the Scandic, despite a name that makes it sound like it is going to be some awful ersatz Italian café, turns out to be a proper, dark-wood bar, warm and inviting (I peep into the atrium next door and find the Piazza FoodFactory, which actually *is* as ersatz as it gets, with the serving stations decked out like shopfronts around a small square). I eat and drink and meet a succession of Finns who somehow make that gloomy Nordic nihilism seem cheery.

The drinks are not dear either, at €4.80 for a 50cl beer. There was a time when I used to keep bar bills from Helsinki in my wallet so that if a friend ever went into cardiac arrest and there was no defibrillator nearby, I could just whip it out so the shock of it might restart his heart.

But at these modest prices, I feel obliged to order another Lapin Kulta, brewed at the Arctic Circle and one of the world's great lagers. It dates from 1963, when the Tornion Olut and Lapin Olut breweries merged to become Lapin Kulta Oy. 'Kulta' means gold, but because there was a mining outfit of the same name, the brewery had to buy it out to secure copyright. Even today, the company charter announces that its line of business is 'prospecting for gold and the manufacture and sales of beer'. Fittingly, in 1964, Lapin Kulta was entered in competition at the Brussels International Beer Festival – and won gold.

I learn all this at the bar, because Finland is so tech savvy, there is free wi-fi throughout the hotel (hey, wi-fi first *happened* in Tampere in 1999) and I'm sitting at the counter on the laptop, talking to people when they grab a stool next to me and, when they leave, hopping online to see if what they have just told me is true or crap.

And there is a lot that is true. In Tampere in 1837, they built the first six-storey building in the Nordic countries. In 1843, they had the country's first paper machine. In 1882, the first electric light in the far north. In 1991, they made the world's first GSM call ('Hi, Riitta? I'm in Tampere – I'm on the train'). In 1999, they tested the first WAP service. Technologies that have revolutionised my life were born here.

The Finns do fabulous breakfasts, and next morning I plough my way through the buffet in the FoodFactory, somehow managing to eat fresh berries with muesli and yogurt, ham and cheese, bacon and eggs, then croissants and jam. Far from being disgusted at my gluttony, I am delighted because, even if I fall now on a frozen, snowy footpath, I am coated in so much blubber I shall probably just right myself straight away. That said, I walk gingerly along the main street, Hämeenkatu, so as not to repeat a performance eight years ago in Helsinki; I ended up severely bruised when I slipped while leaping to avoid flailing snow chains at a junction that looked like *Ben Hur* with SUVs. Eventually, I reach Hämeenpuisto and the Tampere Workers' Hall. I am beyond excited, because this is the very place where, in 1905, the exiled Vladimir Ilyich Lenin met Josef Stalin, the first contact between the two communists whose ideologies shaped the twentieth century for half of Europe's population.

The hall is just like workers' halls everywhere – there are terrazzo floors with curved skirting and an open-plan cloakroom with enough pegs for the coats of a battalion. On the third floor, there is a Lenin Museum, the only permanent one left in Europe now that the Soviet Union has turned its back on the past and embraced the decadent pleasures of the West – designer labels, package holidays and Chelsea Football Club. It is a very old-fashioned museum, full of glass cases with books and pictures, many of them, sadly, just copies of the originals and, in one corner, a couch Lenin may have sat on while living in exile in Finland. There are two main elements to the exhibition, one on Lenin's time in Finland and the other on his childhood, the factors that shaped his philosophy and his rise to power.

I was a cautious socialist as an adolescent but concluded that, like thrice-daily masturbation, it was something best outgrown in my teens. I went to a few meetings of one fairly doctrinaire socialist offshoot party in Dublin in the early 1980s, always convened in the cold, threadbare, upstairs rooms of pubs on slack Monday nights – but I panicked when I realised they wanted everyone brought down to the level of the proletariat. My brand of socialism also demanded equality for all, but only so long as that meant a Mercedes in every driveway and speciality coffees provided free in the workplace. So I went off to be a capitalist. Not alone, as it happens; nowadays, when I see some of the people I knew in the wider socialist family back then, it is on the society pages of the Sunday papers.

In any case, to be absolutely truthful, I really went to the meetings to be near a woman I fancied. She in turn was going only because she fancied another bloke. He actually was an ideologue, though given the fact that he ended up with another woman from the group, who can say for sure why he was there either? It was like *La Ronde*, but with duffel coats and desert boots.

Looking back, my devotion was all the more remarkable given that, with the exception of my sadly oblivious inamorata, socialist women in Dublin in the 1980s didn't exactly, er, make the most of themselves. In Tampere, I find out why when I see photos of their role model, Nadezhda Krupskaya, an activist Lenin married in 1898. Though portrayed as the heroic wet nurse of the Soviet system, standing on podiums and delivering long speeches about tractors to dewy-eyed serfs, there is no denying that were you to think up a single complimentary noun for Nadezhda's looks, you would be performing a Nobel Prize-winning act of charity. Later, I feel a bit of a heel when, on Wikipedia (which in the course of my travels has become as addictive as crack cocaine), I learn that she may have suffered from Graves' Disease, which affects the thyroid and causes the neck to tighten and the eyes to bulge. But why should I worry when the Bolsheviks seem to have found this hilarious, and inside the party codenamed her The Fish – while Lenin allegedly called her 'my little herring' (like a lot of things on Wikipedia, I can find no secondary source for this, but refuse to believe it is the work of a prankster and therefore have decided to take it on faith).

In her book, catchily titled *Memories of Lenin*, Nadezhda very wisely skips over the day she finally snapped and said, 'Herring? I'll give you herring, you bald fuckwit', and instead writes of the Bolshevik conference of 25–30 December 1907, which took place where I am standing: 'What a shame the minutes from this great meeting were not preserved! There was such great excitement in the air! The revolution was then in its hottest phase and every comrade was filled with excitement. Everyone was ready to fight!' The last line really strikes a chord with me, and sounds just like my usual Christmas too. I am fascinated to learn that the forty-one delegates stayed at the Hotel Baijer, on the site of the Scandic Hotel, and therefore walked the same route I did today. The key difference, of course, is that while they were preoccupied with the overthrow of the tsars, the liberation of the peasantry and the dawn of a new political era, I just wanted to get to the Workers' Hall without falling flat on my arse.

I leave the museum and walk to Särkänniemi amusement park, which has wonderful rollercoasters I would love to try out, but the park, understandably, opens only in summer. So I put my fear of heights to one side and take the lift to the top of the 168-metre Näsinneula Observation Tower, the tallest in the Nordic countries, and have a coffee looking out over the beautiful lakes of Näsijärvi and Pyhäjärvi (my Finnish friends always say that the language is very easy to speak because you pronounce it as you see it, but all I ever see is an optician's chart, I'm afraid).

The difference in height between the two lakes is 18 metres, and the Tammerkoski rapids that are created as one flows to the other gave the town a source of power that was first exploited in the nineteenth century. James Finlayson, a Scottish Quaker on a mission to sell Bibles, founded a factory to make industrial machinery in 1820, but it was soon converted to a cotton mill and saw Tampere dubbed 'the Manchester of the North'; it still goes by the diminutive soubriquet, Manse. Textile production moved out of the city from the 1960s onwards and, from 1995, the factories were transformed into a dynamic complex of cinemas, galleries, theatres and cafés. The warm red-brick façade still dominates the main market square and the sign that spells out 'Finlayson' is eerily reminiscent of the original Disneyland California typeface. If you told me I was looking at Willy Wonka's chocolate factory, I would believe you.

I wander around the open-air market but it is getting cold again and I'm clean out of reading material, so I make for the Academy Bookshop off Hämeenkatu and find a ticket system for queuing. I have never seen this anywhere outside of government offices, but the fact that the Finns need to be forced into some sort of orderly line to get to the register, even in a *book* shop, is just about the smallest surprise I've had in Ryanland.

I'm frozen, so I nip to Henry's Pub for a warming drink and find Manchester City playing Newcastle on the television. It is 11 November and, before kick-off, there is a minute's silence for Remembrance Day, which commemorates the dead of all wars but originated in marking the 1918 armistice that ended the Great War. And it reminds me that history is, in a very real sense, close enough to actually smell – because November 1918 was just one year, in the Western calendar, after the October Revolution in Russia that brought Vladimir Ilyich Lenin to power. It was the revolution Nadezhda Krupskaya dreamed of, the one planned and plotted by the forty-one delegates who for six days in 1907 tramped the pavement in front of me, muttering about the new political era that promised so much.

I make my way back to the Scandic, grab my things and take a €30 taxi to the airport.

'It's cold,' I say.

'You should be here when it's minus twenty,' the taxi man replies.

I don't plan for that but I would like to come back in summer, to laze around the lakes and return to Särkänniemi to ride the rollercoasters. I had no expectations of Tampere because, in truth, I had never heard of it, which is probably why I enjoyed it so much. It fits a pattern that has emerged the longer I travel. If I plan excessively, I am disappointed. When I submit to a destination – Porto, Santiago de Compostela, Lincoln – it seems wantonly generous with its favours. And Tampere? Well, I loved it.

At the airport, I learn there are only fifty-two of us booked on the flight. I don't bother with priority boarding, because there really is no queue for the Finns to bunk. It is already late in the evening (we're not due to land until 10.20 p.m.) but that doesn't matter. A friend has flown from Dublin to meet me and we're going on the piss in Riga, the stag-party capital of the new Europe.

RIGA–LIVERPOOL–MANCHESTER

FR2735 • Tampere (TMP) to Riga (RIX)
491 km • €23.67

FR9607 • Riga (RIX) to Liverpool (LPL)
1,740 km • LVL40.10 (€57.06)

FR557 • Manchester (MAN) to Dublin (DUB)
264 km • £25.74

Last month, Britain's Queen Elizabeth II was on a state visit to Latvia and the local Conservative Party invited her down to Riga's old town on a Saturday night in order to witness the antics of her subjects. Leaving aside for a second the rather arresting image of Her Maj stumbling shit-faced from Studio 69 muttering, 'I say, did you clock the bazookas on that blonde?', it is hard not to concede the politicians had a point when they sniffed, 'Sometimes it's hard to believe these people have arrived from cultured and traditionally rich Great Britain.'

Yes, the Brits abroad are loud, noisy and overly fond of the ale – which also makes them great craic. That's why, just minutes after arriving, I have hit the ground running and joined them. I've also met up with Andrew Lohan, an old friend and an architect, a valuable travelling companion as I pick my way through the baroque and art-nouveau treasures of 'the Paris of the North'. (Have you ever noticed, incidentally, how that always seems to work only the one way – Tampere 'the Manchester of the North', Bruges 'the Venice of the North', and so on? No one ever says, 'Ah, Palermo, the Waterford of the South', do they?)

Anyway, if you've ever watched *Grand Designs Abroad* on Channel 4, Andrew and his wife, Jackie, are the ones who converted a church near Westport in County Mayo into a stunning holiday home. Every time I take a long-haul flight, that episode seems to be on.

Having flown directly from Dublin, Andrew has been in Riga for hours before I arrive, and has reconnoitred all the best bars. He has also established that the Latvian for beer is '*alus*', the only local word we need to know. I've been alone on the past eight Ryanland jaunts and I'm enjoying having someone to drink with – though the irony is that so many people here are in such a great party mood, everyone ends up talking to everyone else anyway. I make a mental note that if I ever embark on a tour like this again, my friends will be made to join me in places like Brno, where I was so bored with my own company I almost hired the hotel hooker for a chat ('I just want to talk,' I would have said pathetically, to which she inevitably would have replied in time-honoured tart-with-a-heart style, 'Aw, wife don't understand yer then, ducks?').

The first thing you notice about Riga's bars is that 90 per cent of the tourists are male. They come because of cheap flights, cheap beer, cheap food and, frankly, cheap women. One ad in a listings magazine offers Riga's cheapest private dance at 4.80 lats – that's €6.83, or just £4.58 – which means you can have a real woman naked in front of you for about the same price as *Playboy*.

The Baltic Guide, a very good free tabloid magazine written in English, reports that one Latvian man took offence at the attention a local was paying to tourists.

'How come all our girls are chasing foreign men?' he asked.

'We have standards,' she replied loudly, to a round of applause.

Today is a national holiday, Lāčplēsis diena, or Bearslayer's Day, named after a folk hero but commemorating a more recent event in Latvia's history. (Lāčplēsis is just one example of the Latvian fondness for adorning every letter of the alphabet with psychedelic diacritics – it's taken me about four minutes to type that one word.) The country declared independence from Tsarist Russia after the first revolution of 1918. Following the second revolution, the one that brought the Bolsheviks to power, it was soon under pressure to join the Soviet Union and, at the same time, under attack from forces to the west who wanted to restore the German Empire. In 1919, after fierce fighting at the Daugava railway bridge, the Germanic invaders were repelled and Latvia remained free.

Not for long, sadly, as we shall see tomorrow when, on the recommendation of three Scottish lads, we visit the Occupation Museum. ('It's interesting,' they tell us – and then, perhaps mindful that in a pub literally pulsating with testosterone, professing interest in anything intellectual might be as dubious as asking the DJ to play a couple of tunes from *Hello Dolly*, they add, 'and it gives you something else to do during the day besides drink.')

We have met them in De Lacy's which, precisely as you would expect in the historic old town of a Baltic city 1,950 kilometres from Dublin, is an Irish bar. It is run by a guy from Courtmacsherry in County Cork who plays his cards so close to his chest he must have spades on his skin ('Is business good?' I ask; 'Ah, it's okay,' he shrugs, looking around a bar that is heaving with people). He has a sign hanging over the counter that reads: 'The secret to being a good barman is knowing who is drunk and who is stupid.' To be honest, I'm heading at breakneck speed towards drunk, so while I can still walk, Andrew and I head out into Livu Laukums, a large square.

Immediately, we are pounced on by touts. 'Free drink, free drink,' one shouts. 'Most beautiful girls in Riga,' says a second. Both are effortlessly topped by a youth with lank hair and owlish glasses, sort of Harry Potter meets Bolshevik revolutionary, who holds up a sign for a club called Barfly and asks, 'You want big boobies and crazy pussy?'

We are still laughing five minutes later when we see a quiet bar and decide to extricate ourselves from the madness to recharge. We sit and order two beers and a woman brings them over – and only then do we notice the pole, bright and shiny, on a podium. Another girl arrives. She is very tall and slender. She has a tumble of dark, silky curls, high cheekbones and lacklustre, tired eyes. She is wearing a white bra, very short, white hot pants and white ankle boots.

In a corner, she revs up like the Roadrunner, legs moving but her feet seemingly a centimetre above ground, and she achieves such velocity that when she finally does connect with the floor, she flashes by us like a TGV, launches herself into space and connects with the pole by her fingernails. She swings around about six times while still perfectly parallel with the ground, only gradually allowing herself to fall to the floor like a Slinky. My eyes are watering and my ears have popped with the whoosh still reverberating through the room. If you could capture that and stick it in Sudafed, you could clear every sinus in Ireland. Being a little gauche in the etiquette of such matters, I'm not sure what to do. Andrew is no better, so I offer her a drink.

She fixes me with a businesslike look. 'Do you know the rules?' she asks.

'Rules?' I gulp.

'It is 12 lats for you to buy me a drink, plus the price of the drink. It is 25 lats for a topless dance and 40 lats to go upstairs for an erotic massage.'

'Well, thank you, we'll think about it,' I lie, and she wanders off, probably to spray WD-40 on her knees and elbows before the countdown to her next launch. We finish our drinks and leave, and when I look from the street to the name above the door, I am astonished I could have thought for even a moment it might just be a neighbourhood bar. There aren't many, I imagine, called the Markiza de Sada.

The taxi man who takes us back to the Albert Hotel asks for three times as much money as the driver who brought us to the old town. I'm so sick of being ripped off by taxi drivers I shove half of what he asks for into his hand and say, 'No more fucking nonsense, pal, that's all you're getting from us. You must think we're fucking stupid, do you?' He mutters something colourful in Latvian – there are diacritics zinging past my ears like kitchen knives during a domestic altercation – but he backs down and takes what he gets. And at least he has the good grace not to fart, so he's only my second-most-despised cabbie in Europe.

Next morning, the breakfast room looks like a field hospital on the Somme. Bleary-eyed, battle-weary men, young and old alike, wander dazed from the restaurant tables to the buffet. There is a logjam at the orange-juice counter, and people seem to be scooping grease onto the bacon in the hope that an old wives' hangover cure might actually work. Though there must be a hundred people here, there is a hush as everyone ploughs through the roughage and tries not to think of another day of drinking ahead. Many will be spared duty, as it is Sunday and they are heading home – but Andrew doesn't leave until tomorrow and I'm here until Tuesday, so we're girding our loins for the session ahead. All I can think of is that I'm almost out of Zantac and they probably don't sell it here.

We walk through the park, past the Monument of Freedom, which is manned around the clock by impassive guards, and wander through the old town to the Occupation Museum. It was built in the Soviet era to commemorate the contribution of the Latvian Riflemen to the Red Army between 1917 and 1920 (a contribution which many here feel understandably ambiguous, if not downright hostile, about) and is without question the ugliest building in Riga. The minute the Russians finally left in the early 1990s, the space was given over to a compelling exhibit documenting their oppressive regime. Thankfully, there are also advanced plans to re-clad the exterior.

The listings magazine, *Riga This Week*, says it is 'an objective account of systematic attempts to destroy Latvia and its people by both Soviet and Nazi regimes'. Every time I read that sentence, I laugh – the clash of 'objective' and 'systematic attempts to destroy' is wonderfully arch.

In fact, the museum is as distant from objectivity as it is from Vladivostok – and why not? For, make no mistake, there was not one minute of the fifty-one years of occupation that native Latvians enjoyed. Russian tanks moved into Riga in 1940, the Nazis occupied the country from 1941 to 1944, and the Soviets came back that year and stayed until Mikhail Gorbachev's reforms led to the fragmentation of the Soviet Union and the reclamation of independence by Lithuania, Estonia and Latvia alike. By the end of the Second World War, a third of the population was gone – killed in raids or in battle, executed, sent to the death camps, or held as prisoners of war.

The Russians promptly dismantled the Latvian army, placed farms and private property in collective ownership, repressed all religious practice, determined 'correct' modes of social and cultural interaction, and deported dissenters to the gulags (or, when they couldn't be bothered with that, just shot them). The wickedness of it all is heartbreaking. No one denies that the capitalist system is riddled with flaws, not least in its frequent disregard for the most vulnerable in society – but was there ever a system quite as monstrous as the Soviet one, which institutionalised the denial of the simple human urges to be individual and to be free?

Though it is little consolation for the Latvians who died under the occupation, their refusal to submit to the oppressor and their hunger for the restoration of freedom is deeply humbling and inspiring. By the mid-1980s, they had become organised, and brave enough to hold public demonstrations. Gorbachev rattled the sabres a few times but he must have known the game was up. On 23 August 1989, the fiftieth anniversary of the Hitler–Stalin Pact that left the Baltic states open to invasion, over 2 million citizens of Estonia, Lithuania and Latvia staged the most dignified and moving protest in history. From Tallinn to Riga to Vilnius, they stood on streets, along the shoreline, across farmland, through forests. Then they all joined hands – and they sang.

There was no going back. That was the year the Berlin Wall came down, then the satellite states of the old Warsaw Pact fell like dominoes. In May 1990, Latvia reinstated its constitution. Russia protested, and even sent in the tanks, but a failed coup in Russia that saw Gorbachev removed from power presented an ideal opportunity to break away for ever. In August 1991, Latvia declared full independence and, as was the case in so many cities of the eastern bloc, a rope was slung around the neck of Lenin's statue and he was pulled to the ground. Just two days ago at his museum in Tampere, I traced his life from birth to death and it seems tragic that a philosophy with such fundamental goodness at its core – that the spoils of society should be shared equally by all – so quickly became dour, stultifying and dangerous. And how sad that so many of us were playing at socialism in the dingy upstairs rooms of Dublin pubs, because we were free to do so, while the regimes we admired were suppressing the rights of so many people to choose their own political destinies.

The Occupation Museum practically vibrates with vituperation and an uncompromising hatred of the Russians. To me, an Irishman who has long championed conciliation on my own island, it is startlingly raw, but you would have to be a complete fool not to understand it.

Sober in every sense, Andrew and I find a tourist office, where he notices on the wall a list of the city by-laws. The first municipal prohibition is on breaches of the peace – the second is on witchcraft. Clearly, we are not in Kansas anymore.

The old town nestles warmly in the cold winter air. The spire of St Peter's Church looks like groups of acrobats perched on each other's shoulders; the taller spire of the Dome Cathedral towers over everything else. Colourful shopfronts, cobbled streets, medieval palaces, all add to the fairytale landscape. Groups of lads wander aimlessly, all desperately trying to delay the hour when the only option is to start drinking again. We eat at De Lacy's, which is quieter now that many of the weekend visitors have gone home, then we head out on the beer. Of Harry Potter and the crazy pussy (and what a title that would be if J.K. Rowling went back on her word and wrote an eighth book), there is no sign.

Next day, we go for a meal in a traditional restaurant, where one of the options on the menu is 'chicken spit pickled in greens' – now there's a dish in dire need of a hyphen. We take the glass lift to the Skyline Bar on the twenty-sixth floor of the Reval Hotel Latvija and watch as the twinkling lights come on across town. As an architect, Andrew notices how few cranes are dotted around the city, probably because all the local builders are throwing up housing estates from Lerwick to Limerick. In 1990, there were 909,135 people living in Riga. This year, that figure has dropped to 727,578. After independence, many ethnic Russians just went home – then, when Latvia acceded to European Union membership in 2004, huge numbers of economic migrants sought their fortunes in Britain and Ireland.

In March, Latvia's European Commissioner, Andris Piebalgs, said up to 40,000 of his countrymen might have moved to Ireland alone. Perhaps four times that number have emigrated to Britain, and they are mostly the young who could build genuine prosperity at home. Instead, they are minding the children of Ireland's yummy mummies, picking the mushrooms in market gardens from County Down to Devon, or driving taxis in Dublin or Edinburgh. Freedom, like everything else, can be a two-edged sword.

I leave Riga's shiny international airport and fly to Liverpool. I had expected much more time here but Ryanair changed the flight time by a full day, long after I booked – that's the downside of picking up cheap flights months in advance. I haven't been to Liverpool since 1984, when I was sent by my newspaper to the Royal Court Theatre to cover the first live gig Frankie Goes To Hollywood played after their phenomenal chart success that year with 'Relax', 'Two Tribes' and 'The Power of Love'. It was a run-down city then and, at every shop door, there was someone collecting cash for Britain's miners. They were in the ninth month of the catastrophic strike that destroyed the trade-union movement in Britain and, looking back, this was the moment that also marked the passing of political power from the working class to the middle class.

Over twenty years later, the Liverpool I'm standing in today truthfully doesn't look a whole lot better, with dreary shopping precincts and fast-food restaurants everywhere. Lime Street is filthy, with many buildings shuttered, and if they want a successful reign as Europe's 2008 City of Culture, they need to get their skates on and give the place a good wash. No harm if they cleaned the used toilet roll off the railway tracks too.

I pay an absolutely astonishing one-way, off-peak fare of £9.40 to Manchester Airport. What a mad world we live in – a forty-five-minute train trip in England is the same price as having two Latvian girls jiggle their breasts in your face as they half-heartedly gyrate to some generic Europop tune.

The train never makes it to the airport. Instead, it comes to a halt in Manchester Piccadilly and a muffled voice says some services have been suspended. It seems someone has committed suicide further up the tracks. Everyone grumbles and groans and gets agitated in that modern, snarling way, lashing out at officials who, in all fairness, didn't exactly push the poor unfortunate under the wheels. I sense so much stress, so much tension, that I just want to go to the station announcer's hut, grab the microphone and tell everyone to line up on the platform. I want us all to join hands and sing.

BRATISLAVA–MILAN BERGAMO

FR4282 • Dublin (DUB) to Bratislava (BTS)
1,740 km • €23.45

FR4643 • Bratislava (BTS) to Milan Bergamo (BGY)
626 km • SKK481.23 (€13.98)

FR9429 • Milan Bergamo (BGY) to Dublin (DUB)
1,430 km • €19.43

My round trip from Dublin to Bratislava in Slovakia, onwards to Milan and then home again totals 3,796 kilometres. Based on my train fare between Liverpool and Manchester Airport, which worked out at 25.5 cent per kilometre, it would cost €854.10 to cover that distance by train in Britain. Soaring over Europe on Ryanair, it costs €56.86. That's right, less than forty quid sterling for three flights halfway across a continent. So next time some do-gooder Green bores you shitless at a dinner party about how much more environmentally friendly travelling by train is, remind her of this fare discrepancy with some force and ask her if she would mind chipping in the difference if you choose to go by rail instead. I say 'her' because, well, nine times out of ten, it is a woman.

I'm still smiling at how little my flights have cost when I am first to board in Dublin; I have somehow managed to shoehorn everything I need into a carry-on bag and the BMW jacket, which has now taken on mythic proportions and weighs about half what I do. There are days I expect to unzip a pocket and find Lord Lucan riding Shergar. The flight seems more like a meeting of old friends, as nine-tenths of the passengers are Slovak. They clearly know the steward, as many kiss him when they get on – or perhaps they are looking for a bit of help in the raffle. They are laden with children's toys, deep-fat-fryers and DVD players, the shiny gifts emigrants always bring home to dazzle relatives with.

We land, as most Ryanair flights do, at about twice the speed of any other airline – those twenty-minute turnaround times on which the whole schedule depends mean pilots treat every flight as if they were entering Berlin during the Soviet blockade. I've noticed that Eastern Europeans still do what the Irish used to do years ago, when we first could afford to fly but were still knotted in superstition, and clap energetically when we land. Then I remember I still bless myself on every take-off, so who am I to talk?

The apron at Bratislava is filled with planes in the livery of Sky Europe. This is the home base of the central European low-fares outfit, which was founded just five years ago and already operates ninety-nine routes between forty-two destinations in nineteen countries. Europe is voting with its feet, and Europe wants those feet curled under a seat at 35,000 feet while it sips red wine and gazes at a raffle ticket, hoping to win its next trip for free.

Ryanair calls this destination 'Bratislava (Vienna)' and, indeed, it is less than an hour from the Austrian capital; if you wish, you can even take a high-speed catamaran along the Danube between the two cities. I want to stay here, though; Bratislava is, after all, home city of Kara Milovy, the beautiful cellist portrayed by Maryam d'Abo in *The Living Daylights*, who escaped with James Bond to the West by tobogganing down a mountainside in her open cello case while being shot at by border guards. I still think something like that would have added a lot to the finale of *The Sound of Music*.

First, I must clear immigration, and you can see here the residual suspicion of those brought up during the communist era. The guard takes my passport, regards it intently, tries to outstare me (he's wasting his time – I've been a journalist for far too long not to have a withering glare down pat), looks at the passport again, looks at me, looks at… And I just want to say, 'Listen, pal, I didn't have to vote Yes, *twice*, in the referendums on the fucking Nice Treaty that let you lot into the EU, so if you want to play silly buggers, fine, I'll just write a cheque and *buy* fucking Slovakia, if that's what you want.' Eventually, with a grunt, he hands the document back to me and I'm on my way.

The outskirts of the city look like the other eastern bloc cities I've been to in the past few months, full of utilitarian apartments, tramlines and people huddled at bus shelters. On the way to town, I read the *Favourite Places Guide to Bratislava*, which tells me: 'All the Slovak staff in clubs speak at least one foreign language. English is an obviosity.' It is such an obviosity, in fact, that the guide continues: 'Bratislava's big advantage is almost non-criminality even during the night and no disturbing by street girls in the street.' There is a wide range of music available from the '60ties to the 80ties', and, perhaps best of all for a single man, the guide says: 'The far-famed beauty of Slovak women will definitely ensure a smooth finish to your challenging daylong programme.' Luckily, Bratislava is also a city 'where you can spend a twenty-four-hour day non-stop'.

I also love the advertisement selling a two-day tour of the city, which includes visits to three bars, a beer-tasting session, accommodation, the services of a guide, a visit to a 'big relax centre' and transfers throughout. The price for all this is listed as 'bunch of people'.

I'm staying at the Radisson SAS Carlton Hotel, allegedly the finest in the city, and it would certainly want to be, as I've paid €200 a night for it. I thought about staying on something called the Botel Gracia, which is a floating hotel (Botel – geddit?), but as we drive along the banks of the Danube, which today is grey rather than blue, I see the Botel and am glad I resisted the temptation. I'd say it might be fun in summer, but today it looks bleak and uninviting.

The Carlton is on Hviezdoslavovo námestie (and even I know by now that '*námestie*' means 'square'). It is an attractive cobbled quadrangle on the fringes of the old town, and also home to the State Opera and the concert hall. The Slovak Symphony Orchestra is playing Rachmaninov's 'Variations on a Theme by Paganini' tonight, and though there are no seats left, I manage to pick up a standing ticket for 70 koruny – that's just €2.

I wander around the old town. After Brno and Riga, I'm a bit old towned out, though it is undeniably handsome. The Christmas market is being set up, the streets are full of happy revellers going about their business, the men look like tortured poets and the women are all six feet tall with cheekbones a sparrow could perch on. There are ornate castles, marzipan palaces and elegant spires. It is the very definition of what Mittel Europe should look like – that is, a theme park that can hold the attention of Western European men of a certain age until the lap-dancing clubs open.

The ordinary bars range from the usual suspects (here, it's called

The Dubliner) and chilled cafés like Greenwich Time, which has giant gauze-covered lamps on the footpath, lots of billowing white organza, leather couches, ambient lighting and the unmistakeable chill of Balearic house oozing out onto the footpath.

I wander, and find that Carrefour has beaten Tesco to the prime location in the relentless carve-up of Europe by the supermarket giants – but since I carry loyalty cards for both, I root for neither.

I've hit a bit of a wall, having flown over 10,000 kilometres so far this month alone, and decide to use some of the hotel facilities I've paid €200 for. I make my way to the top-floor spa and sweat in a small sauna. In my robe, I wander to the outside deck for a wonderful view across the old town and the river (and its spaceship-like, cable-stayed bridge which, despite being built in 1972, is still called the New Bridge), then make for the wooden loungers in the rest area.

There is a TV set mounted on the wall and, on screen, there is a woman being mounted from behind by a very enthusiastic swain as she orally pleasures his best mate. In most of the hotel spas I've been to, the televisions have been tuned to something innocuous, like *Sky News* (and, small tip, never fly or do anything dangerous during Kay Burley's shift – that's when all the big stories break), not to some Slavic beauty being given a good seeing to on the double. There may be children around, I think with alarm – what if they stumble accidentally upon this porn? I get very angry about it for, oh, it must be almost forty-five minutes, and leave only when I am sure the woman on screen has enjoyed the hot shower with her kindly best friend, who offers to wash her back but has a very bad aim. Oh, the chaos that ensues when the soap goes missing…

I dress up for the concert hall and arrive to find it already thronged. I wander through gilded halls, one the length of a football field, with acres of parquet flooring and fourteen chandeliers. It's all a little faded and the paint is peeling here and there, but it crackles with atmosphere. Soon, the doors open and when we arrive in the hall, it is intolerably warm, not least because a chandelier the size and shape of an upturned fir tree (think *The Poseidon Adventure*) must contain about 1,000 bulbs; sitting under it is like being a slice of lasagne in a canteen. I have dressed in layers because it's very cold outside and now my eyelids have started to droop alarmingly, a combined effect of the heat and the fact that I was up at 3 a.m. to catch a 6.10 a.m. flight. A woman beckons me to a spare seat beside her and when I explain I have a standing ticket only, she intimates it is fine to sit until someone claims the chair. The orchestra, over ninety musicians in all (how can they sell tickets for €2 and pay even the electricity bill, never mind the performers?), comes on stage to enthusiastic applause, then respectful silence as the conductor taps his baton and the lead violin guides them through the melancholy and occasionally wildly romantic music of Rachmaninov.

I'm not sure if a crescendo or an elbow wakes me, but I do know that when I open my eyes, about twenty other pairs are staring at me and telling me to hush. I have, it seems, been snoring for ten minutes. The woman who gave me the seat looks thunderous, and I am genuinely embarrassed that I spoiled her evening. Shamed, I leave at the interval.

It could have been worse. The Opera House on the same square is staging *Aida*, and there is a lonely-looking man with a bored-looking camel at the foot of the front steps. I saw Franco Zeffirelli's staging of the Verdi opera at the Arena in Verona two years ago and only the scale of the production (at one point, I counted over 300 people on stage) kept me awake then, so things could have been a lot worse tonight if I had delivered an ear-splitting snort during the most tender of arias.

I walk to a traditional restaurant I spotted earlier, all pine furniture and red-and-white checked gingham tablecloths, and order the Slovakian national dish, Bryndzové halušky, a sort of gnocchi, or potato dumplings, with bryndza (a sheep's cheese) and bacon bits on top. It arrives, and my first thought is Polyfilla with pork scratchings. The bacon is crisp and delicious, but there are maybe only a dozen shavings of it – after that, there is just the seemingly endless stodge of dumpling and cheese, with a slightly sharp aftertaste. It is hellish, and I leave three-quarters of it. I protest I was just full when the crestfallen owner retrieves the bowl, but I take comfort from the fact that the plaster crack in the wall over the bar will no doubt finally be filled. And, to be fair, he did come up with an apple strudel of such flaky, light perfection, and a great local beer in Zlatý Bažant, that the game was definitely won in the second half.

I walk the streets again and note with pleasure that, unlike Riga three nights ago, Bratislava seems filled with locals out as couples or in groups; they haven't quite allowed the stag parties to take over. I hope they continue to resist but the thought barely lives past the next morning. As I am walking through the lobby of the Carlton, I hear a group of Irishmen wondering aloud about the quality of the hookers. One of them points to me and laughs, 'Ask him – he looks like a satisfied customer.' They snigger until I say, 'And how was the weather when you left Finglas this morning, lads?' and they all blush like adolescents.

I walk through the old town again, stopping at a bookshop where the titles in the window are all by James Joyce, Jack London, Samuel Beckett and Aleksandr Solzhenitsyn. It is not a surprise. On my eastern European trips to date, Bratislava seems the most studious city. It is unmistakeably the wealthiest, too, and its citizens are the friendliest.

My flight to Milan is not until the late afternoon, so I find a genuine gourmet restaurant called Lebowski in the old town and treat myself to the best meal so far on my travels – grilled prawns in garlic; a fillet steak the size of a spaniel, with earthy, chunky chips and a sauce of green peppercorns that zings with flavour; a chocolate dessert; and half a bottle each of excellent Slovak sauvignon blanc and pinot noir, a double espresso and a Bailey's, and all for slightly less than €30. 'Splendid' does not do it justice and I leave Bratislava a happy agglomerate of veins and arteries slowly silting up with cholesterol.

When we arrive at Milan Bergamo, it is teeming with rain, and what is usually a forty-five-minute coach journey takes almost an hour and a half. I've booked into a Four Points by Sheraton, which was only €75, but have no clue where it is, so when we arrive at the bus terminus beside the Centrale train station, I join the longest taxi queue I have ever seen. As it inches its way along, an Italian man and his wife, ostensibly walking alongside, perform the quickest of shimmies and nip in front of me, and at least 150 others.

'Excuse me,' I say, 'there's a queue.'

And he looks at me and draws himself to full height and says, 'You are in Ee-taly now. Shut up. It will be easier.'

I practically self-combust with rage, but there is little I can do, so I call the Four Points and am assured the hotel is no more than 500 metres away. I risk the walk and dodge the biblical flood, and when I see the room I have been allocated – the bed is bigger than my entire room was in Brno and the duvet like a cloud of cotton wool – I buckle. Tonight is an early night.

The plus side is that I'm up early. The rain has stopped and I take a bus to La Scala Milan and wander across the square to the Galleria Vittorio Emanuele II. Built between 1865 and 1878, its intersecting arcades laid down a basic template for shopping-mall design ever since, though it must be one of the few where you can shop at Prada, then walk across to McDonald's for a quarter-pounder.

I've never taken to Milan before, but there's something in the air today that just seems to assault me. Maybe it's because I've never been inside the Duomo, the vast cathedral dominating the city centre. I finally find out what all the fuss is about. Begun in 1386 and completed (well, as much as it will ever be) in 1965, the close-on 600-year construction period went through almost as many architects as Italy went through coalition governments. Indeed, the Italian expression equivalent to our 'painting the Forth bridge', is '*fabbrica del Duomo*' – 'building the Duomo'.

I can truthfully say that walking into it is one of the most heart-stopping moments of my life. It is so overwhelmingly vast, I actually exhale audibly. The support columns line up like tree trunks in a symmetrical forest. The stained-glass windows, avoiding those look-at-me blues, reds and yellows of most Gothic cathedrals, instead whisper in muted autumnal shades, sending dusty, filtered light about halfway into the church before it is swallowed up by the gloom. The stone is the softest of greys, bordering on beige, with slate, tan and fawn all present in minuscule graduations. I'm trying to think where I have seen all these shades lined up together before, then realise with a jolt that they are the signature colours of Milan's most famous designer, Giorgio Armani. Walk into any branch of Armani Collezioni and look along the rail of men's suits and there you have the essences of the Duomo's colour palette distilled. I later learn that Armani's first job was window-dressing La Rinascente, the department store next to the cathedral. Hmmm…

It takes for ever for me to drag myself from the Duomo. I cannot think of any other building that has left me so overawed. There are many as beautiful, but none quite as spiritual. If you ever really have to talk to God, and your god happens to be the Christian one, then come to the Duomo. It really is His home.

After that, Milan has a lot to live up to so, rather than racing around, I slow down a gear and sit at a table on the pavement of the Corso Vittorio Emmanuele, where I pay €9 for a pint at Esercizio Tre Gazzelle, a café that has something to do with three gazelles but, to my mind, is just too dear.

I walk around the designer shops on the Via Montenapoleone, Via della Spiga and Via Manzoni. From Armani to Prada, Gucci to Pucci, Audemars Piguet to Gianfranco Ferré and Chanel to Dolce & Gabbana, I feel like I should be escorted off the premises by the fashion police. But, you know, everyone is friendly and welcoming, which strikes me as something new in Milan – though maybe I'm just radiating the grace I've pilfered from the Duomo.

After the relative austerity of eastern Europe, I'm revelling in all the bling Milan can throw at me and make for the Piazza san Babila, where I settle myself in at a pavement table under cover at the Café san Babila. I see that beers are €9 or €15 and assume the larger one is a litre, but check with the waitress.

'Si,' she says, 'per uno litro.'

'Si, per favore,' I reply.

Tentatively risking shaky English, she asks, 'Just one?'

And I smile and say, 'Well, for now.'

She smiles and repeats 'for now', as if teaching herself the phrase, then looks at me and says, 'for now' again before bursting into laughter. And then comes the single most unexpected thing that has happened to me in Ryanland – she wends her way through the tables, bearing a foaming litre of *birra alla spina* in a huge frosted glass tankard, and she slams it down in front of me and roars, 'Cheers, big ears!' And I laugh until the tears drip from my chin.

Next day, back at Orio al Serio Airport in Bergamo, I queue behind witless people who look at everyone else taking off watches, mobile phones, belts, shoes, the works, yet it never occurs to them to do likewise until they are at the scanner. We are being held up for twice as long as we need to be by people being inconsiderate and I long to say something in a loud and superior voice.

But one thought overrides all others. It says, 'Philip, you are in Italy now. Shut up. It will be easier.' And you know something? It always is.

WROCLAW–KRAKOW

FR1172
Shannon (SNN) to Wroclaw (WRO)
1,770 km • €43.03

FR1175
Krakow (KRK) to Shannon (SNN)
2,010 km • €21.26

I had a day at home after Milan, and now here I am at midnight the day after, getting out of bed and into the car for the three-hour drive to Shannon Airport, so I can tick the box against another Ryanland outpost. Naturally, I would prefer it if the flight had been in the late afternoon instead of at 6 a.m., but at least Ireland in the small hours is deserted and we rattle across the country so quickly we have time for almost two hours sleep in the car when we arrive. I say 'we' because my sister, Joyce, who is almost six years younger than me, has never been to Poland either and we've planned this as our first European trip together in over twenty years. We both stayed in the family home for about a decade after our older sister and brother had moved out, so we've always been close. Neither of us has a complete sense of humour; when we went our separate ways, we were awarded joint custody of the same one.

I haven't been through Shannon since the mid-90ties, as they say in Bratislava, and it looks old and tired. Every flight bound from Ireland to the USA, and vice-versa, used to have to stop here, and it gave the airport an artificial financial lifeline that had nothing to do with commercial reality. Now, only a couple of US flights a day depart from Shannon (and, oddly, the inbound leg of charters from Orlando, as if to remind you that you might have had a great time, but hard luck, pal, you're home). It is, however, a busy Ryanair hub and has also derived an unlikely boost from the Iraq War, as most US military flights refuel here (including, allegedly, the CIA's so-called rendition flights bringing prisoners to Guantanamo). All this, incidentally, despite the fact that Ireland has pursued a policy of neutrality since independence in 1921 and famously refers to the years between 1939 and 1945 as 'The Emergency'. Hundreds of thousands of US troops en route to Baghdad pour through the duty-free shop, the world's first when it opened in 1947, to stock up on linen tablecloths, Waterford Crystal and, if they have any sense, Aran sweaters with a cable-knit pattern so thick it could repel a direct hit by a Scud missile. If traditional knitters dyed some sweaters orange, they might even get a few orders from the rendition flights.

Thanks to the inflatable pillow that has sustained me since May, and internet check-in that secures Seat 16F, I sleep all the way to Wroclaw, in the Polish province of Lower Silesia (no parsing of vowels here, clearly), where we arrive before 10 a.m. The airport is thronged with people awaiting the homecoming of the émigrés who keep the Irish economic miracle alive, the painters, plasterers and plumbers, the shop assistants, waitresses and hairdressers who are now so ubiquitous that the census in April was conducted not just in English but also in Polish and almost a dozen other languages.

Crying into pints and emotional reunions in Arrivals used to be our gig, when the Irish were the ones who went abroad to build the roads or nurse the sick. The difference was that when the Irish left, they went in significant numbers to countries where English was the first language, because they never bothered learning another. Only those who went to Britain itself had much chance of regularly visiting home. For the rest, who went to America, Canada and Australia, the day they left Ireland was often also the last time they ever saw it, disappearing beneath the clouds as a new life beckoned far away.

But at Ryanair prices, Polish workers can, and do, travel home once a month if they wish, and the low-fares airlines are driving a social revolution unseen in Old Europe, a sort of semi-detached exile that is very much migration rather than emigration. It is easy to have a foot in each country – and, as I find out, probably cheaper to fly home for a weekend on the beer than it is to pay Irish prices for pints.

Maybe that's why the emotion here today is muted. When we were kids, waiting for our overseas cousins to arrive home at the airport, the reunions were raucous and emotional, as people who hadn't seen each other for years melted into joyous embraces. Today in Wroclaw, the parents, the spouses and the siblings might just as well be picking their loved ones up from the train station at the end of a working day.

On the way to the city, a car clips the wing mirror of our Mercedes taxi. Ignoring the fact that he has passengers, the driver goes into road-rage mode and gives chase, narrowly missing other cars, cyclists, pedestrians and trams. Only the last item on that list really worries me, because the trams are not like modern, light-rail units, but hulking, heavy, metal carriages that look as if they could take out a suburb, never mind a cab. Certainly, neither Joyce nor I has located our shared sense of humour by the time we reach downtown. Nor, indeed, has either of us re-established anything resembling a normal heartbeat.

We make for the mock-Bavarian main square (as part of the German Empire, the city was called Breslau), which is colourful and pretty, though just as susceptible as the rest of eastern Europe to creeping colonisation by Western retailers.

There is only one thing I really want to see, though, and that is yet another landmark building, about 3 kilometres from the centre. The Centenary Hall, the Hala Ludowa, was designed by the German architect, Max Berg, and built between 1911 and 1913. It's a UNESCO World Heritage Site because, at the time of construction, the reinforced concrete cupola – 69 metres in circumference, 42 metres high and made up of a series of four concentric terraces – was by far the largest yet built. The engineering involved represented a major breakthrough that made possible much of the arena architecture we see today. Unlike the Villa Tugendhat in Brno, the Hala Ludowa still impresses, because the design itself remains unique; only the principles of its construction were aped by others.

On rare occasions, concrete acquires a patina that makes it attractive rather than brutish, and this building has a patina as attractive as a halo. As lights shines through the windows and picks out the ribs that act as a vault for the ceiling, it looks like something from Fritz Lang's *Metropolis*. For a building so heavy, it feels airy as a soufflé, a secular cathedral rather prosaically being dressed today for a dull trade fair. In the lobby, a fascinating exhibition shows it has played host to many notables over the years. Adolf Hitler held a rally here. Pope John Paul II said mass. And Paul Anka sang here too, in the 1960s, an event that seems to be rewarded with a slightly disproportionate amount of coverage until it dawns on me that he may well have been the only Western entertainer to do so.

After wandering around the belvedere that radiates from Hala Ludowa, Joyce and I make our way back to the station and take a train for Krakow, three and a half hours to the east. The city turns out to be a delight, with the dramatic Wawel Castle looking out over a bend in the Vistula River, quaint side streets, good bars and restaurants, an interesting cathedral (it was Pope John Paul II's parish church when he was plain Cardinal Karol Wojtyla) and a vast main square I remember from *Schindler's List*.

The very thought of that movie makes my stomach lurch, because I really had to question myself many times before I finally decided to do what I plan to do tomorrow. The unavoidable conclusion was that I could not hope to understand Europe without confronting the evil that almost stole its heart. That's why, on this trip, I'm glad I'm not travelling alone – tomorrow, Joyce and I are going to Oswiecim, which you may never have heard of. You are much more likely to know it by its German name, Auschwitz.

On a TV on the coach, a documentary tees up a lot of the history that preceded the establishment of the death camps, which were commissioned by the Nazi hierarchy to carry out the Final Solution, their term for the complete extermination of European Jews. The video shows the fall of the Weimar Republic, the subsequent political unrest and power vacuum in Berlin, the rise of the Nazis, the Kristallnacht pogrom, the deportations of Jews, the invasion of Czechoslovakia and Poland, the outbreak of war – and, finally, the conversion, in May 1940, of a former army barracks into a concentration camp, originally for the detention of Polish intellectuals, members of the resistance, German criminals and homosexuals.

On arrival, we are split into groups of around twenty people and assigned a guide who walks us through the reception area and into the original camp. We have all seen the famous gates – with the words 'Arbeit Mach Frei' worked into the wrought iron – in so many movies that there is the momentary sense of being on a set rather than in the place where the assembly-line techniques of the industrialised world were employed in their unthinkable task. Daily, occupants of the cell blocks would march to work, an orchestra playing to keep them sub-consciously in step as they derived futile hope from the slogan above, promising that work would make them free.

Auschwitz I, as this part of the complex is known, soon began accepting Jews too, and as we tour the blocks, the guide shows us a map of Europe and all the cities where thriving Jewish communities were first ghettoised, then liquidated. Some of the names leap out at me – Paris, Salzburg, Frankfurt, Marseille, Lübeck, Brno, Bratislava, Riga – so many are places I've been to this year.

In one block, behind a glass case about 30 metres long, is a mountain of human hair, shaved from the heads of inmates when they arrived. This is what remains of tonnes of hair sent back to Germany to be spun into yarn – there is cloth on display here that was made from it. In another room, there are suitcases by the thousand, many with names scrawled on them – here a doctor from Danzig, there an orphan from Budapest. Another case is filled with the accoutrements of human frailty – prosthetic limbs, spectacles, crutches.

In another room, and most movingly of all, there is an endless pile of shoes, mostly ageing to a uniform shade of dull grey. On top, towards the back, I see a sandal in a fading red, floral print, with an ankle strap and an open toe. In my mind, I can see the woman who bought the shoes – she was in her early twenties, a looker, with curves that would make men sitting at a pavement café table turn and nod admiringly, maybe even whistle, as she passed. The shoes would have made her feel sexy, desirable, and even when she was being deported, she had paid so much for them she surely was not going to leave them behind. Now, one of them sits on top of a pile of decaying boots, a potent symbol that the '6 million' we always talk about in a vaguely detached way were, in fact, 6 million *people*. They were attractive and ugly, sexy and plain, funny and cantankerous, tall and small, young and old, straight and gay, able-bodied and crippled, blonde and brunette, fair-skinned and sallow. Their individuality became secondary to the fact that they did not meet the Nazi ideal of Aryan perfection, and they died for it.

In Block 11, the full horror of how that happened is brought home when we descend to the cellar. This was a prison for prisoners, and the punishment cells redefine macabre. In the fetid confinement where Fr Maximilian Kolbe (later St Maximilian) perished, the tiny window led to a slow and excruciating suffocation. In another, little more than a metre square, four men at a time were forced through a ground-level aperture that looks like a dog flap, then made to stand all night, pressed up against each other, in the dark, unable to sleep, urinating on themselves and each other when they no longer could hold back. The thought of such claustrophobia is making my chest tight and my throat dry.

Then the guide tells us that this is also the spot where, on 3 September 1941, the first tests of Zyklon B on humans were conducted. On the spot where I am standing, over 800 Soviet prisoners of war were gassed in the first mass extermination. My whole body is gripped by a chill I never wish to experience again. A feeling starts to wash over me, one I'm not sure I've ever felt before. I have known grief, profoundly on occasion, and sorrow, and the pain of loss, but this is the first time I have been introduced to despair in its true sense, an all-encompassing feeling of helplessness, desolation and slack-jawed horror.

We move on to the first purpose-built gas chamber, and the adjacent ovens, where it took days to incinerate the 700 corpses from one kill. To one side, just behind the back wall of what was for years his family home, stands the gallows on which, in 1947, the longest-serving camp commandant, Rudolf Höss, was hanged after being found guilty of war crimes at Nuremberg. I don't agree with the death penalty, but when a man is responsible for murder on this scale, what other punishment fits? Some might argue he should have been held instead for his entire life like his fellow Nazi, and almost namesake, Rudolf Hess, Hitler's one-time deputy *führer*. But by the time Hess died in Spandau Prison in Berlin in 1987, at the age of ninety-three, there were many who felt *he* had been badly treated. As if.

When we move into the chamber itself, and look to the fake shower-heads and the vents in the roof where canisters of Zyklon B were dropped among the people who believed they were here only for delousing, a stillness overtakes me. Instinctively, I know I am in a sacred place, maybe because almost everyone who died here did so surrounded by family. In the last moment of life, would love overcome terror? Would the proximity of someone who gave your life meaning make the end of that life serene? I cling to the hope that it was so.

I look around the others in our tour group and see reflected on their faces what I am feeling, a blank stare of incomprehension, a silent prayer of thanks for our own fortunate lives – and the unmistakeably dull dread that there is worse to come in Auschwitz II-Birkenau, the camp where everything the Nazis had learned was distilled in the most efficient death factory in history.

We drive there parallel to a railway line. I love railways, but I know where this leads to – and *what* it led to. Suddenly, it becomes sinister, because this piece of track is connected to every other in Europe, from the far north of Sweden to the far south of Greece, from the Urals in the east all the way to the English Channel in the west. The Holocaust might have happened anyway if the victims had to be transported here by road, but it would have taken far longer and many lives would have been spared. The railways made it so easy, so seamless. From so many cities on that wall map, the points were relentlessly aligned so that thousands of journeys could end in this one destination, passing under the low, wide arch at Birkenau and drawing to a halt beside the platform in front of me, surrounded by wire, overlooked by watchtowers.

There, the arrivals were screened. Something in the order of the healthiest 10 per cent of the men were saved for camp work, while everyone else, including all the women and children, were marched from the train to the 'showers', made to lay their clothes in neat piles when they undressed – and gassed. Then their gold fillings were removed by the *sonderkommando*, workers selected from the prisoners' ranks to assist in the genocide, and their bodies were shovelled into ovens. When the war started going against the Nazis, the Final Solution was speeded up, and mounds of bodies were doused in petrol and set alight in the open air. Ashes rained down on the rest of the camp, leaving many men wiping the dust of their own wives and children off their prison uniforms. Between May and August of 1944, over 400,000 Hungarian Jews were murdered here – and the camp, stretching into the hazy far distance, is to the last square millimetre an enormous gravesite, and a shrine.

In one of the hundreds of huts that was home to inmates – its design adapted from a cavalry stable and unheated, even in winters when temperatures dropped to minus thirty – the guide stands us in a semi-circle. She leads this same tour every day, yet tears are streaming down her cheeks.

'Look around you,' she says, only moderately successful at clearing her throat. 'Remember one thing when you leave here today. People did this to people.'

I'm terrified to look around, because I know that we're actually all in tears at this stage. But hers is an important point. The victims are not the only ones whose individuality can't be denied – those who killed them were people too. People who, for reasons unfathomable, felt superior enough to their neighbours to set about their annihilation.

Rudolf Höss' father wanted him to become a Catholic priest – has anyone in history ever deviated so far from what was wished for him?

That is the warning from history, the lesson we must learn – the differences that give Europe its energy can also feed its hate. The success of one man can fuel the bitterness of another. A union of the weak can become strong if the strong do nothing to stop it.

I ask the guide if this takes a huge toll on her, conducting people through the camp every day, and she looks at me, the streaks on her cheeks almost dry, and says, 'Yes – as you can see.' In fact, all I see is one of the bravest women I've ever met. Awkwardly, for I'm not sure if this is the right thing to do, I shake her hand and whisper, 'Thank you.' And it strikes me in a flash that I made exactly the same gesture, months ago, when I stepped from the baths at Lourdes – the common denominator being, I suppose, that on both occasions I felt that my own humanity, spirituality, whatever you wish to call it, had been reinvigorated. Auschwitz is obscene, but it is not entirely devoid of hope.

At the meeting point, a group of Israeli teenagers is waiting for a bus. It is a tradition for them to come here on a pilgrimage, but I think they are the people least in need of seeing it – a day in Gaza might be a better idea for them. Instead, every European child should be made come to Auschwitz II-Birkenau, to confront what may be buried deep within, and to ensure that if it exists, it remains forever dormant.

No one speaks on the coach home or, if they do, it is in a hush. Joyce and I walk around Krakow but we're too numb to have fun. We drift from bar to bar, eat a truly awful meal, then have more beers in the hotel. What else can you do after a day out in Hell?

28

KAUNAS

FR2971
Dublin (DUB) to Kaunas (KUN)

FR2972
Kaunas (KUN) to Dublin (DUB)
1,950 km • €82.42 return

The day after flying home from Krakow and driving from Shannon, I am in Dublin Airport for the flight to Lithuania's second city. I have become used to the horrors of Dublin Airport, though not inured to them, and have developed coping mechanisms that are starting to knock on the door of neurosis. As yet, these do not involve ingesting banned narcotics, though I fear the day cannot be far away. For now, I wear only trainers with Velcro straps so I can take them off and put them back on with one hand if needed. I wear a belt that has a clamp instead of a prong and holes – it too can be undone, and fastened again, with one hand. I now bring an attaché case on wheels (this one a corporate gift from Honda), because the walk to the temporary gates is still a half-marathon. As well as my computer, the case is big enough to also carry a shirt, two T-shirts, socks and underwear. The jacket, as usual, takes everything else, including my Ziploc bag full of toiletries and, today, a thin thermal fleece, a warm beanie and gloves dished out last year when we drove Land Rover Discovery 3s to the top of an amazing glacier in Iceland. There are many times, it must be said, when my job beats working for a living.

At the departure gate, it becomes obvious that when it comes to queuing, Lithuanians makes the Finns look as orderly as the English, so I am glad to have only hand baggage with me and to have checked in on the web. I ease into Seat 16F, smile at a crew member I have come to know at this stage of my travels and settle in for the three-hour flight.

When we arrive at Kaunas, we land at the usual breakneck speed. The Lithuanians are no different from their Latvian neighbours and, the instant the wheels hit the runway, half of them jump from their seats to grab their luggage, while the rest applaud like the audience at the Last Night of the Proms. The cabin crew dispense with all decorum – as one grabs the microphone and roars, 'Sit down! Sit down!', two more are running from opposite ends of the aisle and pushing people back into their seats. It's not difficult to see why the Soviets had to shoot a few people every now and then to keep order, because obeying the rules does not appear to come instinctively in the Baltics. Secretly, I admire their foolhardiness; Ryanair flights land so fast, the pilots practically perform wheelies to get off the main runway, and I'm too timid to unbuckle my belt until the engines have come to a complete stop.

When I come down the stairs, the air is freezing, but the terminal is so compact, the queue for passport control snakes out onto the Tarmac. It has been a relatively late and mild winter so far, but it is now making up for in ferocity what it lacked in punctuality, so rather than wait for a bus, I grab a taxi. The McDonald's Index, a non-scientific barometer of how expensive a country is, based on how long it takes the average worker to earn the price of a Big Mac, could never be applied to taxis. No matter where you are, they always cost the same, and I pay 70 litas, about €20, for the 11-kilometre trip.

I was a little worried about the Best Western Santakos Hotel, because the photos on the website made it look the staff quarters at Dracula's castle. Instead, it is warm and welcoming, and so cheap I bagged myself a suite for €65. This boasts a huge double bed, two armchairs, a couch, and separate bathroom and toilet. The furnishings are a little old fashioned but, after the chill of outside, it couldn't be cosier. When I think of some of the places I've paid twice as much for, it's a palace.

I switch on the TV and find a home makeover show in Russian. The way homes are decorated is always a snapshot of a country's evolution, and the designer here errs on the side of what we might call 1980s retro, one part hi-tech to two parts functional minimalism. The family has two sons in their early teens and, despite my total lack of Russian, I can make out that it was essential that the room still had the piano at its heart. The TV was tucked away in a corner, along with the PlayStation, because the parents wanted the boys to persevere with their music lessons.

The Soviet system was predicated entirely on telling everyone what they could and couldn't think, or do – but there are some stages in life when people need to be pushed towards what's good for them, and no one can accuse the Communists of ignoring the classical repertoire. I wish someone had made me play the piano, or the guitar. I wish I could stand up at a microphone and sing, because I love all sorts of music but haven't a note in my head – so I envy the Russian boys who someday will be able to play Gershwin and *Grand Theft Auto* with equal skill.

The hotel is located on a very quiet street immediately parallel to the main drag. And what a main drag it is – Laisves Aleja (it's the Lithuanian for Liberty Avenue) is 1.7 kilometres long, totally pedestrianised, and with a double row of linden trees running the entire length of the central walkway. At one end is the church of Michael the Archangel, a white, Byzantine confection that served as an art gallery during the Soviet era and has now been restored as a place of Catholic worship. At the opposite end is the start of Vilnius Street, which leads to the old town.

That's the best news I've had all day – there's another old town…

I wander to the end of the avenue and back again, noting that Lithuanians clearly love pizza and prescription drugs – I don't think I've ever seen so many pizzerias and pharmacies in one place. At Vilnius Street, the architecture changes and everything becomes much more familiar, in a BrnoBratiKrakoRiga sort of way. But this may well be the prettiest old town yet, because it is more compact and, I suspect, more authentic. It is not difficult to imagine yourself wandering down here 200 or even 300 years ago and seeing very little difference.

Local amber is the big souvenir and this is apparently one of the world's cheapest places to buy it, though I've never understood why any woman would want to wear jewellery that looked like a lozenge.

The hotel has a restaurant that appears very popular with locals as well as guests, so I eat at the bar, as I usually do when travelling alone (I always think a single man eating at a table looks tragic, as if he's been stood up by his date). The barman is very slick and speaks perfect English, so I am not surprised to learn he has spent the past five years working for the Celebrity cruise line. He saw the world, made a few bob, bought himself an apartment and now works at a pace that suits himself, chatting all day to foreigners. He has clear memories of the Lithuania of his childhood and sums up the difference between then and now very succinctly.

'We always had lots of money but nothing to spend it on,' he laughs dryly. 'Now we have lots of shops but very little money, and everyone goes abroad to work.'

I ask if he knows where Ireland is. 'Of course,' he laughs. 'Everyone knows where Ireland is.'

I'm drinking Švyturys lager. The name translates as 'for our land', so I feel a proxy patriotism and have a few. An American, in his late twenties/early thirties, joins me at the bar and we get chatting. He has a buzzcut and clearly keeps himself in shape. He tells me he is based in Germany and uses his free time to see as much of Europe as possible on Ryanair. Inspector Clouseau could work out the obvious, but I ask the question anyway.

'Are you in the military?'

He hesitates. There was a time when denial was restricted to those in the secret service, not people in the regular army. I feel sorry for him, because it must be difficult to schlep around Europe while always dreading this question, when you know that public opinion across the continent is so opposed to the ludicrous, desperate Iraqi war. He says yes, he is a full-time soldier, working in a discipline so specific I'm going to fudge any details that might identify him. Because Brad, which is not his real name, confesses that he and most of his colleagues think the war to be just as futile as the rest of us do, and he has seen too many soldiers die before his own eyes not to have been deeply affected by it.

Because of that, we get the subject out of the way in five minutes flat, but not before he tells me something very sad. He is, he admits, one of the very few soldiers to travel beyond the base in Germany. Most of his friends are too afraid to confront Europeans who might take them to task on US foreign policy. This is not just because the infantrymen don't agree with the mission they have been sent on but also because they don't feel articulate enough to explain their position. Imagine being more comfortable facing a member of the Shia militia toting a rocket launcher in Sadr City than arguing with a mildly hostile backpacker in a German bar. For those of us who love nothing better than a good pub row, the news is little short of tragic.

Soon, we are joined at the bar by a Danish businessman called Henning and, within a couple of hours, we are best mates and deliver ourselves unto Kaunas to be entertained. We walk to Liberty Avenue and find a basement nightclub called Siena, where two distinct dancefloors shielded from each other by double glazing – one playing classic hits, the other pumping out garage and house – are absolutely heaving. The women are beautiful, mostly dark-haired and slim, but nursing a slightly off-putting fascination for high-heeled, white ankle boots worn over jeans. It looks like Essex in 1987.

Brad is a big hit with one woman in particular and, when I leave, they are bumping and grinding in a fashion that suggests neither will sleep much tonight. And, you know, he'll have plenty of time for sleep when he ships out to Iraq next week. For now, I hope he has the shag of a lifetime because, as a soldier, I guess you never know how long a lifetime really is.

Next day, I retrace my steps through the old town, past the Town Hall that is known as 'the white swan' because of its slender tower, and make my way to Kaunas Castle, at the confluence of the Nemunas and Neris rivers. Set in what is now a large park, the red-brick castle has a circular keep and a witch's-hat turret in red tile and sits on top of what was once a vast moat. It has none of the menace of most castles, but instead looks like a renovated Normandy farmhouse with a dovecote. I'd move in tomorrow.

Back on Vilnius Street, I hear a sound I haven't heard for thirty years, that of a Hare Krishna parade wending its way through town. Do Krishnas deliberately target countries on the cusp of prosperity? They arrived in Ireland only when we were making that leap from a religious to a secular state, exploiting the people on the margins for whom materialism did not bring the instant gratification it gave to the rest of us (well, I was instantly gratified, that's for sure). When I look at the Krishnas here – the leaders are well-fed Americans, I suspect, and the stragglers Lithuanians who are still not fully comfortable with their tambourines, layered clothing and the bird-dropping marks splashed on their foreheads – I am back on Grafton Street in 1976, watching the same haphazard procession and the endless quest of those without meaning in their lives to find something that will fill the void. A Big Mac always worked for me.

Back at the airport, I am reminded that, for many, filling the void means leaving Lithuania altogether. There are people crying in the queue, especially mothers with haunted faces here to wave off children who know they should be just as upset but who are buoyed by the prospect of the riches Ireland or Britain have to offer. The signs tell them where Ryanair will take them – to Stanstedas in Londonas, or to Dublinas. The trick here seems to be adding 'as' to every word to make it Lithuanian, or else to spell a word as you say it. Beside me on the plane, a young woman is reading a magazine that looks like *Heat!* and it contains features on Katei Preis (that's Jordan to you and me) and Oscar-winning actress Riz Wizerspun.

The funny thing is, I know how most of these emigrating kids feel because, as we take off, a weight lifts from me too. I've been almost exclusively in eastern Europe for some weeks now and I'm tired of the drabness, and the heavy food, and carved wood, and signs I can't read, in languages I don't understand. Most of all, I'm tired of old towns – so I'm off to Benidorm, which barely existed in 1960, never mind back when Vytautas the Great was planning to do something unspeakable to Boleslaw the Bold, or whichever king was on the Polish throne at a time when the map of central Europe was redrawn as frequently as the screen on an Etch-A-Sketch.

I want vulgarity on a vast scale, and if you can't find it in Benidorm, then I suspect it's not available in Europe.

MURCIA–VALENCIA

FR7094

Dublin (DUB) to Murcia (MJV)

1,790 km

€27.95

The flight from Dublin to Murcia is my 625th. In the course of those travels, pretty much everything bad that can happen to you on an aircraft has happened to me. Once, we hit the runway so hard, all the oxygen masks fell from their covers. Then I had that emergency landing in Copenhagen, when no one was sure the undercarriage wouldn't collapse. I was on a commuter flight from Minneapolis to Rhinelander, in Wisconsin, seated behind the pilot, when there was a huge flash – we had been hit by lightning, the plane nosedived and I watched as the altimeter spun like the hand on a weighing scale returning to zero. I flew over the

Bay of Bengal in a typhoon – 'The weather people told us the storm was somewhere else,' the captain said sheepishly, which was little consolation – and it tossed a 747 around so ferociously even the crew were terrified. Worst of all, I got so bored once between Dallas-Fort Worth and Phoenix that I joined the Mile High Club by myself.

But today is the first time I've been on a plane where someone is so ill we have to make an unscheduled landing to offload him from the plane. Two American girls sitting behind me think this is the most exciting thing that has ever happened; I, on the other hand, am rueing my bad luck. The Federal Aviation Administration in the United States estimates that there will be a severe passenger illness on around one in 1,400 flights. In some 85 per cent of those cases, there will be a positive response to the announcement everyone dreads – 'If there is a doctor on board, could he or she make themselves known to a member of the crew?' – and the situation can be dealt with on the spot. Indeed, while we waited to take off from Sydney earlier this year, a little girl became hysterical and when the appeal for a doctor went out, six people came forward, which I thought pretty impressive. They hovered around her for forty-five minutes until she finally made the whole plane erupt in laughter when she screamed, 'But I don't *want* to go to Melbourne!'

But here's the rub – only one flight in 5,000 actually has to make an unscheduled landing to offload a sick passenger. So here I am, on the receiving end of a 1-in-5,000 chance of something bad happening – yet in six months of drinking Bavaria lager and Red Bull, just to get double tickets in Ryanair's bloody raffle, I still have not cracked the positively puny 1-in-100 odds of winning a free flight. It gets worse. As we come in to land, I see a familiar roundabout, a hamlet of houses and a branch of McDonald's – yes, I'm in Beauvais again, for the forty-fifth time. Of course, this being France, the minute we arrive at the stand, a swarm of firemen, *les pompiers sapeurs*, descends on us. As usual in

France, it seems one person does all the work while the rest contribute nothing more demanding than a group shrug. I have no idea why France bothers holding presidential elections when the heads of the main parties could surely share the gig, given that the country employs at least two people to do every other job.

A young paramedic in oilskins makes his way down the aisle. One of the American girls, finally getting a clear handle on the really important issue, shrieks, 'Oh, he's so cute!', then fumbles for her phone, switches it on and starts filming him. When he quizzes the cabin crew about the nature of the passenger's illness, her legs seem to buckle. Fanning her breastbone like a really bad actress playing Blanche DuBois, she clutches her friend and asks, 'Omigod, o-mi-god, is that, like, *Spanish*…?' I remind myself to log on later to YouTube, that lightning conductor of the moronic, where her little drama will no doubt have been shared with the entire world.

Anyway, no sooner has the sick young man been stretchered off than we have pushed back and finally make for Murcia. The routing takes us straight over Paris and, through a hole in the cloud, we get a fantastic view of the city and can even clearly make out the Eiffel Tower. The silence from behind suggests this has been enough to send the Americans into a faint. In the silence, I watch *Miami Vice* and wonder if there has ever been a darker movie – not in tone, just in the way it's lit. Colin Farrell's stubble is so thick, I can't even tell him apart from Jamie Foxx. The TV series was a riot of cream linen and pastel T-shirts and when you saw a pink shape and a yellow shape in the far distance, there was little doubt it was Crockett and Tubbs. In the movie, I haven't a clue who's a good guy and who's a bad guy or, indeed, what the hell is going on.

We arrive at Murcia over an hour late and I am shuttled to the Hertz desk in a shopping centre 3 kilometres away. Maybe Avis does try harder after all. I'm off to Torrevieja, one of the great shrines of Ryanland, a place that simply could not exist without low-fare travel. The population of the town has doubled in ten years to nearly 100,000, as so many have realised the dream of owning their own properties here. For some, these are holiday homes, but for many northern Europeans, especially Brits and Russians who just don't want to do winter any more, this has actually become a permanent home. With a host of budget carriers and charters flying into airports all along the sunny Spanish coasts and their historic hinterlands – Seville, Malaga, Almeria, Granada, Murcia, Alicante. Valencia, Reus, Girona – it is easy for a wife and kids to live here all summer while Dad commutes at weekends, or for families to visit grandparents for weeks at a time, or for long-term residents to make it back to Britain or Ireland just to meet friends for lunch if they want to. I flew here today for less than €28, for heaven's sake; I would have paid more for a train to Cork.

So many Irish have bought second homes on the Costa Blanca, it has – in a play on the names of two sprawling Dublin suburbs – variously been dubbed Ballymun-in-the-Sun and Tallaghtcantè. As I come into Torrevieja, I can see why the comparison is made. Huge tracts of housing, mostly identikit single-storey and two-storey white villas, spread out in every direction. There are so many, it seems the only difference between living here and in, say, Nottingham is the temperature – but given that it's November and I'm in shirt sleeves, that seems like sufficient lure to me.

I haven't bothered booking a hotel, an omission that feels increasingly foolish. Since everyone who comes here actually has a home to stay in, it's not exactly overburdened with quality accommodation. I eventually find the three-star Hotel Fontana and though it looks gloomy, it's only €60 a night and I have no option but to take it. I dump my bag in the cell that passes for a room and wander around the town centre, which is unremarkable except for a very attractive theatre on a plaza. I hear probably three conversations in Spanish all night – the rest are conducted in English accents. And, you know, it's getting easier to see why they live here. After all, we're only a month away from Christmas, yet I'm sitting outdoors at 8.30 p.m., at the Cafeteria Festival on Plaza Waldo Calero and, after eating a chicken fillet with sauté potatoes and a side salad, and a huge banana split, washed down with a pint of Mahou, I'm presented with a bill for just €15.20. The equity in a northern European home, added to a pension, could go a very long way down here.

When I get back to the hotel, I hear music and make for the bar. I imagine the Fontana was built in the 1980s – the décor, certainly, is of the era. The lounge area is huge, with really uncomfortable green chairs, and it looks as inviting as the third-class bar on the *Titanic*. A man is playing an electric organ to this cavernous, empty room – the only other drinkers are three people sitting at the bar. I order a beer and start getting melancholy again, which is not a feeling I wear well. The closer I get to the end of my travels, the more I realise how much I miss home and how sick I am of cheap hotels. As I make for the exit, the organist flashes a rueful smile that says 'you lucky bastard – I have to stay here for hours yet playing this godawful shite' and steels himself for the inevitable rendition of 'Feelings'. I arrive back at my room to find the radiator has leaked all over the floor. I'm too tired to complain and just slosh my way to bed before going out like a light.

Next morning, I drive to Alicante and find an Alcampo hypermarket. I'm in Spain at least twice a year every year, and always buy my shoes here for about half the price of home. Today, I leave with black leather dress shoes, a pair of trainers (with Velcro straps for ease of airport use) and Converse-style runners, all for less than €100. As I eat lunch, I decide I'm not staying anywhere grotty tonight, so I log on to the net, have a little rummage and find a newly opened Sheraton hotel, the Real de Faula, in Benidorm, offering introductory rates of €80 a night. The reason I didn't have a place to stay in Torrevieja last night was because I hate pre-booking hotels when I'm driving alone, because it means I actually have to go looking for them. There's nothing worse than arriving somewhere new, late in the day, and wasting an hour or more as you get tied up in infernal one-way systems at rush hour, especially when the hotel is in front of you but you just cannot find the road that leads to it (and once, even though I could see it just 100 metres to my right, I kept missing the turn for IKEA in Roissy, north of Paris, and ended up at kerbside check-in for Delta Airlines at Charles de Gaulle). Today, amazingly, the gods are with me and the first motorway exit for Benidorm also has a sign for Real de Faula, and for somewhere called Terra Mítica. This turns out to be a theme park in a former limestone quarry; it is closed for the season, but the rides look terrific, especially Magnus Colossus, which I learn is Europe's longest wooden coaster, with over a kilometre of track and a double drop on the first hill that follows the terraced terrain.

The Sheraton and its sister hotel, the Westin, are at the heart of a new golf and country club designed to look like a Spanish village – there is a plaza between them, and the Sheraton reception area is in the village 'church', where the space falls away down a set of stairs to a huge restaurant area surrounded by a swimming pool. In a showy, new-money kind of way, it's very impressive.

But there is a problem. The receptionist is immediately sorry and regrets there are no rooms in the Sheraton. I am about to go postal when she nervously asks, 'Would Mr Nolan care for a deluxe corner room in the Westin instead, at the same rate, obviously?'

'Oh, I suppose so, if I have to,' I concede mock-grudgingly. I am escorted across the plaza, someone takes my bag, and I'm walked through the pueblo to a guest wing overlooking the golf course and Benidorm itself. The room is huge, decorated in soft creams and whites, with a living area separate from the canopied bed, and with a plasma TV. The front balcony has a table and chairs, the side balcony two sun loungers. As soon as the porter closes the door I let out the 'yippee!' I've been suppressing and jump up and down on the bed like a four-year-old. Already, I know they're going to have to call security to drag me out of here in the morning.

I drive down the hill to Benidorm and make for the Gran Hotel Bali. At 186 metres (210 if you include the mast), it's the tallest building in Spain and the highest hotel in Europe. I pay a fiver and take the lift to the observation deck. They say you can see Ibiza, which is around 160 kilometres distant, on a clear day but, try as I might, I can't make it out (mind you, on one occasion, after pulling an all-nighter in Café Mambo and Manumission, I couldn't see Ibiza from Ibiza itself).

Benidorm is astonishing. I had all sorts of preconceptions that it would be a nasty, high-rise hell full of lager louts (or larger louts, as one website puts it) but, in truth, it is Europe's Copacabana. There are more than 310 buildings here over 35 metres tall, and while the architectural standard varies, there is no doubting that the overall effect achieves a texture that is thrilling. I would stay up here for longer but, on cue, my vertigo kicks in, and when I feel the Bali start to sway, I put my back to the wall, spread my arms and feel my way to the lift in large, exaggerated steps. Back at ground level, my breathing returns to normal and I drive along the promenade of the Levante and Poniente beaches, looking at a cliff face of high-rises. I think it is one of the most extraordinary views in Ryanland, and only a complete snob could remain unmoved by it.

I walk the back streets and idle in the markets, have a pint in the Shamrock and eat a KFC at a table next to some English lads ("Ere, Dave, wot woz the name of that bird you shagged last night, ven?'). I wander around what appears to be an entertainment quarter but decide to pass on the various sexy magic shows on offer. Benidorm is big on sexy magic. The most famous performer is a woman called Sticky Vicky, who pulls scarves, eggs, strings of threaded razor blades and, for all I know, a rill of cabbages from a place not normally used as a storage cupboard. Best of all, though, it seems she can also open bottles of beer in an inventive way – if you're ever washed up on a desert island alongside a lifetime's supply of Budweiser longnecks, you've got to hope Vicky is washed up with you.

But the competing shows all start very late and I'm not sure I want to applaud loudly when a dove manages to escape a very unusual roost and, against all the odds, remains Persil white. No, Benidorm itself is the star and, as the sun sets, I sit on the beach and watch the shadows of the buildings lengthen and the lights go on.

Next morning, I drive the 100-odd kilometres to Valencia. I first came here in 1988 – ironically, on a special Ryanair flight. Hothouse Flowers, a popular band at the time, were loaned a plane to fly all over Europe and make a video to be shown during the interval of the 1988 Eurovision Song Contest in Dublin. Ryanair, a main sponsor of the event, allowed the band to bring along their friends, families and a gaggle of music journalists. We left Dublin on a Saturday morning and flew to Lisbon, from where we were bussed to the coastal village of Sesimbra for a long and very liquid lunch. That's where it all started to unravel. All the hacks knocked back so much vinho verde that we stripped to our underwear and went swimming. Then, on the onward flight to Valencia, everyone on the aircraft performed the safety drill with the stewardesses, as if it was a big game of Simon Says; it was the funniest thing I have ever seen. We arrived into Valencia in the middle of the Falles, the festival where giant effigies are burned on the streets. We joined the whole city in an all-night party, watched the Flowers sing 'Don't Go' in the main square to a crowd of tens of thousands on the Sunday afternoon, then drank all the way home on the flight before hitting the clubs in Dublin. It was the most rock 'n' roll week-end of my life.

Sadly, my visits since have been a little more sedate, because Valencia is another popular venue for car launches. These usually begin or end at the Ciutat de les Arts i les Ciències, the City of Arts and Sciences, designed by our old friend, the native Valencian architect Santiago Calatrava. Built in a dry riverbed, the complex includes an opera house, a planetarium, a science museum and an oceanographic park, surrounded by vast pools. It is like a catalogue of Calatrava's tiresome tics, all exposed ribs and elliptical shapes (the Umbracle walkway looks like a rack of lamb, while the opera house resembles an American football helmet). It is a masterpiece of engineering but emotionally sterile. As I wander around it for the umpteenth time, hoping it will finally win me over, I can't help thinking of Benidorm, haphazard, largely unplanned in the urban sense, yet organically beautiful. I'd take it over this any day.

I drive back to the airport, where building work has left a very confused traffic system in operation. It doesn't really matter, though, because all roads lead to my next destination. I'm off to Rome.

ROME CIAMPINO–VENICE TREVISO

FR9676 • Valencia (VLC) to Rome Ciampino (CIA)
1,130 km • €24.01

FR9408 • Rome Ciampino (CIA) to Venice Treviso (TSF)
433 km • €28.70

FR9451 • Venice Treviso (TSF) to Dublin (DUB)
1,579 km • €26.72

Red wine is today's designated double-ticket item on the snack trolley, and when I hear the flight time is around two hours (a surprise – I always assume everywhere in the Mediterranean is about twenty minutes from everywhere else), I decide to buy two quarter-bottles. I've noticed over the course of my travels that flights from Spain tend to have a much younger passenger profile than any others, and that the young tend to buy fewer snack items than old bastards like me – so, with four tickets in my hand and little by way of competition, all my ducks are finally lined up in a row.

I watch as the crew combine all the tickets they have sold. The pretty blonde announces that the raffle is to begin and tells everyone to watch their tickets. She asks a man in Row 2 to pull the winner and then reads out the six-digit serial number.

'Five.' Yes. 'Four.' Yes, 'Four.' Yes. 'Six.' Yes. 'Eight.' Yes. My stomach lurches. One, I whisper, say one….

'One.'

My head shakes from side to side involuntarily and I blink furiously. One. She said it. ONE!

'Yes!' I shout, and practically punch a hole in the fuselage. I've done it. I've finally done it. On my fifty-third flight in Ryanland, I've won a free trip.

'Do we have a winner?' she asks. I start prodding the call bell like a schoolteacher pressing a pupil for the answer to a question. She looks down and sees me practically levitating with excitement and it's like she knows how much it means to me because she leads the whole plane in a round of applause. The two students beside me shake my hand, the rest of the crew smile and give me the thumbs-up. I'm presented with a certificate and told I must ring the special booking hotline within seven days. It is like getting a golden ticket from Willy Wonka and I spend the rest of the flight on a cloud.

I have deliberately sat on the right side of the aircraft today because, when flying south into Ciampino, you are treated to an amazing view of Rome. I pick out the Vittorio Emanuele monument, the Forum, the Colosseum and Bernini's vast colonnaded quadrangle in front of the Vatican, and mutter a quiet prayer of thanks to whoever has been looking after me.

From Ciampino, which is cramped and horrible, I take a taxi to Via

Portuense, near Rome's much-nicer main airport, Fiumicino. Colleagues are arriving tonight for yet another car launch, and we're booked in to the Cancelli Rossi, which looks like a perfectly adequate three-star hotel on the website, but turns out to be absolutely the worst I have ever stayed in. It is mean, nasty and dirty – just hateful. I wish I'd read TripAdvisor.com first, because when I log on and look at the comments, they are universally scathing. There's no carpet in the corridors, unbelievable in an airport hotel, because people are arriving and leaving all through the night and there is endless banging of doors and trundling of luggage. My room is also adjacent to the lift shaft and, by the time dawn arrives, I am fit to be tied.

Things soon cheer up no end, though. Visitors to Rome seldom check out the area around the city, largely, I suspect, because negotiating the Gran Raccordo Annulare, the notorious ring road, is just so nerve-shredding. When tourists go missing in Italy, I suspect the first thing the cops do is check if they hired a car and pulled out onto this road. Personally, I wouldn't even start looking for them until about the fourth day. I don't think I've ever driven it without getting lost or missing an exit.

We start by driving to Lago di Bracciano, and see the castle where Tom Cruise married Katie Holmes. There is some truly stunning lakeside scenery within an hour of Rome, yet I doubt many who visit the city ever see this other side to its attraction. As well as Bracciano, there is Martignano and, perhaps the most dramatic of all, Albano, in the caldera of a collapsed volcano, overlooked by the small town of Castel Gandolfo, summer residence of the popes.

Near Bracciano, we eat a superb buffet lunch looking out over the lake, before heading back to find the Sheraton Golf Parco de'Medici. I'm navigating and one of my colleagues is driving, but the route map, which has been reliable until now, suddenly becomes ambiguous at precisely the wrong moment – which is just as we attempt to leave the Gran

Raccordo Annulare. Before I know what has happened, we're heading north towards the cruise terminal at Civitavecchia. Sharing duties with the same driver, I made exactly the same mistake last year. After 17 useless kilometres, we get back on track and can see the golf course and the hotel from the motorway, but not the exit. Fearing we will be sucked into city-bound traffic, we pull off the road into a service station to take a deep breath and study the map more carefully.

On the forecourt, I see another Kia cee'd (nice car, stupid name) and as I start chatting to the driver, a third cee'd pulls up, the driver just as baffled as the rest of us. At the same moment, a taxi pulls up too, and we have the brainwave of asking him to lead us to the hotel. Unfortunately, he thinks we want to go to the Sheraton Roma – and leads us straight into the city anyway. I actually am in the car with him, because he wouldn't take the job until he had a hostage and was sure he would be paid, and by the time I get through to him that we actually wanted the Sheraton Golf, we are in a hideous traffic jam. Being Italian, he makes a sudden manoeuvre to escape the worst of it, slips down the hard shoulder of a clogged off-ramp in a Fiat Scudo that's now at a 45-degree angle to true, mounts the pavement to get under a bridge, then manages a sharp U-turn before bolting to the on-ramp in the opposite direction. In his wake, three Kias perform the same action with varying degrees of conviction while all of Italy unites in blowing its collective horn and waving its arms pointlessly in the air. For 10 exhilarating kilometres, we duck and dive and weave through traffic as if in a remake of *The Italian Job*. It is hair-raising, but the best fun I've ever had on the Gran Raccordo Annulare.

At the hotel, everything has a golf theme. Even the soap is the shape and size of a golf ball. I shower gingerly – I don't need any inadvertent practice for a sexy magic show. I need to iron a shirt but I'm told that Italian law now prohibits the use of irons or kettles in hotel rooms because there have been so many fatalities due to fire. So I'm led to a small, bare room with just an iron and board in it, a safe distance from the nearest combustible. When I'm finished, I have to alert the front desk and wait until someone comes along to ensure I have indeed unplugged the potential weapon of mass destruction. Milan during Fashion Week must be a hoot.

After dinner, a few of us head into Rome, and have a couple of beers at doney (the lower case '*d*' is theirs, not mine), the stylish and expensive bar of the Westin Excelsior that fronts onto the Via Veneto. I love Rome, especially after dark, and we have the city almost to ourselves as we walk to the Spanish Steps, descend to the Piazza di Spagna, walk along the designer-label drag of the Via dei Condotti and finally reach the Fontana di Trevi. The fountain is one of those sights you simply must see at night. The crowds have long gone and the lighting gives it a magic completely lacking in the daylight hours. I throw my coin in, to ensure I will return.

Back at Ciampino next day, I pay my €3 for priority boarding, but the Italians are wise to this and lots of them have done likewise. There are two queues, one for priority and the other for everyone else, so I slip in behind the three people already there. My action provokes a stampede that leads to the formation of two lines almost identical in length. I count close on sixty people who seem to have paid for priority boarding, which rather undermines the reason for bothering. Suddenly, a woman walks to the top of the priority queue, lifts the rope and forces her way in. No one in front of me chastises her – and, needless to say, no one from Ryanair is anywhere close by. A familiar red mist swirls around me. When a man follows and attempts to join her, I lean towards him with a stern expression and point to the back of the queue. He says something in Italian and I jab the air again.

'I 'ave priority,' he says dismissively, pointing to his ticket.

'We *all* have priority,' I say, pointing to my own.

He glowers at me and, just like the man on the taxi queue in Milan three weeks ago, says, 'This is Italy', as if that makes everything just dandy.

The red mist becomes a dense fog. 'I'm well aware of where I am, pal,' I say, 'but let me remind you, you're getting on an Irish plane, and I'm Irish and, today, we're making the rules – so be a good lad there and get yourself the fuck to the back of that queue.'

Astonished, he does as he is told.

The check-in staff arrive, take a cursory look at my passport and wave me on. I walk through the door and onto the… bus. Shit! It's one of *those* airports. Because I'm almost first on, I'm gradually pushed to the middle – and in any case, I can't think of anything better to do because no matter which side of a bus you stand on, the other is, nine times out of ten, nearest to the steps when you reach the plane. The gamble might cost me my seat.

Because my foe is now last in the queue, he is also last on the bus, then first off when the doors open. He makes for the front steps, so I frantically elbow people out of my way and make a bolt for the rear steps. He sees me – and starts giving me the finger! – and races to the plane while I take the steps two at a time, giving the finger back. We hit the aisle together, he racing from the front, me from the back, oblivious to the fact the plane is empty anyway. At precisely the same time, he plonks down in 15A and I in 16F; we settle for the draw and never make eye contact again.

When we land, the privately operated ATVO bus service runs us to Venice and drops us at the Piazzale Roma, where I learn there is a public-transport strike. All the *vaporettos*, the city's water buses, are out of service. Having been to Venice before, I know I could buy my own dinghy for the same price as a water taxi, and even if gondolas came up this far – and they don't – the idea of being punted for almost 2 kilometres to my hotel doesn't exactly push my buttons. So I do the only thing I can do, and start to walk, laptop bag hanging from my neck, BMW jacket as warm as a duvet, and wheelie bag dragging across the cobbles behind me.

Thousands of people are forced to take exactly the same action, and because Venice is a labyrinth, all I can see at the end of every alleyway is someone else with a Samsonite, racing furiously in the opposite direction to the one he should be going in. After spotting a third red Samsonite case, the whole pantomime becomes a cross between *Blame it on the Bellboy* and *Death in Venice*. By the time I make it to the Piazza San Marco, that white spume you see on a thoroughbred after it has won a race has covered my neck. I look rabid and demented, which is a little out of step with the elegance of my hotel.

I first came to Venice in 1985 with my friend, Conor Swords, by train from Greece. We were only ten minutes out of Athens when the train caught fire, but since this was also the holiday where I ended up with half a Cretan road embedded in my leg after falling from a moped, I had long since abandoned all expectation of making it back to Ireland alive and could scarcely be bothered to evacuate the carriage. When we eventually arrived in Venice, half a day late, we fell in with a Dane called Charlotte, a force of nature who could brighten up a dull weekend but would set your teeth on edge if you hung out for any longer than that. She was one of those girls who bounces rather than walks and projects confidence in Cinemascope, but always ends up being the neediest of all. I knew it was time to jettison her when she started doing accents.

We stayed at a cheap *pensione* and I vowed I would someday treat myself to a room in one of the grand hotels that occupy the city's finest palazzos. And tonight, because it is low season, I've picked up a room at the Danieli for €215, on the net.

The lobby of the hotel may be the most beautiful in the world, especially today, as the main staircase is garlanded for Christmas. Built in 1400 for Doge Dandolo, the palazzo passed through the hands of many aristocratic families before the first floor was rented out in 1822 to a hotelier named Dal Niel, and the hotel was established as an almost-anagram of his own name. He bought it out completely in 1840 and, over the years, his descendants annexed the next-door palazzo and built a third. It is certainly the only hotel I've stayed in where, to get to my room from the lobby, I must walk across an enclosed bridge over a canal. 'Magical' doesn't come anywhere near describing it adequately.

My room is a slight disappointment and way too chintzy for its own good – but the public areas, especially the American Bar, are wildly sophisticated. There are Murano glass chandeliers, stained-glass windows, marble floors and pink-marble columns, and gold leaf everywhere. A night here has been a Christmas present to myself, and my choice has proved impeccable.

The next day goes by in a whirl. Venice is a very walkable city, and one best approached without a plan. Any attempt to locate somewhere specific will end in failure, and surrendering yourself to the capriciousness of the maze is the only guaranteed way to find the city's treasures – a narrow alley that opens into a gracious square, an arched doorway that frames a scene of impossible beauty, a café window heaped with sand- wiches stuffed with Parma ham and mozzarella. Walking by one doorway, I hear an unmistakeable sound, so I slip through and pass a sublime hour listening to Vivaldi's 'Four Seasons' being played by a chamber orchestra in a church, the acoustics so amazing that the music is almost overwhelmingly intense.

Of all the seasons, this is actually the best time to visit. Forget summer, when it is packed with tourists and the canals are smelly. Venice in winter is ethereal, a chiaroscuro masterpiece of washed-out colour and blurred edges, often decaying, occasionally decrepit, yet still the most glorious city ever built.

Though most of its traditions are centuries old, one is more recent. The Bellini, a cocktail of puréed peaches and prosecco, the Italian sparkling wine, was invented at Harry's Bar by Giuseppe Cipriani in the 1930s and no visit to the city is complete without a visit and a sample. It turns out to be a limp exercise – the tiny bar is packed with braying English women on a hen weekend, and the €14-a-pop drinks are poured as if on an assembly line.

Instead, I find a simple neighbourhood café, the Gelateria Sommariva, where I eat a simple penne arrabiatta, drink a half bottle of Chianti and, because this is Italy, finish with a bowl of ice cream that looks like a scale model of the Dolomites. With a pint of beer thrown in, the meal comes to less than the price of two Bellinis at Harry's.

Because my flight is early out of Treviso, I decide to spend the last night there and arrive with lots of time to walk the city. As has so often been the case, it is not entirely worthy of the detour, but it is full of per-sonality anyway. Unusually decked out for Christmas – the streets are festooned with pink dolphins, green polar bears and blue penguins – and thronged with shoppers, it has attractive streets and a buzzing main square in the Piazza dei Signori. And, just like Venice, water flows through the centre of town here too.

I have checked in to the Hotel Carlton, decent value for €80, where I turn on the television and find Italy glued on a Saturday night to the local equivalent of *Strictly Come Dancing*, a format that appears to have been seized on by every country in the world. One of the judges is Lina Wertmüller, who found brief international fame in the 1970s as the first woman to be nominated for an Oscar for direction, for *Seven Beauties*. She also directed *Swept Away by an Unusual Destiny in the Blue Sea of August*, a title shortened to *Swept Away* so it would fit on cinema marquees; it was remade in 2002, disastrously, by Guy Ritchie as a vanity vehicle for his wife, Madonna.

I'm saddened to see Wertmüller here. She always had an inflated reputation, but she was, nonetheless, a serious artiste, a communist, a feminist and an anarchist – and while none of those ideologies should by definition be incompatible with having a bit of laugh, I find it staggering that she would end her days holding up scorecards for a celebrity paso doble. But she is emblematic of the new Europe. Much of what we used to rail against has disappeared in a hail of prosperity. We have gone from intellectual snobs to intellectual slobs in just quarter of a century, and have become complacent, even decadent. Celebrity is more important than ideology or talent, and now a generation of Italians will remember Lina Wertmüller as the dodgy old bint sitting between the two camp guys on *Strictly Come Ballroom*, just as British kids will remember Ken Russell, not for directing *Women in Love* and *Tommy*, but as the geriatric bloke who walked out of *Celebrity Big Brother* after Jade Goody shouted at him because he wouldn't stop snoring.

Venice Treviso Airport is so packed next morning that the queue snakes out the door of the terminal and, flushed with my success in Ciampino, I take it upon myself to police it, very successfully, as it happens. An American woman is the only other passenger to have bought priority boarding, so instead of a whole bus being wasted on us, we are put in a car and chauffeured to the plane. Then we get to Dublin, land very precariously in a tempest and are held on the plane for forty-five minutes because the stairs keep blowing over. I'm beginning to think there's something to this global warming after all.

31

BERLIN SCHÖNEFELD

FR8558

Dublin (DUB) to Berlin Schönefeld (SXF)

FR8559

Berlin Schönefeld (SXF) to Dublin (DUB)

1,320 km • €45.59 return

The phone answers. 'Hi, I won the raffle on a flight between Valencia and Rome, and I want to book my free flight,' I say.

'Oh, right, yeah,' says a female voice.

Hmm, not quite the cheery 'congratulations' I was expecting, but then this is Ryanair.

'Where do you want to go and when do you want to travel?'

'I want to go to Madrid on the ninth of January and back on the eleventh, please.'

'No, problem, we have flights those days.'

I knew that, because I've already checked, and they're 99 cents each.

'Now, I need a credit-card number,' she says.

'For what?'

'Well, that comes to €54,' she says. 'For taxes, insurance and a bag.'

'But I won a free flight,' I say.

'The flights *are* free,' she says, 'but if you check the certificate there, it says you have to pay the taxes and charges.'

'Hang on,' I protest. 'When I was invited to buy a snack and get a ticket for a draw for a *free* flight, no terms and conditions were announced before I took part. No one said, buy a snack and get a ticket for a draw that will win you a flight where all you have to do is pay the taxes and charges. For heaven's sake, Ryanair has so many sales, I hardly ever pay more than this for flights anyway – and I have no doubt that if I wanted to book something now that was more than about €9.99 a sector, you'd tell me there was no availability.'

There is a silence.

I continue. 'What you're saying is that my prize here is €1.98, but to avail even of that miserable value, I have to pay €54. That's outrageous.'

I hear a sigh. 'What would you like me to do?' she asks.

I have a suggestion, one which involves taking the words 'arse', 'it', 'stick', 'your' and 'up' and rearranging them into a well-known phrase. But it is not the girl's fault and I just tell her to cancel the booking. I take legal advice but, guess what, because I didn't pay for the ticket itself but was given it as a bonus with a bottle of wine, and because it is unlikely I could establish jurisdiction in a case involving an Irish airline at an indeterminate point high over the Mediterranean, I am effectively screwed.

When added to the fact that I've been travelling non-stop for so long, the episode leaves me wanting to give Ryanair a miss for a while. I am booked to go to Balaton in Hungary tomorrow and then to Dinard in France, but the thought of driving around a lake in eastern Europe for three days and happening by chance upon half a dozen old towns finally breaks my resolve. My wife takes a look at me and says, 'You're burned out – don't go.' The decision is made.

It's a shame, because the tourist literature for Balaton showed great promise. It had advice on where to stay: 'The number of the rooms is in accordance with the quality of the hotel, which is roomy enough to hold your home-folks.'

It carried a veiled warning for geriatrics: 'No matter how young you are in your heart, if you have white hair and a walking stick in your hand, do not try to get in! Hostels are really designed for spry youngsters, who can even fight for some hot water.'

Best of all was this advice: 'If you like swimming-pools and chloric water, then go to Fûzfõ. Many people like the stretched water-surface, and the limits of the swimming pool. Women like above all the athletic swimming pool attendant. He gorges his whistle while he watches your butterfly-strokes.'

These unrivalled attractions – the final one unique, as most countries have laws against public whistle-gorging – will have to wait for another day. After the free-flight débâcle, I wait a week until my blood is merely simmering rather than boiling, then travel to Berlin as planned. My sister, Joyce, has travelled with me again, and as soon as we arrive, we decide to go to the revolving restaurant, 207 metres above ground, in the Alexanderplatz TV Tower to get our bearings on the city.

This turns out to be a huge mistake. It's only 11 a.m. but we order two glasses of champagne as the city spins around us. And we get mellow. So we have a beer, and another.

'Is it just me,' I ask Joyce, 'or has this started to go quicker…?'

The waitress comes over. 'You would like another, ja?' she asks. 'Ja,' we say. The greeter, who is used to seeing most tourists head upstairs for a light lunch or maybe one drink and one circumnavigation of the city, arrives and smiles and says, 'This German beer is gut, ja?'

And we giggle like teenagers and reply 'ja' and have another.

Four hours later, the restaurant is spinning like the drum in a washing machine on spin cycle. I've been around Berlin more often than an Allied bomb squadron in 1945 – I could draw a detailed map of it from memory. I can see all three airports, Tegel, Tempelhof and Schönefeld. I can distinguish the dome of the Pergamon Museum from the one on the Reichstag. I have even given the angel in the Tiergarten a nickname. But above all else, my eye has settled on a Christmas funfair on the Schlossplatz, next to the skeleton of the Palast der Republik, once the East German parliament building and now slowly being demolished. That was inevitable after the discovery of asbestos forced its closure in 1990, just twenty-four years after it opened – that and the fall of communism, of course. Nearly forgot.

At the base of the TV Tower, a woman is offering handwriting analysis. I scribble: 'I am here in Berlin', which gives some idea of my state of mind, and the machine tells me I am intuitive, even-tempered (never true, but even less so since I started flying Ryanair all over Europe), lacking in self-confidence, one who likes to be seen as unique, who is open-hearted and welcome everywhere, and someone 'who makes use of good and purposeful breaks to recover his energy'. Well, I've had about thirty good and purposeful breaks this year and I'm knackered.

We walk towards the fair and come to that cluster of treasures known as Museum Island, another UNESCO World Heritage Site (I think I nearly have the full set at this stage – if I'd been given a stamp for every one I visited, I'd surely be entitled to a free kettle at least). The finest museum is the Pergamon, which houses the reconstructed Ishtar Gate, built in the sixth century BC in Babylon, and once considered a wonder of the world. There is the Mshatta façade, from a fort near Amman in Jordan – it forms the centrepiece of the wing known as the Museum für Islamische Kunst, not a name you should type when drunk. Above all, there is the Pergamon Altar itself, a frieze over 100 metres wide and built in Turkey in the second century BC to honour Zeus. Though its arrival here predated the First World War, it later became an object of fixation for the Nazis, and it gives Museum Island a wonderful echo of *Raiders of the Lost Ark*.

From the Pergamon, we shuffle in the biting cold to the funfair. The Germans have historically done two things very well – Christmas and surrendering. Here, they show their prowess at the former, as *glüh-wein* is dispensed by the pitcher from wooden huts garlanded in fir branches. We knock back a couple and, once we are warm, hop on the chair-o-planes and soar out over the Kupfergraben, a short arm of the River Spree that forms a perimeter of the island, before rejoining the main river course. We take a trip on a wild mouse rollercoaster (it's called the Wilde Maus – see, I speak German, too) and move on to a vicious ride where seats affixed to the end of a hydraulic arm are turned upside down about 40 metres in the air. The most nervous man in Berlin sits opposite me, wondering just how long I can hold on to beer and *glühwein*.

We move on the Gendarmenmarkt, and the most beautiful Christmas fair I have ever seen. It is held in this square in the old French quarter of Berlin (I know, that's almost as implausible as a Catholic quarter on the Shankill Road, but there was a thriving community here once). It sits in front of the concert hall, between the matching German cathedral on one side and the French Huguenot one on the other. If you saw the execrable recent remake of *Around the World in Eighty Days* with Jackie Chan, the German cathedral played the Bank of England – or maybe you saw Lola do here what it says on the tin, when she crossed the square in *Run, Lola, Run*.

Tonight, it is filled with huts and tents selling quality Christmas gifts – hand-carved wooden toys, hand-painted china, intriguing lampshades, clothing, everything you can think of. There is a superb juggler on the main stage, and beer tents with musical acts of their own. There is mulled wine, and stalls selling sauerkraut, frankfurters and sinful pastries. My senses are murmuring in pleasure – it looks great, the food is fabulous, the music is evocative and the smell divine, a mix of fir, spices and wholesome cooking. In short, it is the very distillate of Christmas spirit. If you could bottle it and bring it home then, just like Tabasco, a drop or two could add piquancy to the most mundane of festive seasons. It proves a perfect end to a wonderful day.

Next morning, we walk to the top of Unter den Linden, the beautiful main boulevard of the former eastern sector of the city controlled by the Russians after the Second World War. The last time I was here, this was a wasteland with the Brandenburg Gate at the centre. In front of it, there was a temporary marquee that held about 7,000 guests for the inaugural MTV European Music Awards. Behind the gate was a tented Hard Rock Café, beside a huge press centre where we got to interview 'the talent' during rehearsals. These sessions are usually incredibly dreary, as fans with typewriters ask inane questions like, 'Where did the inspiration for your song, 'Barbie Girl', come from?' (The dumbest question I ever heard asked, though, was backstage at the Oscars in 1994, when someone put it to the winning cinematographer, Janusz Kaminski of *Schindler's List*, that maybe the naked people in the Auschwitz scenes looked a little overfed.)

In the MTV media centre at Berlin that year, we happened upon a room full of unattended phones. 'What's the most expensive phone call we can make?' an English guy asked.

'Ring the speaking clock in Sydney and leave the phone off the hook,' I volunteered.

A Romanian woman I had befriended looked at me witheringly. 'No,' she said. 'Ring my mother…'

All talk that night was of a secret gig Prince was playing in an old gymnasium near Museum Island. I got my hands on a ticket and he came on stage at 3 a.m. and performed a blistering set for about two hours to no more than 300 people. It was a privilege to be there until, about five minutes before the end, I was grabbed by a man with no neck, five feet tall and just as wide, and hurled into a corner, just to make way for Michael Hutchence and Helena Christensen, who were dating at the time.

The memories come flooding back today as I look at a very different Pariser Platz, the square in front of the Brandenburg Gate, which wears its almost two-decades-old freedom by hosting the French and US embassies, and a Starbucks. For mediocre coffee, so many died. We're here to take the New Berlin Tour, an innovative walking excursion which ostensibly is free – you pay at the end only if you have enjoyed it.

We do enjoy it, even though it lasts four and a half hours – and we pay generously too. Our guide, a moonlighting young English juggler who has settled here with his German girlfriend, not only knows his subject inside out, he knows how to build suspense and how to breathe life into history.

Following the evolution of Berlin from its origins in a swamp, he takes us through the era of Frederick the Great to the Prussian Empire, the expansionist plans of Kaiser Wilhelm and defeat in the Great War. He moves on to the decadence of the Weimar Republic, centred on the cabaret clubs and brothels of Friedrichstrasse, to the rise of Hitler and the chaos at the end of the Second World War, when the city was divided between the victors (in this case the USSR, Britain, the US and France) and when West Berlin was kept alive by an Anglo-American airlift launched while the Russians blockaded the other three-quarters of Berlin in 1948.

He moves on to the construction of the Wall, which isolated West Berlin completely in 1961, and to John F. Kennedy's famous speech beside it, 'Ich bien ein Berliner' – 'I am a Berliner' – delivered on 26 June 1963, just ten days before I was born. In historic terms, this might as well be yesterday.

The guide takes us past Checkpoint Charlie, scene of a near calamitous diplomatic stand-off in 1961, when US and Soviet tanks faced each other for a day just 100 metres apart, and the world held its breath. We are brought to a faceless apartment building which, it transpires, sits on the site of the bunker where Adolf Hitler and Eva Braun took their own lives. We see the new Memorial to the Murdered Jews of Europe, almost 5 acres of concrete slabs of varying heights, laid out in a geometric maze that gets deeper and deeper and seems to signify how a horror as huge as the Holocaust started small and became stifling in scale before anyone noticed what was going on.

We wander through the Gendarmenmarkt again and come into Bebelplatz, where we find a Perspex trapdoor over a subterranean 'library' with empty shelves. This is the spot where, in May 1933, the Nazis burned books by, among others, Thomas Mann, Sigmund Freud and the nineteenth-century Romantic poet, Heinrich Heine. The plaque bears a quotation from Heine: 'Wherever they burn books, eventually they will burn people too.' Joyce and I look at each other and shiver. It's barely three weeks since we were in Birkenau.

The tour ends on the steps of the natural-history museum, overlooking the eerie Palast der Republik, where the guide has saved the best until last – the story of 9 November 1989, the day the Wall was breached. Pressure had been building in East Germany as its satellite states, including Czechoslovakia and Hungary, had already relaxed border controls. The government of the German Democratic Republic, as the East was ironically known, decided that limited movement to the West was to be permitted. Günter Schabowski, the East German propaganda minister tasked with telling the world this, was just back from holiday and badly briefed. When asked at a press conference how soon the new measures would be implemented, and not wishing to look foolish by saying he didn't know, he replied, 'I think immediately.'

Thousands of East Berliners heard this live on television and radio. They made their way to the border posts and attempted to cross. Surprised guards rang superiors to see if they should start shooting, but the military chiefs feared not just a riot but a full-blown insurrection. Sense prevailed. The barriers were lifted and thousands and thousands of East Germans swarmed into the West for the biggest party in history. Though there was a wide disparity in value, the shops – and, mostly, bars – in the West accepted the East German mark at parity with their own. Families separated for years hugged each other. Strangers danced together all night on top of the Wall. Even more amazingly, they all went home convinced, correctly, that the genie was never going back in the bottle.

Pain and suffering don't usually make me emotional – but show me the triumph of the human spirit and I'm blubbing in a second (this is noble in a situation that is epoch-defining, but less easy to explain when I bawl for a kid who overcomes nerves or a stammer and gets through a whole song on *The X Factor*). The night the Wall fell, I remember watching the television with tears streaming down my face. Thinking about it today still moves me. It was the defining moment in recent history for my generation of Europeans because it wasn't just the day Germany was reunited, it was the day Europe was united. The fissure at the heart of a continent was sealed, the frontline of rival ideologies disappeared, the tensions of the Cold War evaporated.

You know, if I have learned anything on my travels around Ryanland, it is that Europe is far from perfect. The older countries have grown fat and lazy, especially their children. The fledgling states to the east are attracting most of the new investment, but they're using it only to ape what the rest of us already have – Tesco and Carrefour, H&M and Zara, *Pimp My Ride* and *Punk'd*.

Yet for all its flaws, for all its new cultural and religious tensions, for its wariness of mass migration, the fact remains that Europe is still the beating heart of all that is civilised. Discourse is expected and welcomed. Anyone who is not with us is not, by definition alone, against us. We don't, as a matter of course, attack countries that haven't attacked us. We love our own gods – and, between us, we have a few of them – but we don't expect everyone else to. We don't think that those who are against us hate freedom. It's entirely possible they just hate us because of how we treat *them*. Most importantly, we are free for the most part to say what we think without fear of censure, and we have enough media outlets to ensure many voices are heard.

In the 2006 index of world press freedom, compiled by the Reporters Without Borders organisation, four countries tied as the freest of all – Finland, Iceland, the Netherlands and, to my great pride, Ireland. But look who's in the Top 10 – the Czech Republic, Estonia, Slovakia, Hungary, Latvia and Slovenia. These are six countries which, scarcely a generation ago, had the most restricted press in the world, unable to report the simplest of news without official approval. Yet, instinctively, they always understood what freedom was, and the responsibilities that went with it, and they never stopped craving it. Once the German Democratic Republic disappeared, it seemed anything was possible – certainly, the fragmentation of the Soviet Union could not have happened without the existence of a unified Germany.

Looking back, it feels strange that the Wall stood for just twenty-eight years – but then it seems odd, too, that it's just a blink ago since Latvians, Lithuanians and Estonians held hands for freedom, or that

Lech Walesa led the Solidarity trade union in Gdansk, or that Nicolae and Elena Ceausescu were shot like dogs in Romania, bringing to an end the regime most resistant to the exhilarating path of change in Europe in the magical year of 1989.

As we look down into the parliament chamber from the new dome on the Reichstag, we remember the evil that once emanated from here and briefly consumed a continent. But when we walk out on the rooftop terrace and look across the rooftops of east Berlin – the '*e*', importantly, now just a lower-case one, and a geographical locator, not a political statement – we see that same continent not only reclaimed, but reborn.

If we look back on the past century, Berlin was at the heart of Europe's troubles but was also the scene of its redemption. It is the continent's most significant city, the only one that approaches New York for vibrancy and energy, the only one that exudes that same feeling that every corner has a history. But, like New York, it is not sentimental. Just as the Freedom Tower will occupy Lower Manhattan, rather than the remnants of the World Trade Center, the Wall too has gone for good. Other countries might have preserved it, but the Germans waited twenty-eight years for their chance to go at it with pickaxes and they took that chance with gusto. If you want to find the Wall today, the best thing to do is look down – a strip of stones inlaid in paths and roads will tell you where it once stood.

Of a thousand-year Reich, there is no sign whatever. Nor, indeed, of a socialist Utopia.

Both of these outcomes seem very worthy of a beer. Joyce and I hop in a taxi to make the invisible crossing from west to east. The taxi driver is unusually loquacious, laughing and joking until he misses a turn.

'I'm sorry,' he says with a giggle. 'It's not easy to drive after four beers...'

Slightly rattled, we ask him to drop us off at the Gendarmenmarkt.

We thread our way through the people preparing for Christmas. We buy two glasses of *glühwein*, we clink them and we hug – and we drink to Berlin, to freedom and to life itself.

EINDHOVEN–
BRUSSELS SOUTH CHARLEROI

FR1964 • Dublin (DUB) to Eindhoven (EIN)
818 km • €28.93

FR047 • Brussels South Charleroi (CRL) to Dublin (DUB)
808 km • €17.05

I arrive in Eindhoven, which seems to have been almost completely rebuilt after a pummelling in the Second World War. It is very, very dull. Certainly, I didn't exactly have to dip into deep reserves of strength to give the Philips Lightbulb Museum a miss. Now that I have passed on it, though, I have niggling questions: Is it arranged chronologically or by wattage? Is there one room for screw tops and another for bayonet heads? What are the exhibits lit by? And is there a special section for lightbulb jokes, my favourite of which is: How many mystery writers does it take to screw in a lightbulb? Two – one to screw it almost all the way in and the other to give it a surprising twist at the end.

Darn. Probably should have gone there.

The architecture in Eindhoven – pedestrian precincts with shops faced in a fairly anonymous light brick – reminds me of those rows of shops you see in Britain. You know the ones that are on a road running beside, and parallel to, a bigger road, and have flats above them? Well, the whole town here looks like that. What is surprising is that, in the middle of these low-rise units, there are blocks maybe thirty storeys tall. I know the Netherlands are densely populated, but flying in, I saw lots of green space. Why not just move a little further out? It's not like they would destroy any areas of great natural beauty, given that everywhere is as flat as a model lying back on an airbed.

I hear on the news that there is a ferocious storm headed our way, so I cut my losses and decide to take an earlier train to Brussels than I had intended. Rain is sheeting against the windows and it is impossible to see a thing outside, a state of affairs less annoying here than anywhere else in Europe, since there is nothing to see anyway. I'm supposed to change at Dordrecht, with a twenty-minute stopover, but two hours pass and still there is no sign of, or information on, the Brussels train. The wind has started gusting severely and a Dutchman – who has reduced his risk of flying by talking shelter in a waiting room – eventually tells me that a platform announcement (it sounds like 'Och yahr bfnicht leer-dammer chnuck') basically has suggested we all try to make our own way to our destinations or just go back home.

At his suggestion, I join him on the local train to Roosendaal, which I have never heard of, and therefore I have no idea if I am in the Netherlands or Belgium. Mind you, the storm has become so intense, it is hard to tell whether it is day or night. We change there for Antwerp, and leave that station just as the wind blows a large chunk of the ceiling down on the train. By the time we finally make it to Brussels, an as-the-crow-flies journey of 137 kilometres has taken nearly eight hours. That said, I am merely inconvenienced; for others, it is much worse. The storm, the worst in twenty years, claims seven lives in the Netherlands and dozens across Europe.

I like Brussels but today it is not at its best (though, storm or no storm, as we slow before the Gare du Nord, I notice a street where the windows are lit with red lights, each with a woman peering hopefully from within – I suppose there are worse ways to see out a shower).

After the Netherlands, Brussels is welcomingly hilly, and a taxi takes me to my hotel just off the Avenue Louise, passing the impressive Royal Palace on the way. The Belgian royal family were probably the ones who put me off the concept of monarchy. In May 1968, when I was almost five, I was teed up for weeks for a trip to Arbour Hill, burial place of most of the leaders of the 1916 Easter Rising, which saw the first shots in a five-year countdown to the Irish Free State. King Baudouin of the Belgians and his wife, Queen Fabiola (a name any drag act would be proud of), were to lay a wreath during a state visit and we were all to go along with little Tricolours and wave. My limited knowledge of what a king should look like was rather coloured by the storybooks I had been given, so I was expecting a Henry VIII figure who would leap from a carriage and, draped in ermine, lop off a couple of heads with a broadsword before spiriting a maiden to his bedchamber.

Instead, a car pulled up and an accountant got out, followed by the lady captain of the golf club. And I thought, right, if they can't be bothered, why should I be? The only time I waved my flag all day was when a volley of rifle-fire rang out over the graves of the republican dead.

It is now quite late, but I had earlier spotted a pub called the Michael Collins on the corner of the Avenue Louise. Since Collins was a hero of the Easter Rising, having fought beside Padraig Pearse in

Dublin's General Post Office, I interpret this as a sign to go drinking (though, to be fair, it seldom takes more than a neon sign flashing the word 'open'). I can hardly see to the back of the bar, such is the fug. When Ireland announced a total ban on public smoking in 2004, I realised the game was up and quit a forty-a-day habit. On my travels in Ryanland, I have been amazed at just how much I now detest second-hand smoke. I never ask people to put a cigarette out when they're blowing smoke in my direction – I did it to others for so long myself, carping now would be repugnantly hypocritical – but I really hate it and, especially, the smell of my clothes the next morning. Smell was a sense I lost for the twenty-two years I smoked and, except for the occasional morning in Sardinian taxis, I like having it back.

Next morning, I walk the Avenue Louise – or Louiza, if you speak Flemish. Brussels (Brussel, or Bruxelles, take your pick) really is a poly-linguistic city, not only because of its own political and cultural schizo-phrenia, but also thanks to its role at the heart of the European Union. As I stand before the Berlaymont building, home of the European Commission and its secretariat, I am reminded that Irish recently became the twenty-first official language of the union. That's why I've never understood Britain's fear of a United States of Europe – such a thing simply isn't possible without simple communication. Equally, when the vast majority of the EU's 493,119,161 people who speak a second language choose to speak English, then that seems to me to represent a great opportunity to promote British culture and values. Here is a country that could be at the very heart of Europe, but instead chooses to stay emotionally as cut off as it is geographically, defending its precious pound while the rest of Europe gets to grips with real issues, like how to make the perfect camembert, or grow the perfect olive.

The British should instead do what the Irish and the French do, which is to accept all the good the EU offers and enact legislation it doesn't like, just to keep everyone happy – then ignore it all anyway, and just pay the fines.

By the time I reach the Grand Place, the wonderful square that defines the city, it is time to eat, and I grab a bowl of the national dish, *moules frites*. On my first school tour, the one to Middelkerke near Ostend in 1976, I discovered not only mussels and chips, but had mayonnaise on the chips too. I reckon this has been responsible for at least two of the three excess stones I carry to this day.

I walk to the Galeries St Hubert, a lovely shopping arcade, and stop at the intersection with the Rue des Bouchers. With its pavement tables, colourful awnings, kerbside fish tanks and anxious greeters desperately trying to get you into their restaurants, the street is delightfully stereotypical. If someone from Mars said, 'I have ten seconds, what does Europe look like?', I would say, 'Get yourself to the Rue des Bouchers and you have it sorted.'

I enjoy going back to the Mort Subite, which translates as Sudden Death. It's one of the best bars in the city, with walls yellowed by nicotine, and I linger over a *croque monsieur*, a toasted cheese and ham sandwich, and one of their own craft beers. I remember being here on a media visit with maybe twenty others back in 1989 when my friend, Margaret Ryan, walked up to the bar and said, 'Cent bières, s'il vous plaît.'

'Mais, Madame,' the barman replied, 'that is a hundred beers.'

'That's right,' said Mags. 'Now get pouring…'

It remains the classiest line I've ever heard.

When I finish my beer (and, God, don't the Belgians know how to make it), I visit the *Mannikin Pis*, the statue of a little boy taking a leak. It's the first time I've seen him and I regret that today is not an anniversary or special occasion. Apparently, they dress him up, and I have missed Elvis' birthday by two weeks; the sight of a juvenile Elvis having a non-stop piss would, I reckon, have trumped a lot of what I believe to have been surreal on my travels.

Brussels has ridden out the worst of the storm, but the weather is still bad and I have no appetite for walking around, so, even though I have lots of time, I head to Charleroi, an hour away by bus, and take the flight home. I need some sunshine and some heat. Malta, the newest destination in Ryanland, beckons.

MALTA LUQA

FR7242

Dublin (DUB) to Malta Luqa (MLA)

FR7243

Malta Luqa (MLA) to Dublin (DUB)

2,530 km • €58.53 return

The night before I'm due to leave, the forecast warns of early snow, so I book a hotel at Dublin Airport. On the shuttle bus the next morning, I meet a retired couple from Nantes in western France who wanted to travel from Paris to Malta but found it cheaper to fly to Dublin from Nantes with Ryanair, stay overnight, buy dinner, fly on to Malta, and then do the whole thing again in reverse. That's what po-faced environmentalists will never understand – the easiest way to cut down greenhouse gases is to encourage people to fly in a straight line, but passengers will never do that unless the flag-carrier airlines reduce their prices. Until then, we would fly from Luton to Stansted, via Greenland, if it was only a fiver.

The flight to Malta is the longest of my entire trip, over 2,530 kilometres; it still surprises me that the former Soviet Union countries of Latvia and Lithuania are nearer. Today is also the inaugural flight. The last time I was on one of these was as a guest of the airline in 1993, when Ryanair launched a route to Birmingham. The company chairman then was Ray MacSharry, a former EU commissioner, but did that stop the police at immigration holding us all for ten minutes? Don't be ridiculous. I discovered on many occasions, nipping over to London for a day to do something important like interviewing the cast of *Ballykissangel*, that a Paddy travelling to the UK with no luggage whatsoever was even more suspect than one who arrived with a ticking suitcase.

Flying into Malta is one of the great approaches in Europe. It is the seventh most densely populated country in the world, with 1,282 people per square kilometre (the equivalent figure in the UK is 243, and in Ireland a paltry 60) and the clusters of limestone houses dotted all over the island glisten like honey as the plane lines up to land. When we descend to the tarmac, we are met by camera crews and photographers and, inside the modern terminal, a band is playing to welcome us. Women dressed in the national costume are handing out flowers and wine and the clear message is that Malta is overjoyed to become the latest outpost of Ryanland (the flight is the lead story on all the papers next day).

This is the southernmost Ryanair destination in what broadly constitutes Europe – on the network as a whole, only Marrakech, in Morocco, and the Canary Islands are farther south. This means that, even in February, the temperature is a lovely 19 degrees, and I peel off the layers of clothing before driving in a T-shirt, with the window of the car rolled down, to my hotel in St Julian's. I love Malta and know it well, thanks to a family connection with the island, so I skip the dual-carriageway that links the never-ending towns of the north of the island and instead drive through Floriana (yes, it is filled with flowers) to the city of Valletta. The lookout from the Upper Barrakka Gardens, over the three cities of Senglea, Vittoriosa and Cospicua, offers one of the finest urban views in the world.

Later, I drive inland to the old walled citadel of Mdina, known as the Silent City, a perfectly preserved fortress you will have seen in many movies, including *Gladiator* and *Troy*. The climate and the low cost of living have seen Malta become one of the busiest film-production centres in the world. It is versatile too, having played everywhere from Turkey in *Midnight Express*, to Tel Aviv in Steven Spielberg's *Munich*. In fact, a couple of years back, my wife panicked while having coffee in the lobby of the Hilton Hotel when she heard a man muttering words to the effect that 'they've killed our people, and now we must hunt them down and kill them too'. Fortunately, it was just Geoffrey Rush, who played a Mossad paymaster, learning his lines for the movie.

I meet friends in Portomaso, a very ritzy marina development where you can pay a million pounds sterling for a good apartment, and we go for dinner at Zest, an Asian fusion restaurant that challenges anything in London for the quality of the food, especially the sushi. We end the night at TwentyTwo, a bar and club on the twenty-second floor of the tower in Portomaso, where very elegant women and sharp-dressed men chatter over cocktails and champagne. The smell of newly minted money is intoxicating; people here work hard and few nationalities will exploit EU membership as effectively as the Maltese.

Next day, I take the ferry to Gozo, the unspoiled sister island that looks like the west of Ireland, but with sunshine; it is my favourite place in all of Europe, wild and unspoiled. When I return to Malta (it's the name of the island as well as the country; the third outcrop in the archipelago is Comino), I join the locals on the *passeggiata*, a gentle walk along the promenade. I call in at the Dubliner Bar and chat to Carl, the Anglo-Maltese owner, who welcomes the Ryanair route. Malta has pursued a strategy of attracting low-volume, high-spending tourism, but the money seems to have stayed in the five-star hotels. A lot of people here are hoping that mass-market tourism is back as low fares entice those who have never been here to sample the island, and that the dividend will be shared a little more widely.

After I leave Carl, I should really go back to the hotel. Instead, I make my way to Paceville, the entertainment hub of the island, loved by younger tourists and younger Maltese, though frowned upon by the older generation, who are conservatively Catholic and see the bars and clubs as the font of all licentiousness.

I'm here to celebrate. This is my last night in Ryanland, the end of a journey that has taken me to nineteen countries, and I want to celebrate on my own. Malta is a good place to end my travels, because it is in many ways symptomatic of all of Europe. It has, at various times, been ruled by Phoenicians, Carthaginians, Romans, Byzantines, Vandals, Moors, Sicilians, Aragonese, the Knights of St John, French and British. It took a hammering in the Second World War from the Germans, who persistently bombed the Allied Mediterranean fleet as it sheltered in Valletta's Grand Harbour.

This is the story of so many countries I've been to – endless colonisation, new rulers every other day, languages blending into one, with words borrowed from here, there and everywhere, and repression that never could break the resilience of the people. In fact, the Maltese were so defiant during the war, the entire island was awarded the George Cross for bravery; it's still in the corner of their flag.

I make my way to Footloose, a music bar where the hits of the 1970s, 1980s and 1990s are belting out. This is the music of my era – these songs are the soundtrack to my life. The crowd is half my age, but they know all the words; culture is relentlessly recycled nowadays. Everywhere, people are dancing – on the floor, on chairs, on tables. The atmosphere is wild and uninhibited.

These are the children of the new Europe. They are fearless. They have almost limitless opportunities to be what or who they want to be. They are not held back by their sex; in fact, the girls in the room are now statistically more likely to be smarter and forge better careers than the boys. They are not hidebound by religious tradition, they are not oppressed by the ideologies forged in Europe that caused such misery but, fortunately, were sealed in the twentieth-first century as if it was a capsule.

Because of the mobility offered by budget airlines, they are becoming stateless – they all look H&M and they all speak MTV. When I was their age, it was a big deal to travel to a nightclub on the northside of Dublin, but the people here think nothing of taking a three-hour flight for a weekend away, using Ryanair as a magic bus to all the far-flung corners of the continent, to places most of us have never heard of and can't pronounce.

The DJ starts roaring. 'Is England in the house?' A cheer goes up. 'Is Belgium in the house?' Another roar.

'Is Italy in the house?' Yeeessss.

He works his way around the map and there are people here from so many of the countries I've visited that I soon lose track.

I think he has forgotten, but eventually he asks the question. 'Is Ireland in the house?' A few people down the back of the bar cheer. I look at myself in a mirror, raise my glass and smile the sort of smile old Rik, the itchy Belgian, smiled when I met him eight months ago in Santiago on the night he finished his altogether more altruistic pilgrimage.

Yes, I think to myself, Ireland is in the house – but it's time Ireland went home.

Next morning, I pack my bag for the last time, pull the Velcro straps across my trainers, buy priority boarding and settle into 16F. By the time a Spaniard is telling us that if we buy a Bullseye Baggie, we get '*el segundo gratis*', I am fast asleep.

THANKS

My mother and father always made sure we had a holiday – so I owe not just my existence but also my love of travel to Nuala Nolan and the late Bill Nolan, a perfect dad. Fortunately, Nuala is as full of life as ever and we continue to have travel adventures to this day. No son could love a mother more.

Many of my happiest holiday memories are, of course, shared with my brilliant sisters, Anne and Joyce, and my brother, Mark, the wisest man I know. The fact that we all get on as well today as we did as kids is one of the great joys in my life. I have been very fortunate to have a wonderful sister-in-law in Claire Nolan, and highly entertaining and interesting nephews and nieces in Luke, Marcus and Alva Nolan, and Katy and Alex Gash.

Special thanks to my parents-in-law, Godfrey and Emily Plunkett, for kindnesses too many to enumerate, and to John Brereton, for making Mum smile.

Thanks also to my incomparable friends – Jonathan Nolan (who read the manuscript and laughed in all the right places), Conor Swords, Aengus Cummins, Brendan Seaver, William Brereton, Arthur Doran, Mark Courtney, Denis Houton and Andrew Lohan.

Ted and Ursula O'Brien are good neighbours who became best friends and my first port of call in many a storm. I love them like family. Ditto the other Nolans – Brian, Rosaleen, Fionnula and 'young' Brian.

From my college days, Elaine Cobbe, Brenda Power, David Robbins, Margaret O'Brien and Eddie Coffey – and, of course, Jacinta O'Brien and Pat Ward – can still make me feel eighteen again. The enduring friendship of Marty and Maria Whelan is another valued treasure. For minding my wife while I travelled, I am deeply indebted to our great friends Caroline Dooley, Sharon Kiely, Ruth Allen, Jackie Lohan and Rita O'Reilly (and her cherubians). Special thanks go to Andrew Cody and Eva O'Brien, the proof that holiday friendships really can last a lifetime.

Every child should be blessed with at least one inspirational teacher. Mine was Pacelli O'Rourke, at CBS Eblana Avenue in Dún Laoghaire, who taught me English to Inter Cert level and who did me the simple but wondrous favour of allowing me play with words.

In twenty-six years as a professional journalist, I have had the privilege of working with many of the finest talents in the industry. It would be remiss of me not to single out the following people, in chronological order, whose support and encouragement has meant so much – Eamonn McCann, Micheline McCormack, Celine Naughton, the late Niall Hanly, Mary Glennon, Bairbre Power, Michael Brophy, Colm McGinty, Paul Russell, Vincent Doyle, Michael Denieffe, the late Michael Hand, Vincent Browne, Sean Ward, John Boland, Noeleen Dowling, Patrick Madden, Frances O'Rourke, Michael Keane, the late Steve Wrottesley in Cape Town, Liam Mulcahy, David Lawlor, Frank Coughlan, Danny Wheeler, Maurice Gubbins, Dan Linehan and, especially, Peter Carvosso, who gave me my first big break.

At the *Irish Daily Mail* and *Irish Mail on Sunday*, Martin Clarke showed me that it's never too late for an old dog to learn new tricks, while Ted Verity reminded me that my oldest trick – writing – still is the one that gives me most pleasure. His encouragement was crucial to this book.

Above all, my thanks go to Paul Drury, who has been my editor for over a decade, on three different newspapers. It is surprisingly rare for colleagues to become friends, but I am happy to count him as a true friend. Another who leaped the invisible line is the peerless, funny and loyal Liz Ryan. Helen Rogers and Brendan Farrelly have been around the longest, and still are always there for me, twenty-four years later.

On a practical level, the following people operated elastic deadlines during the writing of *Ryanland* and never grumbled when I said work would be late 'because I'm in Lithuania' – Marianne Power, Robert Mayes, Alex Moffatt, John Cooper, Sebastian Hamilton and Roslyn Dee. Thanks also to Tom Mooney, Pat McGoldrick, Ronan O'Reilly, Jack White, Ciarán O'Tuama and Lorrie Bennett.

My sincere gratitude to everyone at Hodder Headline Ireland, especially Breda Purdue, who said yes, and my lovely editor, Claire Rourke, whose cheery 'hello, love' telephone greeting turned many a dismal travelling day instantly brighter. Also to Terry Foley and Karen Carty of Anú Design for, respectively, the terrific cover and the inventive typesetting. Special thanks to all at Plunkett Communications for the sterling publicity work.

For sowing the seeds of the idea for *Ryanland*, I thank my Mexican friends Fhernanda Suarez Castaños, Nicole Molina Camou and, especially, the wonderful Jimena Gamboa Baragaño.

Finally, and this is the one place where words do fail me, my thanks and my boundless love go to Sharon for being in my life for twenty years now. No matter how far I travel, I know for sure that the loveliest sight I have ever seen, or ever will see, is the one that greets me at the door each time I come home. This book is for her.

Philip Nolan, March 2007